About the Front Cover Design

The antique Bible in the cover photo is an heirloom belonging to my husband's family. It was in the Craggs family and was passed down to us from his mother, Freda Jean Craggs Roeger (1909 - 2007). The Bible contains records of family marriages, births and deaths back to the early 1800's. Pressed between its yellowed pages is the original 1857 marriage certificate of Francis Craggs and Anna Longstaff – my husband's great grandparents who immigrated to America from Durham County, England. The antique pocket watch was also in the Craggs family and is believed to have belonged to Freda's father, Francis Arthur Craggs (1868-1954).

Books by Deborah Roeger

God Still Speaks (paperback [978-1-63199-795-2]
and e-book [978-1-63199-796-9])

Other Titles in Lost in Translation Series

The Power of Obedience: Reading Scripture Through the Lens of Obedient Discipleship (Released July, 2022)

The Power of Hope: Reading Scripture Through the Lens of Hope (Released February, 2023)

The Power of My Spirit: Reading Scripture Through the Lens of The Holy Spirit (Forthcoming)

The Power of Testing: Reading Scripture Through the Lens of God-Ordained Testing (Forthcoming)

PASTOR AND MINISTRY LEADER INTRODUCTIONS

Debbie and Derf Roeger are not new to their calling to teach, however they are newcomers in their assignment to publish studies Debbie has written. Allow them to introduce themselves to you through the words and experiences of some of the Pastors and Ministry Leaders who know them.

Few couples have dedicated themselves to personal discipleship, to listening for Divine direction, and to preparation for Kingdom service as have Derf and Debbie Roeger. Their partnership for many years in the family of Worthington Christian Church was a great encouragement and blessing to the whole congregation. Debbie is a careful thinker, a diligent student of the Bible, and a skillful teacher with well-prepared and delivered lessons. She and her husband share a devotional life and a commitment to prayer, as the primary equipment for their service.

Dr. Marshall Hayden
Retired Sr. Minister, Worthington Christian Church
Worthington, Ohio

I have known Debbie and Derf Roeger for nearly 20 years. Over the years our friendship and ministry relationship grew into several prison ministry assignments, numerous prayer walks, and various worship assignments both in Ohio and Washington, D.C. Debbie is a devoted disciple of Christ, an effective leader, and mentor, filled with a passionate love for Christ and others. She is a bright, innovative, prolific teacher of God's Word and she reaches a multicultural audience. Her classes are informative and challenging creating a hunger for more. Her teachings are solid and sound! They set a foundation on which one cannot only stand but build greater understanding to facilitate greater participation and a greater expression of God's desire on the earth as it is in heaven. Her consistency in her commitment to the

Lord, her husband, her family, and the expansion of God's Kingdom is unchanging. All would benefit from her insightful teachings, which I highly recommend.
Carolyn A. Quinichett, M.A., Prayer Life Ministry/Ministry Leader, Rhema Christian Church, Columbus, Ohio

Debbie is very gifted in organizing and creating a complete Bible-based study on many subjects. She and her husband both have the gift of presenting Bible studies in an interactive way that engages the participants to grow in their knowledge, understanding, and faith. They are both deep prayer warriors!
Pastor Tom Sharron, Chumuckla Community Church, Pace, Florida

I am one blessed ministry leader to have Debbie Roeger on my teaching team at Calvary and in my life personally! Her knowledge of God's Word is deep and is reflected in her writing, and her teaching. She is diligent to record her sources and takes no credit for her ministry. As iron sharpens iron, her sensitivity to Holy Spirit, encourages me, excites me, teaches me, and loves me. Debbie strives to seek God's face every day, and it shows!
Carol DeBlasis, Senior Director of Women's Ministry, Calvary Chapel, Melbourne, Florida

Debbie and Derf Roeger love the Lord and love His Word! They both have been gifted by God to teach His Word. As you study with them, expect fresh insights and a deeper understanding and desire to follow the One who first loved us!
David Roberson, Retired Sr. Pastor, Worthington Christian Church, Worthington, Ohio

Debbie and Derf are not only our dear friends, but they are also amazing leaders and mentors who are filled with a passionate love for the Lord and others. They are devoted disciples of Christ and are intent on leading others to be disciples as well. They teach from the core of Christianity in a manner that is not only relatable, but is also life changing. They live their lives as beautiful examples of ones who know true intimacy with God. And their international ministry, "Hope of the Nations" is to draw others into that same close relationship with our Lord and Savior. Truly it is men and women like Derf and Debbie who personify the 'Hope of the Nations'!

Diane Daniels, Women's Ministry Leadership, Worthington Christian Church, Worthington, Ohio

As a successful lawyer, now retired, Debbie Roeger has developed and mastered key transferable skills such as organization, research, analysis, critical thinking, and the like, which she utilizes as she studies God's Word from a historical, socio-economic, cultural, and spiritual perspective. She articulates profound biblical principles in a way that is simple for readers and students to comprehend. Throughout the years I have witnessed the humility she and Derf embody, their love for people, and their passion to make disciples for God's Kingdom. As prayer warriors, they have developed a keen ability to "hear" God's voice, producing a lifestyle of obedience and worship unto the Lord. I recommend their teachings and classes without reservation as they offer a roadmap for discipleship and the development of a deeper relationship with the Lord.

Dorcas Hernandez, MS, Hannah Ministries, Inc./Overseer

I know Debbie Roeger to be a woman of integrity. Our church is blessed that she is using her teaching gifts in our Small Group Ministry. I know her to be sensitive to the voice of the Holy Spirit and having a passion for intercessory prayer. Her walk with the Lord is an encouragement to the church body as well as myself. She allows God to move through her in every gifting. It is a blessing to know her.

Pastor Bob Russell, Calvary Chapel, Melbourne, Florida

My Dwelling Place

Reading Scripture Through The Lens Of God's Desire To Dwell Among Us

Lost in Translation
Bible Study Series
#3

Energion Publications
Gonzalez, Florida
2024

Copyright © 2019, edited 2023, Deborah L. Roeger. All rights reserved worldwide. No part of this book may be reproduced or used in any manner without the written permission of the copyright owner except for the use of quotations in a book review.

Unless otherwise noted, Scripture throughout this study is quoted from New American Standard Bible (NASB 1995) Copyright © 1960, 1962, 1963, 1968, 1971, 1972, 1973, 1975, 1977, 1995 by The Lockman Foundation. Used by permission. All rights reserved www.lockman.org

Scripture quotations marked HCSB are from the Holman Christian Standard Bible®, Used by Permission HCSB ©1999,2000,2002,2003,2009 Holman Bible Publishers. Holman Christian Standard Bible®, Holman CSB®, and HCSB® are federally registered trademarks of Holman Bible Publishers.

Scripture quotations marked KJV are from The Authorized (King James) Version. Rights in the Authorized Version in the United Kingdom are vested in the Crown. Reproduced by permission of the Crown's patentee, Cambridge University Press.

Scripture quotations marked NET are from the NET Bible® http://netbible.com copyright ©1996, 2019 used with permission from Biblical Studies Press, L.L.C. All rights reserved.

Scripture quotations marked ESV are from the ESV® Bible (The Holy Bible, English Standard Version®), copyright © 2001 by Crossway, a publishing ministry of Good News Publishers. Used by permission. All rights reserved.

Scripture quotations marked CJB are from the Complete Jewish Bible, Copyright © 1998 and 2016 by David H. Stern. Used by permission. All rights reserved worldwide.

Scripture quotations marked AMP are from the Amplified® Bible, Copyright © 2015 by The Lockman Foundation. Used by permission. www.lockman.org

Scripture quotations marked NLT are from the Holy Bible, New Living Translation, copyright ©1996, 2004, 2015 by Tyndale House Foundation. Used by permission of Tyndale House Publishers, Carol Stream, Illinois 60188. All rights reserved.

Scripture quotations marked MIT are from MacDonald Idiomatic Translation, translated by William G. MacDonald. Copyright (c) William G. MacDonald.

ISBN: 978-1-63199-883-6

eISBN: 978-1-63199-884-3

Library of Congress Control Number: 2024935379

Lost in Translation – 1241 Conference Rd – Gonzalez, FL 32560 – pubs@energion.com

An Imprint of Energion Publications

The *Lost in Translation* series of Bible Studies is dedicated to Henri Louis Goulet and Messianic Studies Institute located in Gahanna, Ohio. You taught us that an inherently Jewish perspective of the Messianic worldview and way of life is the principle that all learning is for living. Through your teaching and encouragement my husband and I became lifelong learners!

DISCLAIMER: In this Bible Study I will cite a wide variety of references. While I am comfortable citing the identified source for the specific point referenced, that does not mean that I have read, understand, or necessarily agree or disagree with that source on other points of theology or doctrine. Therefore, referencing various scholars, authors or Study Bibles is not intended to be a blanket endorsement of that work. On this point I appreciate the wisdom of Trevin Wax, Vice President, Research and Resource Development at the North American Mission Board, who rightly noted that "authors who may be wrong in some ways may be reliable and even helpful in other areas. We can benefit from their works as long as we read carefully."[1]

NOTE: The presentation of Hebrew and Greek words I have used is designed to make those words easier to read and pronounce. As a result, some letters are not precisely represented.

---

1 Wax, Trevin, *After You Believe by N.T. Wright: A Review*, March 22, 2010. Retrieved from https://www.thegospelcoalition.org/blogs/trevin-wax/after-you-believe-by-n-t-wright-a-review/ (last accessed June 16, 2023)

Table of Contents

Acknowledgements vii
Introduction To *Lost In Translation* Series ix
Preface xiii

1 God's Desire to Dwell Among Us 1
2 The Resting Place God Desires 15
3 From the Tabernacle of Moses to David's Tent 31
4 From David's Tent to Solomon's Temple 43
5 From Solomon's Temple to Exile 55
6 God's Presence During the Period of the Exile 67
7 Promised Return of God's Presence 87
8 A Rebuilt Temple Without a Dwelling Presence 101
9 A New Covenant Type of Presence among God's People 113
10 Christ as King and Temple 127
11 Building God's Temple, The Mission of the Church 141
12 The Clash of Kingdoms 163

How to do basic WORD STUDIES
when you don't read Hebrew or Greek 189
Index to the Word Studies 203
Meet the Author: Deborah L. Roeger 205

Acknowledgements

In September 2019 I had the privilege of teaching the first draft of this study at Rhema Christian Center in Columbus, Ohio through the invitation of Hannah Ministries Inc. I am so grateful to have been supported in that endeavor by Dorcas Hernandez and Carolyn Quinichett. I am watching God's plan unfold in a consistent way as I write the studies He calls me to write. After a draft of the study has been completed, He opens the door for me to teach it and that experience serves to improve the study in meaningful ways. Sometime after that, He sets the study in line for publication. Thank you to all those who participated in that first teaching of *My Dwelling Place*! What a gift of grace to have studied with you.

The manuscript for this study has benefitted from the careful read of Kelly Russell who volunteered her time and turned lessons around with lightning speed. The end result is most certainly an improvement over the original manuscript. Thanks so much Kelly!

Diane Daniels continues to be uppermost in my list of those to thank. I am so grateful for her seemingly inexhaustible supply of encouragement. She has stayed the course month after month, year after year as I have written draft upon draft of this study and many others. She never fails to inspire with her words, her love and her prayers! "I wouldn't be me if I didn't have you as a friend."[1]

I am also grateful for the faithful prayers of our other prayer partners. I have absolute confidence that I remain standing because you are on your knees praying!

---

[1] I don't take credit for this friendship quote. However, the author is unknown.

My continued respect and gratitude also belong to Henry Neufeld and Energion Publications. Henry's knowledge of original Hebrew and Greek continues to be my safety net in the studies I write. I would not have the confidence to publish these studies without that safety net! Thank you, Henry for graciously sharing your gifts for the benefit of our readers.

This is the third study Energion Publications has released in the Lost in Translation series. Publishing that first study became a marathon as we experienced nothing short of an all-out spiritual battle. Henry and Jody stayed the course with patience and grace. Your persistence in addressing every detail in that study set the course for every study to follow. For that I am humbled and thankful.

And lastly to my husband, Derf, my best friend and the love of my life for more than 50 years. You know how much I mean it when I say, "Thank you!"

To God be the glory, great things He has done.

Introduction To
Lost In Translation Series

God instilled in me a love for digging deep into His Word. He added to that a passion for "getting it right" and the ability to assimilate a wealth of diverse material into an understandable lesson. Those gifts have enabled me to write well-researched meaningful studies. Each one incorporates numerous "Word Studies" along the way to ensure that original word meanings which have been largely lost in translation are brought to life again. The end result is a series of Bible Studies that have a scholarly emphasis on rightly dividing God's Word while highlighting personal application for spiritual growth and transformation. When asked, I succinctly describe *Lost in Translation* as connecting biblical scholars with the rest of us who sit in the church pews. However, I have come to understand that these studies also move toward providing a bridge between conservative evangelicals and pentecostal/charismatics. An explanation of that last statement will be helpful.

Through my research mentor I am able to reach into the best and most current scholarship of the subject matter of the study. With diligent research I become equipped to culturally and historically contextualize Bible passages. Doing so provides relevant background to aid the reader in their understanding of original language word meanings and concepts. My goal is never about increasing intellectual knowledge. My orientation is always a right understanding of God's Word with a focus on personal application and discipleship.

At times God adds to my research with revelation and understanding that does not come directly from the pages of the Commentaries, Bible Dictionaries or other sound scholarly materials I customarily reference. At those times, He simply speaks His heart to me on the matter. Often what He says answers a question I had been pondering but had been unable to draw to a satisfactory conclusion.[1] It wasn't until I started fine-tuning the manuscripts to begin the publication process that I caught a glimpse of what God had been doing through this combination of research and revelation. Here I'll need to insert a bit of background information.

In 2014 R. T. Kendall released, *Holy Fire: A Balanced, Biblical Look At The Holy Spirit's Work In Our Lives*. In it, Kendall wrote about an unplanned "divorce" that had silently taken place in the church between God's Spirit and God's Word.[2] Using broad brushed descriptive strokes he defined two separate and distinct categories of churches.

- Denominations majoring on the written Word of God. Their focus is on the inerrancy of the written Word, expository preaching and sound doctrine. They may be virtually silent about the Holy Spirit. Generally, these congregations are labeled: *conservative evangelical* – strong in Word, much less emphasis on Holy Spirit.
- Other congregations seeking to experience the power that was present in the book of Acts. Their desire to see the gifts of the Spirit operating in the church today leads to an active pursuit of signs, wonders and miracles. Generally, these congregations are labeled: *charismatic/pentecostal*

---

[1] In our international teaching/discipling ministry I have been asked to deliver sermons during a Sunday morning worship service. I imagine my preparation for those messages most likely happens in a way that is similar to those who are called to be Preacher/Pastors. The end result from sound prayerful preparation is a combination of searching out the Word through other resources and the divine guidance of Holy Spirit to bring greater understanding. It's a good example of the way in which God has led me to write Bible Studies.

[2] I had already come to recognize an invisible but distinct separating line between groups of Christ-followers. Thankfully Kendall's book equipped me with a way to articulate what I had observed.

– major emphasis on power manifestations of the Spirit, often much less emphasis on God's written Word.

There is nothing in what Kendall says that intends to indict either evangelicals or charismatics for their respective passionate pursuits. Kendall's point is that Scripture presents a clear and compelling picture of the early church as being *simultaneously strong in both Word and Power*. He credits some congregations with having found that proper balance between Word and Spirit which existed in the early church. Kendall stresses the need for that to be the goal of *every* church.

In his first epistle to the Corinthians, Paul identifies two groups of people, but the distinction he makes is *not within* the body of Christ, it is between those who are *in Christ* and those who are *outside of Christ*. To all of those *in Christ* Paul urged unity in the midst of their diversity.[3] The encouraging conclusion of Kendall's book is that he envisions a day when God will sovereignly *remarry* His Word and His Spirit. As that happens, proper first-century balance will be restored to the body of Christ.

It occurs to me that the *Lost in Translation* Bible Study series works towards that coming remarriage. To that end, the reader may find the series somewhat unique in its orientation – a well-researched Bible Study inseparably joined with Holy Spirit inspired counsel and revelation.

To God be the glory for what He has done, is doing and will yet do!

---

3   "For even as the body is one and *yet* has many members, and all the members of the body, though they are many, are one body, so also is Christ. For by one Spirit we were all baptized into one body ... God has placed the members ... just as He desired.... now there are many members, but one body. And the eye cannot say to the hand, 'I have no need of you'; or again the head to the feet, 'I have no need of you.'... But God has *so* composed the body, giving more abundant honor to that *member* which lacked, so that there may be no division in the body, but *that* the members may have the same care for one another." 1 Corinthians 12:12-25, italics in original

[B]ut just as it is written, "Things which eye has not seen and ear has not heard, And which have not entered the heart of man, All that God has prepared for those who love Him." For to us God revealed them through the Spirit; for the Spirit searches all things, even the depths of God. 1 Corinthians 2:9-10

In His Service by His Grace,

Deborah L. Roeger

Preface

A Word from the Author: My goal for this study is to enable participants to have a life-transforming encounter with God. Our Western culture values *knowledge* for the sake of knowledge, but the culture of the Bible valued knowledge for the sake of guiding righteous behavior. J. I. Packer who is considered to be among the most influential evangelicals in North America has asserted that attempts to interpret God's Word without personal application do not deserve the title "Interpretation."[1] In the world of the ancient Hebrew, the goal of *every* student of *every* rabbi was to go well beyond learning what the rabbi knew and to be like the rabbi – to walk the way the rabbi walked through life. The purpose of education was not to gain head knowledge and become more intelligent but to inform perspective which would transform behavior. May the cry of your heart with every page of this study be, "O God, change me from the inside out, let me be more like you!" As your cry ascends and joins with my prayers for you, I am trusting God will hear and answer in unimaginable ways! Let the change begin!

Use of Yahweh: In the study I may use "Yahweh"– the most frequent Name for God in the Hebrew Bible. It is composed of four Hebrew letters: Yud (Y), Hey (H), Vav (V) and Hey (H) which combine as *Yahweh* or *YHVH*.

---

[1] "…. Exegesis without application should not be called interpretation at all." J.I. Packer quoted by Dr. Grant C. Richison, Website Homepage *Verse-By-Verse Commentary by Dr. Grant C. Richison*. Retrieved from https://versebyversecommentary.com/ (last accessed September 15, 2021)

Yahweh is the personal Covenant Name by which the ancient Hebrews knew God. The first biblical reference is found in the exodus story.

> Moshe said to God, "Look, when I appear before the people of Isra'el and say to them, 'The God of your ancestors has sent me to you'; and they ask me, 'What is his name?' what am I to tell them?" God said to Moshe, "*Ehyeh Asher Ehyeh* [I am/will be what I am/will be]," and added, "Here is what to say to the people of Isra'el: '*Ehyeh* [I Am *or* I Will Be] has sent me to you.'" God said further to Moshe, "Say this to the people of Isra'el: '*Yud-Heh-Vav-Heh* [Adonai], the God of your fathers, the God of Avraham, the God of Yitz'chak and the God of Ya'akov, has sent me to you.' This is my name forever; this is how I am to be remembered generation after generation. Exodus 3:13-15 CJB, italics in original

With this answer, God announced His eternal Name to Moses. As noted in the *Complete Jewish Bible* translation quoted above, the Hebrew verb *'ehyeh* can be translated as "I Am" *or* "I Will Be." Notice in this more Jewish rendering of Exodus 3:13-15 how the four Hebrew letters mentioned above are used in this translation, "Say this to the people of Isra'el: '*Yud-Heh-Vav-Heh* [Adonai], the God of your fathers, the God of Avraham [Abraham], the God of Yitz'chak [Isaac] and the God of Ya'akov [Jacob], has sent me to you.'"

In context, the primary focus of God's answer to Moses is His promise *to be with* Moses and with the people Moses is sent to lead out of Egypt.[2] In the setting of the Old Testament, a name served a much greater function than simply an identification marker. A name communicated that which was essentially true of the one it

---

2   *ESV Study Bible* (Crossway Books 2008) study note Exodus 3:14, p. 149

identified.³ Yahweh equates His Name with His character as being "absolute and unchanging. This immutability provides inflexible reliability that the [promises He makes] will be realized."⁴ To the Hebrew mind, Yahweh above all else meant the God who faithfully keeps Covenant with His people.⁵

Yahweh (often translated as Jehovah or LORD in most modern Bible translations) is the most intensely sacred Name to the Jewish people and many will not even pronounce it. In its place, they may say the four-letters Yud-Hey-Vav-Hey (YHVH) or will often simply use *Hashem* (literally "the Name"). Because of this sacredness, "God" is often written "G-d" in Jewish writings to avoid writing/saying the Name.⁶

Use of "the" Holy Spirit and Use of Holy Spirit: Throughout this study I will interchangeably refer to "the Holy Spirit" (His title) and "Holy Spirit" (His name). Because some might find that objectionable an explanation will be helpful. It is notewor-

---

3   Motyer, J. Alec, *The Prophecy of Isaiah: An Introduction & Commentary* (InterVarsity Press 1993) Isaiah 65:15-16d, p. 528
4   Sarna, Nahum M., *Exploring Exodus: The Origins Of Biblical Israel* (Schocken Books 1986, 1996) p. 52
5   "The verb form used here is אֶהְיֶה (*'ehyeh*) the Qal imperfect, first person common singular, of the verb הָיָה (*haya* 'to be').... [W]hen God used the verb to express his name, he used this form saying, 'I AM.' When his people refer to him as Yahweh, which is the third person masculine singular form of the same verb, they say 'he is.'... The idea of the verb would certainly indicate that God is not bound by time, and while he is present ('I AM') he will always be present, even in the future ...." *NET Bible Notes*, translator's note 47, Exodus 3:14. The source for this information is "Net Notes" however it will be descriptively cited as "Net Bible Notes" throughout the study."
6   The Jewish people understand Deuteronomy 12:4 as a prohibition against "erasing, destroying or desecrating the name of G-d." Jewish Community Center, *Writing G-d*. Retrieved from https://www.jccmb.com/templates/articlecco_cdo/aid/1333937/jewish/Writing-G-d.htm (last accessed August 9, 2021). As a result, many special precautions are taken both when writing the Name and when eliminating any documented format on which the Name has been written.

thy that in the original Greek of John 20:22, for example, the phrase "*pneuma hagion*" (translated Holy Spirit) could properly be a name or a title, depending on how one reads the Greek. Similarly, we find in Scripture references to "Jesus" as His name, while "Christ" (Messiah) is His title. We alternate between name and title often in the English language. For example, we say, "When Lincoln was the president" or "President Lincoln." If we are thinking of Holy Spirit as a name, it is already definite without the use of "the" because a name does not need to be preceded by a definite article. I suggest discomfort with a reference to "Holy Spirit" may be due to lack of familiarity with using His name. However, using His name rather than His title emphasizes the personal nature of the Holy Spirit. And that's my point.

Use of Hebrew word *Talmid* (singular) or *Talmidim* (plural): By the time of Jesus, discipleship was well-established within the Jewish culture. All the great sages, rabbis and teachers of Torah had *talmidim* (disciples). A *talmid* (a disciple) was on a pilgrimage that was far more than an intellectual pursuit. The *talmid's* goal was to be *like* the rabbi – he wanted to assimilate the essence of who the rabbi was into his own life. This was radical discipleship – it was a complete re-making of the one who was being discipled so as to become like his rabbi in knowledge, wisdom and ethical behavior.

In other words, a *talmid's* deepest desire was to follow his rabbi so closely that he would start to think and act just like his rabbi. Jesus summed up the goal of discipleship this way: "*[A]fter [each disciple] has been fully trained, [he] will be like his teacher.*"[7] A *talmid's* behavior would be a reflection on their teacher's reputation – either positively or negatively.[8] That means perseverance

---

7   Luke 6:40
8   Keener, Craig S., *The Gospel Of John: A Commentary*, Volume Two (Hendrickson Publishers 2003) John 13:34-35, citing e.g., Aeschines Timarchus 171-173 among others, pp. 926-927

was a standard requirement for every *talmid*.[9] Once a *talmid* was fully trained, he would become a teacher and he would disciple *talmidim* of his own. What Jesus had begun by making *talmidim* of His first followers, the body of Christ now does as they make new *talmidim* of Jesus. We see the apostle Paul following this established rabbinic pattern when he says, "*Imitate me, as I also imitate Christ. Now I praise you because you always remember me and keep the traditions just as I delivered them to you.*"[10]

When we understand disciple-making in its first-century context, most of us would have to admit that Jesus' (and likewise Paul's) idea of making disciples is vastly different than many self-designated "Christians" or what we often call a "follower," a "believer" or even a "disciple" today.

Throughout the study when I use the phrase "Christ-follower" or the word "Believer" I intend those word choices to be synonymous with the definition and culturally relevant understanding of a *talmid*.

About Word Studies: Hebrew scholar Tremper Longman refers to Bible translations as "commentaries with no notes."[11] I think he is spot on! Because no language easily and accurately translates word-for-word one to another, every translator makes judgment calls as to which word best fits the context as he sees it. Longman calls these "interpretive decisions" and that's why he suggests that any translation amounts to that translator's commentary on the text.[12] Even so, by the very nature of translation,

---

9 Keener, Craig S., *The Gospel Of John: A Commentary*, Volume Two (Hendrickson Publishers 2003) John 13:34-35, p. 926
10 1 Corinthians 11:1-2
11 Longman, Tremper III, *How To Read Proverbs* (InterVarsity Press 2002) p. 18
12 Longman, Tremper III, *How To Read Proverbs* (InterVarsity Press 2002) p. 18

the person translating typically leaves no notes behind for future readers to follow his line of reasoning.[13]

"Our sacred literature does not use obscure language, but describes most things in words clearly indicating their meaning. Therefore, it is necessary at all times to delve into the literal meaning of words to achieve complete understanding of what is actually meant."[14] To that end, from time to time in our lessons it will be advantageous to stop and do a "Word Study" which will allow us to consider the contextual meaning of that word from its original Hebrew or Greek language.

A diligent assessment of original word meanings relies on several factors. Both the authors and the original audience of the Scriptures lived in a different world than today's modern world. Politics, culture(s), ethics, worldview, theology as well as the realities of daily life were all radically different from what we know and experience. Those factors shaped the thoughts and expectations of the biblical writers which in turn shaped their words. An important task in biblical understanding is to discern, as much as possible, what any given word meant to the *original* audience. Therefore, the more we are able to appreciate the ancient mindset of the Bible the better equipped we are to understand what God was trying to communicate in a given text.

When we work to understand the Greek language of the New Testament, it is critical to realize just how much Hebrew thought impacted the New Testament authors. Most recent scholarship suggests *all* of those authors were Hebrew men who grew up in Jewish homes and were educated in the Old Testament writings.[15] As a result, the Hebrew thought-world of the Old Testament is

---

13 In my research experience, the *New English Translation* (NET) seems to be the exception to this rule in that according to netbible.com it contains 60,932 translator notes.
14 Rabbi Samson Raphael Hirsch (1808-1888). Retrieved from https://www.thiss.org/ (last accessed August 8, 2021)
15 According to Henri Goulet, my research mentor, recent research suggests that absent evidence otherwise even Luke must be held to be Jewish. Henri

the beginning source for proper understanding of New Testament Greek words. Although those men wrote in Greek, the thinking behind their writings was informed by their Hebrew heritage making the Old Testament the best starter dictionary we have for the New Testament.

To understand Greek words in the New Testament we may also need to consider ordinary everyday word usage in the first-century Greco-Roman world. Paul authored approximately 50% of the books in the New Testament. As an apostle to Greek-speaking Gentiles, he desired to shape those who had begun to follow Christ into new social communities. He understood that God's way is a whole new way to live, not a simple re-ordering of the *world's* way. Therefore, Paul was intent on providing direction to new Christ-followers about how they should re-orient their lives to walk out life according to their new identity *in* Christ.[16] To quote scholar Teresa Morgan, "New communities forming themselves within an existing culture do *not* typically take language in common use in the world around them and immediately assign to it radical new meanings.... This is all the more likely to be the case where the new community is a missionary one [as it was in Paul's case]. One does not communicate effectively with potential converts by using language in a way which they will not understand."[17] Paul "writes with what he assumes will be shared cultural assumptions regarding language and concepts that he uses without detailed explanation."[18] In other words, Paul, along with the other New Testament authors, would have chosen Greek words which already had common meaning to their audience. That cultural consideration may also supply important interpretive guidance

---

Louis Goulet, Email to Deborah Roeger March 27, 2022, citing the work of Isaac Oliver on Luke

16 Tucker, J. Brian, *Reading 1 Corinthians* (Cascade Books 2017) p. 4

17 Morgan, Teresa, *Roman Faith and Christian Faith: Pistis and Fides in the Early Roman Empire and Early Churches* (Oxford 2015) p. 4

18 Keener, Craig S., *Romans*, New Covenant Commentary (Cascade Books 2009) Introduction, p. 2

which will aid in our proper understanding of New Testament word meanings. When we fail to put biblical words in their proper historical, cultural context they end up getting lost in translation.

No matter what language we are discussing, it is common for words to have more than one meaning. The semantic range of a word is observed by its usage in various contexts. The more times a word is used in different ways, the broader its semantic range. As a result, scholars often advise that words do not mean anything outside of a context. My friend and research mentor Henri Goulet, shares this example he uses at the Messianic Studies Institute in Gahanna, Ohio. Take the English word "trunk: It could mean a host of things from an elephant's [nose], a suitcase, an ornamental chest, the rear compartment of a car, the main stem of a tree, the main part of a human body to which the head and appendages are connected, the principal channel of a tributary, or a circuit between two telephone exchanges."[19]

In the lessons in this study, Word Studies are not intended to explore the entire semantic range of a given word. Every author determines the meaning of a word by how he uses it within a context. The focus of each word studied will be narrowed by the specific context in which the author originally used that word in the particular passage we are studying. To that end, I will always seek to place Word Studies in original literary context as well as to add relevant cultural context where possible.

Refer to the supplement at the end of this study for helpful guidance on how to complete your own research of Hebrew and Greek words using free internet resources.

The Bible's Use of Ancient Near East Background: Because our lessons, where applicable, will seek to point out the histori-

---

19 Henri Louis Goulet, Academic Dean, Executive Director, & Faculty Messianic Studies Institute; Ph.D. Studies (Unfinished), University of Cape Town, Biblical Studies, 2007–2010; S.T.M., Capital University, Biblical Studies, 2007; M.A., Ashland University, Biblical Studies, 2003; B.S., The Ohio State University, Pharmaceutical Sciences, 1984

cal context for Scripture, I will include references to ancient Near Eastern[20] beliefs as appropriate. As Jewish scholar Nahum Sarna points out: "modern scholarship has shown that the Torah made use of very ancient traditions which it adapted to its own special purposes."[21] For example, there are poems in Proverbs that clearly depict creation in imagery and expressions drawn from ancient pagan myths.[22] When a biblical author used ideas and concepts from the ancient culture around him the purpose was to borrow from the imagery to make his communication clear. That does not mean that the author endorsed the original pagan theology.[23] As Sarna noted, "the [pagan] materials used have been transformed so as to become the vehicle for the transmission of completely new ideas" which are entirely consistent with the nature and character of Yahweh.[24] In fact, some scholars believe that the very purpose of "borrowing" from ancient Near Eastern concepts was to demonstrate the absolute superiority of Yahweh over every false god.[25] According to Jewish scholar Joshua Berman, "For weak and oppressed peoples, one form of cultural and spiritual resistance is

---

20 The ancient Near East is the region which includes modern Turkey, Syria, Lebanon, Israel, Palestine, Jordan, Egypt, Iraq and Iran. Important ancient civilizations in this region were the Egyptians, Arameans, Babylonians, Assyrians and Persians. Power, Cain, *Kingship in the Hebrew Bible*. Retrieved from https://www.sbl-site.org/assets/pdfs/TBv3i3_PowerKingship.pdf (last accessed August 8, 2021)

21 Sarna, Nahum M., *Understanding Genesis Through Rabbinic Tradition and Modern Scholarship* (The Jewish Theological Seminary 2015) p. 39

22 See for example: Proverbs 3:20; 8:29; 30:4; Waltke, Bruce K., *The Book of Proverbs: Chapters 1-15*, The New International Commentary on the Old Testament (Eerdmans 2004) Theology, p. 68

23 Waltke, Bruce K., *The Book of Proverbs Chapters 1-15*, The New International Commentary on the Old Testament (Eerdmans 2004) Theology, p. 68

24 Sarna, Nahum M., *Understanding Genesis Through Rabbinic Tradition and Modern Scholarship* (The Jewish Theological Seminary 2015) p. 4

25 See for example: Longman III and Garland, general editors, *The Expositor's Bible Commentary: Psalms*, Vol. 5, Revised Edition (Zondervan 2008) Reflections: Yahweh Is The Divine Warrior, p. 734

to appropriate the symbols of the oppressor and put them to competitive ideological purposes."²⁶

It is worth noting that not all scholars embrace the use of ancient literature outside the Bible itself to assist in biblical interpretation. Some argue that it is a dangerous practice. I am inclined to agree with Professor Jon D. Levenson, Harvard Divinity School, who rightly warns on the one hand that historical criticism should never replace "the more traditional modes of study within religious communities." On the other hand, he advises that neither should modern research of the Bible's historical context be "disregarded or neutralized." Instead, he advocates: "[T]he worthiest course … is one that combines the modern and the traditional modes of study in an intellectually honest and theologically sophisticated way."²⁷

---

26 Berman, Joshua, *Ani Maamin: Biblical Criticism, Historical Truth, and the Thirteen Principles of Faith* (Maggid Book 2020) p. 55. Berman points out during much of its early history "ancient Israel was in Egypt's shadow." Ibid., p. 55

27 Levenson, Jon D., *The Shema and the Commandment to Love God In Its Ancient Contexts*, TheTorah.com, August 14, 2016, last updated June 20, 2021. Retrieved from https://www.thetorah.com/article/the-shema-and-the-commandment-to-love-god-in-its-ancient-contexts (last accessed June 29, 2021)

LESSON 1:

GOD'S DESIRE TO DWELL AMONG US

"[Adam and Eve] heard the sound of the LORD God walking in the garden in the cool of the day ...." Genesis 3:8

IT IS NOT uncommon for our thoughts about God to be filled with notions about His holiness which often leads to a belief that God is far away, distant, lofty and unreachable. To many Christ-followers, God lives somewhere up there in heaven, while we struggle down here on earth. However, such views are entirely inconsistent with the biblical view of God.

Our Key Scripture describes God as personally *walking* (*halak* {haw-lak'}) in the garden with Adam and Eve. The original Hebrew text conveys the idea that God is engaging in this activity because He "*passionately desires* the perceived benefits (*personal* profit) connected with the action."[1] It also reveals that God's walking with Adam and Eve is a repeated action, not a one-time occurrence.[2] What is notable for purposes of our study is that this

1 Hill, Gary, *The Discovery Bible*, HELPS Ministries, Inc., explanation of Hithpael

2 When *mithallēk* in used in the *hithpael*, as it is in Genesis 3:8 (the actual form of the word *halak* used in Genesis 3:8 is *mithallēk*), it "indicates an intensive act of walking, one which is also iterative [repetitive]." Okyere, Kojo, *The Rhetoric Of Work In Provers [sic] 24:30-34*, University of Cape Coast, January 2013, p. 169, online PDF version provided by Research Gate.net. Retrieved from https://www.researchgate.net/publication/268518284_THE_RHETORIC_OF_WORK_IN_PROVERS_2430-34 (last accessed October 13, 2023). Original article "The

same Hebrew word is also used in the Bible to describe God's Presence in the Tabernacle.[3] Scholars suggest that when Genesis was written the author's intention was to picture Eden as the first temple where God met with man.[4]

Israel frequently recorded her memory of God's Presence among them throughout her history. "The memory of God's presence was persistent—but never static. Sometimes God [was] present in pillars of cloud and fire. Sometimes just in fire or a cloud. Sometimes God [was] present in an angel. Sometimes as the weight of God's glory.[5] Sometimes God [was] present in [what was called] God's face. And sometimes those agents [were] combined."[6] Moses rhetorically asked Israel, "For what great nation is there that has a god *so near* to it as is the LORD our God whenever we call on Him?"[7] Paul repeats the same truth when he introduces the men of Athens to the one true God.

> So Paul stood in the midst of the Areopagus and said, "Men of Athens, I observe that you are very religious in all respects. For while I was passing through and examining the objects of your worship, I also found an

---

Rhetoric of Work in Proverbs 24:30-34" printed in *Theoforum*, Vol. 44, Issue 1, 2013, pp. 157-171

[3] Beale, G. K., *The Temple and the Church's Mission: A Biblical Theology of The Dwelling Place of God* (InterVarsity Press 2004) p. 66, pointing out that *mithallēk* (used in Genesis 3:8) is also used in Leviticus 26:12; Deuteronomy 23:14[15] and 2 Samuel 7:6-7 to denote God's Presence in the Tabernacle

[4] Beale, G. K., *The Temple and the Church's Mission: A Biblical Theology of The Dwelling Place of God* (InterVarsity Press 2004) pp. 66-80

[5] In Lesson 4 we will further define the concept of God's glory, here I'll simply provide a quote from scholar Brevard Childs: "The glory of God (k^e *bôd YHWH*) is that aspect of the divine image which is made visible to human perception." Childs, Brevard S., *Isaiah*, Old Testament Library Commentary (Westminster John Knox Press 2001) Isaiah 40:3-5, p. 299

[6] Levison, John R., *The Holy Spirit Before Christianity* (Baylor University Press 2019) p. 8

[7] Deuteronomy 4:7, italics added

> altar with this inscription, 'TO AN UNKNOWN GOD.' Therefore what you worship in ignorance, this I proclaim to you. The God who made the world and all things in it, since He is Lord of heaven and earth, does not dwell in temples made with hands; nor is He served by human hands, as though He needed anything, since He Himself gives to all *people* life and breath and all things; and He made from one *man* every nation of mankind to live on all the face of the earth … that they would seek God … and find Him, though He is not far from each one of us …." Acts 17:22-27, italics in original

In reality, the Bible does much more than merely speak of God's nearness. The Bible repeatedly records God's desire to *dwell* among His people. The first instance is found in the exodus narrative.

> The LORD said, 'I have surely seen the affliction of My people … I am aware of their sufferings. So I have come down to deliver them …. They shall know that I am the LORD their God who brought them out of the land of Egypt, that **I might dwell among them**; I am the LORD their God.'" Exodus 3:7,8; 29:46, bold added

Throughout Israel's history God continues to communicate openly about His desire to dwell among them. We find other examples in such verses as:

> "… **I will dwell among the sons of Israel**, and will not forsake My people Israel." 1 Kings 6:13, bold added

> "…Sing for joy and be glad, O daughter of Zion; for behold I am coming and **I will dwell in your midst**," declares the LORD. Zechariah 2:10, bold added

> Thus says the LORD, "I will return to Zion and **will dwell in the midst of Jerusalem**. Then Jerusalem

will be called the City of Truth, and the mountain of the LORD of hosts *will be called* the Holy **Mountain**." Zechariah 8:3, italics in original, bold added

Let's use a Word Study to learn about the Hebrew word translated as *dwell*. Because this is our first Word Study in *My Dwelling Place*, I think it is important to remind you of something I pointed out in the Preface. "A primary principle in [biblical interpretation] is that the meaning of a passage is found in what the original author intended it to mean."[8] Word Studies are *not* intended to explore the entire semantic range of a given word. The focus of each word we study will be narrowed by the specific context in which the author originally used that word. "Of course, if we are seeking the meaning intended by the author to the original recipients, that meaning *must* be the meaning they could understand at the time, not the meaning we would determine based on our position of advanced historical developments."[9]

WORD STUDY

In each of these quoted verses, the Hebrew word translated as **dwell** *is shakan {shaw-kan'}. It means to settle down, abide, tabernacle, reside.*[10] *Shakan emphasizes the idea of "nearness and closeness" as opposed to "loftiness."*[11]

---

8 Firth and Wegner, "Introduction," in *Presence Power And Promise The Role of the Spirit of God in the Old Testament*, edited by Firth and Wegner (IVP Academic 2011) p. 18

9 Firth and Wegner, "Introduction," in *Presence Power And Promise The Role of the Spirit of God in the Old Testament*, edited by Firth and Wegner (IVP Academic 2011) p. 18, quoting Klein, Blomberg and Hubbard, *Introduction to Biblical Interpretation*, 2nd edition (Word 2004) p. 11, italics in original

10 Baker and Carpenter, *The Complete WordStudy Dictionary of the Old Testament* (AMG Publishers 2003) word #7931, p. 1140; Hill, Gary, *The Discovery Bible*, HELPS Ministries, Inc., [H]7931 shāḵan

11 Harris, Archer, and Waltke, editors, *Theological Wordbook of the Old Testament* (Moody Press 1999) word #2387, p. 925

My Dwelling Place

> *"This same root provides the core for the name of the transient presence of God that later Judaism would identify as the Shekinah (šĕkînāh)."*[12] *Shekinah is not found in the Bible but is introduced in other Jewish literature such as the Talmud.*[13] *It refers to the visual manifestation of the Presence of Yahweh often seen as fire, cloud or light. Shekinah describes the cloud of God's glory over the Holy of Holies which was first present in the wilderness Tabernacle and later in the Temple. It is indicative of the nearness of God.*[14]

Shakan is a verb. Its noun form is *mishkan* {mish-kawn'}. While we may not be familiar with this Hebrew word, we most likely recognize the English translation "tabernacle." The place where God chose to tabernacle with His people was the Tent structure Moses was commanded to build in the wilderness (called the Tabernacle). Until the more permanent Temple was built by King Solomon, the Tabernacle was viewed as the dwelling place for God's Presence among His people. In fact, the term *"mishkan* places the emphasis on the representative presence of God."[15]

---

12 Meier, Sam, *Eden-Tabernacle-Temple-Community*, Messianic Studies Institute, Lesson 4 written summary received via e-mail November 17, 2022. Dr. Meier holds his Ph.D., Harvard University, Hebrew & Semitic Languages and Literatures, 1987; Th.M., Dallas Theological Seminary, Old Testament and Semitics; B.A., UCLA, Ancient Near Eastern Civilization. Dr. Meier began teaching at the Ohio State University in 1986 in the Department of Near Eastern Languages and Cultures. He also serves as Adjunct Professor of History, where he teaches the History of Ancient Israel.

13 The Talmud is the written version of the Jewish oral Law along with written commentaries on that Law.

14 Keener, Craig S., *1 Peter: A Commentary* (Baker Academic 2021) 1 Peter 1:7, p. 79

15 Vines, W. E., *Vine's Expository Dictionary of OT Words* (1940) entry for *Tabernacle*. Retrieved from https://www.studylight.org/dictionaries/eng/vot/t/tabernacle.html (last accessed November 25, 2022)

> Moreover, I will make My dwelling [*mishkan*] among you, and My soul will not reject you. I will also walk [*halak*] among you and be your God, and you shall be My people. Leviticus 26:11-12

Recognizing the fact that *mishkan* and *shakan* derive from the same Hebrew root deepens our understanding of the concept of God's dwelling. At a time in history when God's Covenant people lived in desert tents, God instructed Moses to pitch a tent for Him so He could reside among them in a tent!

The concept of God dwelling or tabernacling with His people is also found in the New Testament. The Apostle John picks up the theme in both the Gospel of John and Revelation. In each case, John uses the Greek word *skenoo* {skay-no'-o}. It has a meaning similar to *shakan* and is found in verses such as:

> And the Word became flesh, and **dwelt** [*skenoo*] among us, and we saw His glory, glory as of the only begotten from the Father, full of grace and truth. John 1:14, bold added

> For this reason, they are before the throne of God; and they serve Him day and night in His temple; and He who sits on the throne will spread His **tabernacle** [*skenoo*] over them. Revelation 7:15, bold added

> And I heard a loud voice from the throne, saying, "Behold, the tabernacle of God is among men, and He will **dwell** [*skenoo*] among them, and they shall be His people, and God Himself will be among them ...." Revelation 21:3, bold added

My Dwelling Place

WORD STUDY

*As noted, the Greek word in these verses which is variously translated as **dwelt, tabernacle,** or **dwell** is skenoo {skay-no'-o} from skenos {skay'-nos} meaning tent, abode. The verb skenoo means to live or dwell in a tent, to reside, encamp, to have an abode.[16]*

Skenoo is used in the Greek Old Testament for the Tabernacle of God. That Tabernacle was viewed as a symbol of God's protection as well as a place of communion with Him.[17]

John is the only New Testament author to use the word *skenoo*.[18] Interestingly, *katoikeo* {kat-oy-keh'-o} is a more common Greek word for dwelling.[19] The fact that John doesn't choose that common word suggests he had a specific purpose in mind for choosing *skenoo*. As noted in our Word Study, *skenoo* is derived

---

16 Zodhiates, Spiros, *The Complete Word Study Dictionary: New Testament* (AMG Publishers 1992) word #4637, p. 1294; Bromiley, Geoffrey W., *Theological Dictionary of the New Testament*, Abridged in One Volume (Eerdmans 1985) entry for *skene* under *skenoo*, p. 1043; Mounce, Bill, *Greek Dictionary*, entry for σκηνόω, *skēnoō*. Retrieved from https://www.billmounce.com/greek-dictionary/skenoo (last accessed September 23, 2022)

17 Hill, Gary, *The Discovery Bible*, HELPS Ministries, Inc. Cognate: [G]4637 *skēnóō*; *John 1:14-18 Commentary*, Precept Austin. Retrieved from http://preceptaustin.org/john_114-18_commentary (last accessed July 17, 2021)

18 *Skenoo* is employed five times in the New Testament, all by the apostle John. See: John 1:14, Revelation 7:15; 12:12; 13:6; 21:3

19 The Greek verb *katoikeo* {kat-oy-keh'-o} means to live, dwell, inhabit. According to Mounce it is used 44 times in the New Testament (as compared to John's five uses of *skenoo*). Mounce, William D., editor, *Complete Expository Dictionary of Old & New Testament Words* (Zondervan 2006) entry for *Dwell*, p. 201

from the word that means "tent" and is used in the Greek translation of the Old Testament to refer to the Tabernacle of God. John apparently bypasses *katoikeo* and chooses *skenoo* because it provides the precise association he is looking for.[20] This association with the Old Testament Tabernacle is critically important and is easy to get lost in translation. According to John 1:14, "[Jesus] become flesh and *tabernacled* among us."[21] In the exodus from Egypt to the Promised Land, Moses and the Israelites pitched a tent for Yahweh to dwell among them in the wilderness. Centuries later, God "pitched a tent" for Himself to dwell among His people by sending Jesus.[22] John wants his readers to see that Jesus became the new earthly point or place of God's dwelling with Israel just as He had dwelt with them in the Tabernacle in the desert.[23] In other words, John declares that the *Shekinah* glory of God which had previously been limited to the physical Tabernacle (Exodus 40:34) became visible in Christ (John 1:14b).[24]

This is a good place to park for a moment and discuss the biblical notion of God's Presence. In this study, we will be focusing on God's Dwelling-Presence, however, His Dwelling-Presence is not the only Presence described in Scripture. The Bible actually denotes two other types of divine Presence, God's Omnipresence and His Manifest-Presence. A.W. Tozer points out that the manifestation of God's Presence is not the same as His Omnipresence.

---

20 Köstenberger, Andreas J., "John," in *Zondervan Illustrated Bible Backgrounds Commentary*, Vol. 4, edited by Clinton E. Arnold (Zondervan 2002) And made his dwelling among us (John 1:14) p. 10
21 Italics added
22 "Dwelt among us means more literally 'pitched his tent' (Gk. *skēnoō*), an allusion to God's dwelling among the Israelites in the tabernacle (cf. Ex. 25:8-9; 33:7)." *ESV Study Bible* (Crossway Books 2008) study note John 1:14 under *Dwelt among us*, p. 2020
23 Beale and Carson, editors, *Commentary on the New Testament Use of the Old Testament* (Baker Academic 2007) The Prologue (John 1:1-18) p. 422
24 *What does it mean that the Word became flesh?* ZA blog, Zondervan Academic, March 26, 2018, *post adapted from Gary Burge's online course on the book of John*. Retrieved from https://zondervanacademic.com/blog/word-became-flesh (last accessed July 17, 2021)

My Dwelling Place 9

"God is [Omnipresent] when we are wholly unaware of it. He is manifest only when and as we are aware of his presence."[25] God's Omnipresence speaks of the fact that He is fully Present everywhere in His creation at the same time (Psalm 139:7-10).[26] On the other hand, His Manifest-Presence refers to God making His Presence known to us by revealing Himself in "sensory form."[27] That is, His self-manifestation is in a form which is recognizable by one or more of our human senses. Old Testament examples include the smoking firepot and flaming torch that walked through the blood-filled trench to make Covenant with Abraham (Genesis 15:17-18) and God's self-revelation to all of Israel in fire and smoke at Sinai (Exodus 19:17-19). God answered Moses in the thunder of Mt. Sinai (Exodus 19:19) and centuries later He revealed Himself to Elijah in a whisper on that same mountain (1 Kings 19:12-13).

Now, let's turn our attention to God's *Dwelling*-Presence. As we have already pointed out, the Garden of Eden is pictured as the place where God initially dwelled among His creation. However, the first biblical instruction regarding God's dwelling place is recorded in the Exodus narrative. When God speaks to the issue, the original Hebrew text makes clear that His desire to have a habitation among His people is not an afterthought on His part. It is a central theme of His Covenant relationship with Israel.

---

25 *The Presence of God*, Broadcast Christ Church Manchester, thebroadcastnetwork.org. Retrieved from https://thebroadcastnetwork.org/the-presence-of-god/#:~:text=Manifest%20Presence%20A.%20W.%20Tozer%20Quote%3A%20%E2%80%9CThe%20presence,and%20as%20we%20are%20aware%20of%20his%20presence.%E2%80%9D (last accessed January 13, 2022)
26 The prefix omni means all. God is all present. To say God is Omnipresent means He is simultaneously present at all times with all His fullness to every part of creation. He is always available to us. We are not able to escape from His Omnipresence. Hanegraff, Hank, *Explaining God's Omnipresence*, The Bible Answer Man, 8/5/2015. Retrieved from https://www.youtube.com/watch?v=KfsfupNwEoA (last accessed January 13, 2022)
27 Bromiley, Geoffrey W., *Theological Dictionary of the New Testament*, Abridged in One Volume (Eerdmans 1985) entry for *morphe* under *C. The Form of God in the OT and Judaism*, p. 608

Let them construct a **sanctuary** [*miqdash*] for Me, **that I may dwell** [*shakan*] among them. Exodus 25:8, bold added

In Exodus 25:8 God commands Moses to construct a Sanctuary that will become God's dwelling place among Israel. Here we will be aided by a short Word Study.

> ## WORD STUDY
>
> *The word **sanctuary** is the Hebrew word miqdash {mik-dawsh'}. Miqdash comes from the root word qadash which means to be hallowed, sanctified, holy.*[28] *Thus, a miqdash is a "'set apart space,' or a 'holy place' that represents something treasured." It is a place of refuge and rest.*[29]
>
> *Biblically, miqdash denotes the place of God's Presence.*[30]

This command to build a dwelling place for God's Presence reflects "a heartbeat (peak) of the spiritual plotline"[31] in the exodus narrative. What is being highlighted for the reader is the fact that God's desire to *shakan*/dwell among His people is the whole crux

---

28 Harris, Archer, and Waltke, editors, *Theological Wordbook of the Old Testament* (Moody Press 1999) word #1990f, p. 786
29 Parsons, John J., *Sanctuary of the Heart, Further Thoughts on Parashat Terumah*, Hebrew for Christians. Retrieved from http://www.hebrew4christians.com /Scripture/Parashah/Summaries/Terumah/Sanctuary/sanctuary. html (last accessed July 10, 2021)
30 *Easton's Bible Dictionary*, entry for *sanctuary*. Retrieved from https://www.blueletterbible.org/search/dictionary/viewtopic.cfm?topic=ET0003213 (last accessed September 5, 2023)
31 Hill, Gary, *The Discovery Bible*, HELPS Ministries, Inc., explanation of Conjunctive Perfect

of the command! Throughout the biblical record we see that the intensity of God's desire to dwell among us is so powerful that He makes great and repeated effort for its provision.

Before we conclude this lesson, I want to point out the obvious. God's desire is described as "dwelling" not as visiting, vacationing or momentarily stopping by. In our English language the word "dwell" carries an ordinary meaning of a longer or more permanent stay rather than the activity of coming and going or the brevity of a "visit." The Greek word choices for "dwell" which were used by the interpreters who first translated the Old Testament Hebrew into the Greek language reflect this notion of security and longevity. We have already learned that one Greek word that is used biblically to translate *shakan* is *skenoo*. However, the Old Testament translators used the intensified verb *kataskenoo* twice as often as *skenoo*.[32] Why does that matter to us? It is important because *kataskenoo* can refer to settling permanently.[33] In a number of its' uses the word is intended to stress the security and lasting nature of the stay.[34] That is to say, the translators understood that the original Hebrew text describes God's dwelling as much more than an occasional overnight stop!

In the ancient Near East, the land of the Old Testament, there was nothing unusual about a deity setting aside sacred space

---

32 Harris, Archer, and Waltke, editors, *Theological Wordbook of the Old Testament* (Moody Press 1999) word #2387, p. 925

33 *Kataskenoo* (from *kata* = down + *skenoo* = pitch one's tent) is frequently found in the Septuagint and generally stresses the thought of a longer stay. Bromiley, Geoffrey W., *Theological Dictionary of the New Testament*, Abridged in One Volume (Eerdmans 1985) entry for *skene* under *kataskenoo*, p. 1043; Harris, Archer, and Waltke, editors, *Theological Wordbook of the Old Testament* (Moody Press 1999) word #2387, p. 925, concluding that *kataskenoo* is used approximately twice as often as *skenoo* to translate *shakan*, perhaps to stress the idea of a longer, more permanent stay

34 Bromiley, Geoffrey W., *Theological Dictionary of the New Testament*, Abridged in One Volume (Eerdmans 1985) entry for *skene* under *kataskenoo*, p. 1043, citing e.g., Numbers 14:30; Deuteronomy 33:12; Psalm 16:9; Proverbs 1:12

for habitation. In fact, the concept of sacred space was universally important for those societies.[35]

> It was the place where heaven met earth and had to be treated accordingly. What we call temples are typically referred to as the 'house' of a deity[36] .... These houses served partly as a visible reminder to the members of a society that their patron god or goddess was present with them.

God's desire has been to take up permanent residence among His creation. He wants to make His eternal abode among His people. Notably, as we will see, the main purpose of His dwelling among us is not so we can care for Him, but that He might fellowship with us and provide for us! In our next lesson we will consider the *place* God chose to dwell.

Hear What The Spirit is Saying to the Church: *Since the beginning of time it has been my desire to dwell among my creation. It is for that very purpose that I created. The earth and the fullness thereof is mine; but man has not thought so. Man, those I have created in my very image, have persisted in their rebellion. If only he knew, if only he understood that what would bring the satisfaction he seeks is found in me alone. How my heart longs to be present in the midst of my creation. The longing of my heart can only be satisfied as I dwell among my people. Does man not understand my longing? Does he not see that I desire to be with him? Does he not care that it is so? But I will move heaven and earth, I will move the very mountains I have made in order to fulfill the longing of my heart. It is not that I am a selfish God, it is that I created man in such a*

---

35 Wells, Bruce, "Exodus," in *Zondervan Illustrated Bible Backgrounds Commentary*, Vol. 1, edited by John H. Walton (Zondervan 2009) Exodus 25:8, p. 247

36 In keeping with this ancient understanding there are times in the Bible when the Tabernacle is referred to as "the house of Yawheh." See for example: Exodus 23:19; 34:26; Deuteronomy 23:18; Joshua 6:24

way that only by his dwelling with me will he find satisfaction. And my greatest joy is to see my creation delighted. I will be the delight of my creation. The time has come for it to be so. I will once again come down to dwell among my people. Not in a Tabernacle or Temple made by hands, no that is too small and insufficient for what I desire to do. I will make my dwelling place in the midst of those who have made me not only savior, but Lord. I will dwell among those who have chosen me above all else. I will dwell in the midst of those who delight in doing my will. Those are the ones who know me, truly know me and because they do I will abide with them. I will come and make my home with them and they will take great delight in what delights me. And I shall make my permanent dwelling place among them. Never again will I send them out of my Presence. I will meet every need. Will you hear what the Spirit is saying to the church? What will your response be?

Lesson 2:

The Resting Place God Desires

 "[Israel] set out from the mountain of the Lord on a three-day journey with the ark of the Lord's covenant traveling ahead of them for those three days to seek a resting place for them." Numbers 10:33 HCSB

IN OUR FIRST lesson we learned that contrary to popular opinion, God is not a distant, far off God. He is a God who draws near to His people and desires to tabernacle among them. In this lesson we will consider "the place" God chooses to dwell. As we will see, the resting place He seeks for His Covenant people mirrors the resting place He desires for Himself among them.

If we are going to understand God's plan to dwell among His people, then we need to go all the way back to the creation story. In Genesis we learn God created the heavens and the earth. He prepared the Garden as a dwelling place for Himself on earth and He created man to dwell there with Him. After God finished creating, the Bible tells us "He rested." He ceased creating because He had created the dwelling place where He intended to rest forever among His creation. In this we learn a foundational truth about the place God chooses to dwell. God desires a *resting place* if He is going to dwell among His creation.

> ### WORD STUDY
>
> *The Hebrew word for* **resting place**, *as used in our Key Scripture, is menuha {men-oo-khaw}. The root nuah denotes absence of movement and the presence of security.[1] It can refer to a condition/state of rest or to the fact of being settled in a particular place.[2] Menuha describes the presence of peace, quietness and trust.*
>
> *It denotes a particular place where work and wandering have ceased so the condition of rest can be enjoyed in the sense of stillness and rejuvenation.[3] In 1 Kings 8:56, for example, menuha refers to the land being at rest because Israel was at rest from all her enemies.*
>
> *The rest of God cannot coexist with uncleanness and corruption.[4]*

Our Key Scripture refers to the resting place Yahweh desired to give His Covenant people. When Yahweh announced the resting place He had chosen for Himself among Israel, He used the same word *menuha*.

> For [Yahweh] has **chosen** [Jerusalem]; He has **desired** it for His habitation. "This is My resting place

---

[1] Harris, Archer, and Waltke, editors, *Theological Wordbook of the Old Testament* (Moody Press 1999) word # 1323f, p. 562
[2] Harris, Archer, and Waltke, editors, *Theological Wordbook of the Old Testament* (Moody Press 1999) word # 1323f under *menuha*, p. 562
[3] Baker, David W., "Isaiah," in *Zondervan Illustrated Bible Backgrounds Commentary*, Vol. 4, edited by John H. Walton (Zondervan 2009) Isaiah 66:1, p. 186; Hill, Gary, *The Discovery Bible*, HELPS Ministries, Inc., [H]4496 *menuḥâ*
[4] Baker and Carpenter, *The Complete WordStudy Dictionary of the Old Testament* (AMG Publishers 2003) word #4496, p. 628

My Dwelling Place

[*menuha*] forever; Here I will dwell, for I have **desired** it." Psalm 132:13-14, bold added

The word "chosen" which is highlighted in bold is the Hebrew word *bachar* {baw-khar'} which infers that God's choice resulted from a thorough examination, taking a "keen look at" the options in order to make His selection.[5] Both uses of the word "desired" in these verses from Psalm 132 are a translation of the Hebrew verb *'avah* {aw-vaw'}. While *'avah* can refer to preferring or being inclined, it can also mean covet or long for.[6]

God's rest refers to "the place where He fixes his presence."[7] Scholars view God's resting place and His dwelling place as being synonymous.[8] As a result, it will be helpful for us to dig a little deeper into the concept of the resting place God desires for His Covenant people and the mirror image that it provides for His own resting place. The Bible teaches that the ultimate rest God seeks for His Covenant people is not limited to physical rest. He also desires them to find spiritual rest in Him.[9] Only as they rest *in* Him can He rest (dwell) *with* them! In short, His Covenant people enter the rest He offers them through a lifestyle of enduring faith and obedience.[10] When those characteristics are present

---

5 Harris, Archer, and Waltke, editors, *Theological Wordbook of the Old Testament* (Moody Press 1999) word #231, p. 100
6 Harris, Archer, and Waltke, editors, *Theological Wordbook of the Old Testament* (Moody Press 1999) word #40, p. 18
7 Bromiley, Geoffrey W., *Theological Dictionary of the New Testament*, Abridged in One Volume (Eerdmans 1985) entry for *katapauo* under *katapausis*, p. 420
8 Longman III and Garland, general editors, *The Expositor's Bible Commentary: Psalms*, Vol. 5, Revised Edition (Zondervan 2008) Psalm 132:7-8, p. 927
9 See in particular Psalm 95 (the word "rest" in verse 11 is Hebrew *menuha* translated into Greek in the LXX as *anapausis*); Hebrews 4:1-11 (the word "rest" in verses 1,3,5,10,11 is the Greek word *katapausis* which is also used in the LXX to translate *menuha*)
10 Cockerill, Gareth Lee, *The Epistle to the Hebrews*, New International Commentary on the New Testament (Eerdmans 2012) Hebrews 4:1, p. 202 and 4:2, p. 203

in His Covenant people, God is able to find His resting place – His dwelling place – among them. He will fix His Presence in that place.

As we consider the biblical understanding of God's desired resting place it becomes easy to see why the Garden of Eden could no longer be God's dwelling place after Adam and Eve chose Satan's plan over God's plan. Trust had been broken and darkness had come into the place that was previously only filled with Light. Because of sin, the Garden was no longer a place where God could rest. The consequences are well known as it relates to God's action concerning Adam and Eve. They were cast out of the Garden and their re-entry was blocked forever by cherubim and the flaming sword that turned every direction guarding the way to the tree of life.[11]

Have you ever considered what changed for God? It appears that His abode was thereafter made in the heavens[12] and the concept of "holiness" is first introduced to creation. Thereafter the Old Testament supplies more than sufficient foundation to identify God's heavenly dwelling place as the true Sanctuary which is merely replicated on earth by the Tabernacle or Temple.[13] In fact, as a side note, I'll mention here that in ancient Jewish thought, after Adam and Eve sinned and were banned from the Garden of Eden, "this Edenic paradise was then taken up to heaven" and is awaiting God's eternal plan for those who are faithful.[14] The main

---

11 Genesis 3:24
12 In the ancient Near East it was commonly thought that the temple for a god was "rooted in the cosmic realm (either in the realm below the earth's surface or in heaven)." Hilber, John W., "Psalms," in *Zondervan Illustrated Bible Backgrounds Commentary*, Vol. 5, edited by John H. Walton (Zondervan 2009) Psalm 78:69, p. 386
13 Cockerill, Gareth Lee, *The Epistle to the Hebrews*, New International Commentary on the New Testament (Eerdmans 2012) Hebrews 8:2, p. 352, citing the following Old Testament references in footnote 12: Psalms 11:4; 18:7; 29:9; Isaiah 6; Micah 1:2; Habakuk 2:20
14 Osborne, Grant, *Revelation* (Baker Academic 2002) Revelation 22:1-5 under *C. New Jerusalem as the Final Eden*, p. 768, citing *T. Levi* 18.10-11; *T. Dan* 5.12-13; *2 Bar.* 4:3-7

point I want to make here is that the first time we see the concept of holiness in the Bible is *after* the mention of the first sin.

The Hebrew word *qodesh* {ko'-desh}, commonly translated as "holy," fundamentally refers to that which is separate or set apart.[15] God's holiness is a theme which runs through the Old Testament denoting that "which separates him from all that is not in harmony with his character."[16] The first time we are formally introduced to the notion of God's holiness is at the beginning of the exodus narrative. As Moses approached the burning bush to see a fire he had never seen before, God called out to him from the middle of that bush. The Hebrew verb used to forbid Moses from *approaching* too closely is the same word that was often used in the Old Testament as a "technical term to describe an approach to the Presence of God in worship."[17] Moses was told to remove his sandals because the place on which he was standing is "*qodesh* ground."[18] The only thing that made the dirt under his feet any different than all the other dirt in that area is that God Himself was present in the midst of that burning bush! His Presence is what made that place *qodesh*.

Before sin, there was no need for holiness. Everything God had created was good and without the stain of sin. After Adam chose to do what God had specifically forbidden, a distinction had to be made. God needed to distinguish between that which is impure, cursed, wicked, polluted, evil, worldly, unholy and that which is pure, undefiled, clean, lacking in corruption – in sum, that which is set apart by Him for Him. Because sin was intro-

---

15 Williams, J. R., "Holiness," in *Evangelical Dictionary of Theology*, 2nd edition, edited by Walter A. Elwell (Baker Academic 1984, 2001) entry for *Holiness* under *In the OT*, p. 562
16 Harris, Archer, and Waltke, editors, *Theological Wordbook of the Old Testament* (Moody Press 1999) word #1169, p. 497
17 Durham, John I., *Word Biblical Commentary: Exodus*, Volume 3 (Word Books 1987) Exodus 3:4-5 under *Comment*, p. 31
18 Exodus 3:5

duced on earth, "creation is affected by divine abandonment."[19] As a result, the things of earth began to be ordered in a new way. God put in place a non-negotiable and unyielding distinction to differentiate between that which is holy and sacred, where He could rest, and that which is common or profane. People can dwell in the profane, but God cannot. "For I am God and not man, the Holy One in your midst."[20]

God's dwelling embodies peace, order, tranquility and perfect rest. On the other hand, whenever sin is present there is chaos, turmoil and confusion. God is resolute and persistently faithful so His plan to dwell among His creation did not stop at the edge of the Garden. However, we begin to see in the biblical account that the distinction between holiness and unholiness must now be taken into consideration in God's plan to create a dwelling place for Himself among His people. Because of "God's total apartness"[21] from all that is evil and unclean, He can only dwell where there is accommodation for His separateness from that which is now ruled by the kingdom of darkness.[22]

With man's dwelling place on earth and God's dwelling place now in heaven, God begins His plan of restoration – a return to Eden where He can find a resting place among His people once more. In fact, that's the unfolding biblical story from Genesis Chapter 4 all the way through Revelation where we read:

> Then I saw a new heaven and a new earth; for the first heaven and the first earth passed away, and there is no longer *any* sea. And I saw the holy city, new Jerusalem, coming down out of heaven from God, made ready as a bride adorned for her husband. And I heard a loud

---

19 Longman III and Garland, general editors, *The Expositor's Bible Commentary: Psalms*, Vol. 5, Revised Edition (Zondervan 2008) *Reflections: Anger In The Psalms*, p. 645
20 Hosea 11:9b
21 Elwell, Walter A., editor, *Evangelical Dictionary of Theology*, 2nd edition (Baker Academic 1984, 2001) entry for *Holiness* under *In the OT*, p. 562
22 Isaiah 60:2; Acts 26:18; Colossians 1:13

My Dwelling Place

voice from the throne, saying, "Behold, the tabernacle of God is among men, and He will dwell among them, and they shall be His people, and God Himself will be among them, and He will wipe away every tear from their eyes; and there will no longer be *any* death; there will no longer be *any* mourning, or crying, or pain; the first things have passed away.' And He who sits on the throne said, 'Behold, I am making all things new.'" Revelation 21:1-5a, italics in original

What John saw and recorded in Revelation is God's finished plan. Once again, a resting place has been created for His Presence to dwell among His people. All things are new. It is a return to Eden and there is no longer a need to maintain the distinction between holy and unholy. There is nothing to be set apart from. Everything is once again perfect and filled with the goodness of God. There is no sin. The rule and reign of the Kingdom of Light, God's eternal Kingdom, is uncontested. There is no more darkness. But we're not there yet! There are important lessons for us as we trace God's Dwelling-Presence from Genesis to Revelation. So, let's begin. As we do, it is helpful to keep in mind that throughout this study the terms "kingdom" and "Kingdom" will be used as verbal nouns.[23] I intend them to refer to "*act* of ruling" – the rule, reign, authority and sovereignty of a king rather than a geographic place.[24] When I capitalize the "K" in "Kingdom" I am

---

23 France, R. T., *The Gospel of Matthew*, New International Commentary on the New Testament (Eerdmans 2007) Matthew 4:23, p. 151. In the New Testament "kingdom" refers to the "reign [of a king]". It is used as a "verbal noun to describe God ruling." Ibid. See also: France, R. T., *Divine Government: God's Kingship In The Gospel of Mark* (Regent College Publishing 1990) pp. 12-13

24 "It is a scholarly commonplace to point out that whereas 'kingdom' in English is today primarily a 'concrete' noun, with a clearly identifiable 'thing' to which it refers (whether a place of a community), the biblical nouns are abstract, and refer to the *act* of ruling, the situation of being king – as did the word 'kingdom' in the sixteenth-century English from which it has entered our biblical tradition." France, R. T., *Divine Government: God's*

referring to the *Kingdom of God* which "points to *God* in control, *God* working out his purposes."[25]

The biblical account describes God's plan for a Covenant people. He begins with Abraham, who is called out from among his people. Abraham (then called Abram) was set apart by God and sent to the place God had chosen.[26] Abraham then became the father of Isaac, who became the father of Jacob, who became the father of 12 sons, each of which was the head of a tribe in the family of Israel (Jacob's new name). According to God's plan, Jacob took his entire family to join Joseph in Egypt to find salvation and rest during a severe famine in the land. They grow and multiply and become a mighty nation of people. Pharaoh enslaved them, but God came to redeem them, lead them out to the Land of Promise and make them His Covenant people. His desire was for them to be His *segullah*[27] – His treasured people, His bride. In the exodus story we begin to see clear expressions of God's dwelling desire. Every memory recorded by the Hebrew people about the exodus experience included the appearance of God's Presence.[28] The Hebrew people were convinced beyond any doubt that it was Yahweh who acted on their behalf to release them from Egyptian captivity and destroy the Egyptian army at the Red Sea. They knew Yahweh was leading them as they walked out of Egypt headed for the Promised Land. In "a fluid interchange between symbol, representative, and God himself,"[29] the Bible identifies

---

Kingship In The Gospel of Mark (Regent College Publishing 1990) p. 12, italics in original

25 France, R. T., *Divine Government: God's Kingship In The Gospel of Mark* (Regent College Publishing 1990) p. 13, italics in original

26 Genesis 12:1

27 *Segullah* denotes that God cherishes Israel because of "His personal stake in her." Tigay, Jeffrey H., *The JPS Torah Commentary: Deuteronomy*, The Traditional Hebrew Text with the New JPS Translation Commentary (The Jewish Publication Society 1996) Deuteronomy 7:6, p. 87

28 Levison, John R., *The Holy Spirit Before Christianity* (Baylor University Press 2019) p. 7

29 Durham, John I., *Word Biblical Commentary: Exodus*, Volume 3 (Word Books 1987) Exodus 3:2-3 under *Comment*, p. 31

the angel of God along with an alternating day cloud pillar and a night fire pillar as guiding Israel's safe passage.[30] That is to say, Israel was able to travel by day or night and God's Presence was always with them to lead the way.

God's glory then manifested at Mt. Sinai where He met with Moses and all the people. It is the only time in recorded history that God's voice was heard by an entire nation of people at the same time! God provided the terms of His Covenant relationship with all of the people while they were standing at the foot of the mountain. He spoke His marriage vows to them and in one accord they all said "we do!"[31] Describing the relationship between Yahweh and Israel in wedding terms is a common biblical theme.[32] Israel is referred to as a "bride" ten times in the Bible – Song of

---

30 Exodus 14:19; "The LORD was going before them in a pillar of cloud by day to lead them on the way, and in a pillar of fire by night to give them light, that they might travel by day and by night. He did not take away the pillar of cloud by day, nor the pillar of fire by night, from before the people." Exodus 13:21-22

31 " All the people answered together and said, 'All that the LORD has spoken we will do!' And Moses brought back the words of the people to the LORD." Exodus 19:8. See also: Exodus 24:3 "Then Moses came and recounted to the people all the words of the LORD and all the ordinances; and all the people answered with one voice and said, 'All the words which the LORD has spoken we will do!'"

32 "The likening of ADONAI's taking Israel as his nation to a marriage is significant. See for example, Isa 16:59–60, 54:5; Hosea 1:1–3:5; Mal 2:11–12; Jer 3:3–20, 31:32; Ezek 16:59–60." Hillel, Vered, *The Wedding at Cana and the Glory of God*, Kesher Journal, Issue 39, Summer/Fall 2021, footnote 16. Retrieved from https://www.kesherjournal.com/article/the-wedding-at-cana-and-the-glory-of-god/ (last accessed October 17, 2023). Dr. Vered Hillel is the Academic Dean of Messianic Jewish Theological Institute. She holds a PhD and an MA in Second Temple Jewish literature from the Hebrew University of Jerusalem. Her areas of interest are Second Temple Judaism and literature, the Backgrounds to Early Christianity, Jewish/Christian Relations, and Messianic Jewish Theology. Kesher is a journal of Messianic Judaism, published by the Messianic Jewish Theological Institute.

Solomon: six times; Isaiah: three times and Jeremiah: one time.[33] The Jewish wedding custom that the bride and groom symbolizes the marriage of God and Israel stems from viewing Israel's Mt. Sinai encounter with Yahweh as a wedding ceremony.[34]

In our Word Study we looked at the Hebrew word *menuha* translated as "resting place." Interestingly, the Bible uses this same word to speak of a resting place in the context of marriage. In Ruth 1:9a we read: "May the LORD grant that you [my widowed daughters-in-law] may find rest (or a resting place) [*menuha*] each in the house of her husband." In a marital context we could say that the idea of a resting place includes marital provision and fidelity. As God and the people recited their "marriage vows" at the foot of Mt. Sinai, God was setting forth the terms of a resting place for Himself as a Husband for the Hebrew people.[35]

"Exodus 19 is replete with wedding imagery, especially according to Second Temple wedding customs."[36] However, thinking of Israel's Mt. Sinai experience as a wedding ceremony might be an entirely new thought to you. As a result, it's worth taking a few minutes to look at just a few of the details that correspond with what is known about ancient Jewish wedding custom. We'll begin with a detail found in Exodus 19:

---

33 Hillel, Vered, *The Wedding at Cana and the Glory of God*, Kesher Journal, Issue 39, Summer/Fall 2021, footnote 17, citing *Yalchut Shimoni* on Isaiah 61:10. Retrieved from https://www.kesherjournal.com/article/the-wedding-at-cana-and-the-glory-of-god/ (last accessed October 17, 2023)

34 Hillel, Vered, *The Wedding at Cana and the Glory of God*, Kesher Journal, Issue 39, Summer/Fall 2021. Retrieved from https://www.kesherjournal.com/article/the-wedding-at-cana-and-the-glory-of-god/ (last accessed October 17, 2023)

35 These wedding vows are more commonly referred to as the Mosaic or the Mt. Sinai Covenant.

36 Hillel, Vered, *The Wedding at Cana and the Glory of God*, Kesher Journal, Issue 39, Summer/Fall 2021. Retrieved from https://www.kesherjournal.com/article/the-wedding-at-cana-and-the-glory-of-god/ (last accessed October 17, 2023)

The LORD also said to Moses, "Go to the people and consecrate them today and tomorrow, and let them wash their garments; and let them be ready for the third day, for on the third day the LORD will come down on Mount Sinai in the sight of all the people...." So Moses went down from the mountain to the people and consecrated the people, and they washed their garments. He said to the people, "Be ready for the third day; do not go near a woman." Exodus 19:10-11,14-15

In preparation for her betrothal or wedding ceremony, a Jewish woman enters a *mikveh* which in Hebrew refers to a gathering or pool of water for the purpose of ritual cleansing. That's exactly what takes place in God's wedding story. Moses made his second ascent up Mt. Sinai to tell Yahweh that Israel accepted His marriage proposal. When Moses came back down he instructed Israel to prepare herself to meet her Bridegroom. At this point in the exodus story we see Israel washing her clothes to consecrate herself for the betrothal ceremony that will take place on the third day. However, this is not a picture of Israel doing her laundry. To begin with, the phrase "and consecrate them" (other translations "and sanctify them") is a translation of the original Hebrew *kidashtem*. It is related to *kiddushin* which is the Hebrew term for the wedding. More specifically, *kidashtem* "refers to an ethical sanctification that includes … immersion in a mikveh."[37] Ezekiel seems to understand Israel's sanctification in Exodus 19:10 as a *mikveh*, a part of the marriage process: "I made my vow to you and entered into a covenant with you, declares the Lord GOD, and you became mine. Then I bathed you with water …. (Ezekiel 16:8b-9 ESV)." There is scholarly support to interpret the reference to Israel bathing with water as part of

---

37 Hillel, Vered, *The Wedding at Cana and the Glory of God*, Kesher Journal, Issue 39, Summer/Fall 2021, citing *Seder Eliyahu Rabbah*, ch. 18. Retrieved from https://www.kesherjournal.com/article/the-wedding-at-cana-and-the-glory-of-god/ (last accessed October 17, 2023)

an ancient wedding ritual.[38] The Talmud likewise understands that a *mikveh* (an immersive bath) is what is meant here.[39]

When the betrothed woman entered a *mikveh* it symbolized a separation from a former way to a new way of life. In the case of marriage, her water immersion indicates leaving her old life for a new life with her bridegroom. Marriage was viewed as a spiritual bonding, not merely a contractual relationship. God was not just asking Israel to wash her clothes, He was looking for an inward consecration of her heart – after all it is the eve of their betrothal ceremony! No other god they had served in Egypt had ever asked for their hand in marriage. Those other gods had simply *demanded* to be served; but Yahweh yearns for whole-hearted intimate relationship.

Having been consecrated according to God's instruction, we find Israel standing under the ancient wedding canopy ready for the ceremony to begin. Ancient Jewish commentary explains that Moses addressed Israel early that morning (Exodus 19:15) saying, "Arise from your sleep; the bridegroom is at hand and is waiting to lead his bride under the marriage canopy."[40] In Hebrew that marriage canopy is called a *huppah* (or *chuppah*). It symbolizes or

---

38 Block, Daniel I., *The Book of Ezekiel: Chapters 1-24*, The New International Commentary on the Old Testament (Eerdmans 1997) Ezekiel 16:9, p. 484, see especially footnote 123, citing several ancient texts which support the conclusion that the reference to washing comes from marriage rites

39 Jacob, Benno, *The Second Book of the Bible: Exodus*, translated from German by Walter Jacob in association with Yaakov Elman (KTAV Publishing House 1992) p. 533, citing *Mechilta, Yeb* 46b. See also: Hillel, Vered, *The Wedding at Cana and the Glory of God*, Kesher Journal, Issue 39, Summer/Fall 2021, citing the fact that "The Talmud testifies to this understanding, but 'how much more should immersion be required where washing of the garments is required?'" b. Yebam. 46b. Retrieved from https://www.kesherjournal.com/article/the-wedding-at-cana-and-the-glory-of-god/ (last accessed October 17, 2023)

40 Talmon, Shemaryahu, *Literary Studies in the Hebrew Bible: Form and Content* (Magnes Press, The Hebrew University, Jerusalem 1993) p. 240, citing the Midrash, Pirqe R. El. 41; Midrash Cant. 1:12; 5:3; Deut. Rab. 3:12; Ag. Ber. 41:126). Cp. L. Ginzberg, *The Legends of the Jews* (IPS 1955) 3.92

illustrates God's protective care.[41] The customary *huppah* is still in use today. It is festively decorated and commonly attached to the tops of four poles (or sometimes held up by attendants during the ceremony). It functions as a roof or covering for the bride and groom during their wedding ceremony.[42] Dr. Vered Hillel, Academic Dean of Messianic Jewish Theological Institute, recognizes that the word Hebrew word *huppah* (the traditional wedding canopy) is not found in any of the biblical accounts which record the events of the Mt. Sinai Covenant ceremony. So, she asks the question, "[W]here is the huppah at Mt. Sinai?" Her answer is, "It is the 'heavy cloud' that covered the mountain [Exodus 19:16]. Hence, the glory of [God] is the huppah. Since a huppah represents the couple's new home, the analogy fits well; Israel's new home or place of dwelling is to be eternally in him."[43]

Bible teacher Ray Vander Laan, well known for his Focus on the Family teaching series, *That the World May Know*, also views the cloud covering the mountain as a possible *huppah*. However, he notes that it is conceivable Mt. Sinai itself provided the *huppah*. That's because Israel is described as standing *underneath* Mt. Sinai during the Covenant ceremony.

> And ye came near and *stood under the mountain*; and the mountain burned with fire unto the midst of heaven, with darkness, clouds, and thick darkness. Deuteronomy 4:11 KJV, italics added

---

41 Vander Laan, Ray, *Fire on The Mountain,* The Faith Lessons™ Series with Ray Vander Laan, Volume 9 (Zondervan 2009) Session Five: I Led You Like a Bride: A Wedding at Sinai

42 Hillel, Vered, *The Wedding at Cana and the Glory of God*, Kesher Journal, Issue 39, Summer/Fall 2021. Retrieved from https://www.kesherjournal.com/article/the-wedding-at-cana-and-the-glory-of-god/ (last accessed October 17, 2023)

43 Hillel, Vered, *The Wedding at Cana and the Glory of God*, Kesher Journal, Issue 39, Summer/Fall 2021. Retrieved from https://www.kesherjournal.com/article/the-wedding-at-cana-and-the-glory-of-god/ (last accessed October 17, 2023)

I've quoted from the King James Version because it accurately renders the Hebrew word "*tahat* {takh'-ath}" used in this verse as "under" the mountain. Most translations read that Moses brought them to the "foot" of the mountain which gives us the idea that they were simply standing at the base of Mt. Sinai. However, *tahat* in this context more accurately means "beneath" the mountain.[44] We can understand the dilemma faced by the translators here – it seems absurd to say Israel was standing underneath Mt. Sinai. Unless of course you look at the picture through the marriage lens and see that Mt. Sinai functioned as the *huppah*, the Jewish wedding canopy!

Now let's return to our study of God's desire to dwell with Israel. After Israel heard all God had to say and agreed to abide by His Covenant requirements, God gave Moses the instruction: "Let them construct a sanctuary for Me, that I may dwell among them."[45] By this command God made clear that His primary purpose for construction of the wilderness Tabernacle was to provide a dwelling place for Himself among His people. Moses was shown the reality of the Tabernacle in heaven when he was on the mountain and instructed not to deviate from what he saw.[46] The earthly constructed Tabernacle and its furnishings were meant to be the exact representative likeness which reflected the original. Not only was it the "authoritative ideal" of God's dwelling place,[47] God intended it to be an earthly model which pointed to the heavenly

---

44 Harris, Archer, and Waltke, editors, *Theological Wordbook of the Old Testament* (Moody Press 1999) word #2504, p. 967. The Hebrew text literally says they stood underneath the mountain as if the mountain itself was the *huppah*. Vander Laan, Ray, *Fire on The Mountain*, The Faith Lessons™ Series with Ray Vander Laan, Volume 9 (Zondervan 2009) Session Five: I Led You Like a Bride: A Wedding at Sinai
45 Exodus 25:8
46 Exodus 25:40; Hebrews 8:1-5; Revelation 15:5
47 Durham, John I., *Word Biblical Commentary: Exodus*, Volume 3 (Word Books 1987) Exodus 25:8-9 under *Comment*, p. 355. Durham points to the fact that Yahweh prescribed the plan for both the Tabernacle and all its furnishing and equipment as supporting evidence that He intended it to be "the authoritative ideal."

original.⁴⁸ The notion of there being a Temple or Sanctuary place for God in heaven is firmly rooted in ancient Near Eastern culture. Temples of the gods were thought to be "either in the realm below the earth's surface or in heaven [which was] a poetic way of affirming [the] secure and enduring qualities [of those temples]."⁴⁹

When Moses and the people had completed the Tabernacle according to the plans they were given, a cloud covered the Tent of Meeting and the glory of Yahweh filled the Tabernacle.⁵⁰ To Israel the description of the cloud descending is a now familiar one. The exodus narrative regularly associates God's Presence with a cloud.⁵¹ There is to be no misunderstanding among Israel – Yahweh Himself entered the completed Tabernacle. Scholar John Durham described the perceived eagerness of God, "The impression is given of a Yahweh waiting with impatience for the completion of the symbolic place of his Presence and descending upon it the moment it is finally ready."⁵²

It was known to all of Israel that God's Manifest-Presence had entered the Tabernacle. It became known as the dwelling place of God. This was the same Presence that was in the Garden and walked with Adam and Eve. It was the same Presence that led Israel by fire and cloud and the same Presence that manifested in itself in lightning and thunder, fire and smoke on the top of Mt.

---

48   Bromiley, Geoffrey W., *Theological Dictionary of the New Testament: Abridged in One Volume* (Eerdmans 1985) entry for *deiknymi* under *hypodeigma* p. 142
49   Hilber, John W., "Psalms," in *Zondervan Illustrated Bible Backgrounds Commentary*, Vol. 5, edited by John H. Walton (Zondervan 2009) Psalm 78:69, p. 386
50   Exodus 40:34. In this context the glory of God (Hebrew *kabowd* {kaw-bode'} or *kabod* {kaw-bode'}) "relates to the visible manifestation of [Yahweh's] majesty in acts of power, whether in the realm of nature … or in history." Hillel, Vered, *The Wedding at Cana and the Glory of God*, Kesher Journal, Issue 39, Summer/Fall 2021. Retrieved from https://www.kesherjournal.com/article/the-wedding-at-cana-and-the-glory-of-god/   (last accessed October 17, 2023)
51   Exodus 13:21-22; 14:19,24; 16:10; 24:16-18; 33:9-10; 34:5
52   Durham, John I., *Word Biblical Commentary: Exodus*, Volume 3 (Word Books 1987) Exodus 40:34 under *Comment*, p. 500

Sinai. Now this very Presence had entered the Tabernacle. God had once again come to dwell among His people.[53]

The Tabernacle that Moses built had three distinct sections each separated by a thick curtain. The people were permitted to enter the outer court. The priests were permitted to enter the center section. However, the most holy place, the Holy of Holies, could be entered only by the high priest once per year. This is the place which housed the Ark of the Covenant where God was said to be seated between the cherubim. Whereas God walked with Adam and Eve in the Garden, in the wilderness Tabernacle His Presence was now set apart from the people in a *holy* place. Dr. Sam Meier points out that the Tabernacle is an ever-present reminder to Israel of the access that was lost in the Garden of Eden. On the other hand, it is an ever-present reminder of God's desire to dwell among His Covenant people.[54]

Hear What The Spirit is Saying to the Church: *Do you not know how I long to dwell among you? Do you not understand that it has always been my heart's desire to do so? But I cannot live among a people who are not resting in me. I desire to dwell in a place where I can rest. In doing so I bring my rest with me and that rest is shared with you. Will you create for me a place where I can rest among you? If you will, the rest I promised to my servant Abraham will be the blessing that will come among you and we will dwell together in that place forever. Will you choose me over the ways of the world and in doing so become my holy people? Then can I dwell among you and fulfill the desire of my heart.*

---

53 "Let them construct a sanctuary for Me, that I may dwell among them." Exodus 25:8

54 "Like the Garden, Israelites cannot enter the Tabernacle. This structure is a constant reminder that all is not as it should be: humans cannot freely walk with God as did Adam and Eve in the Garden. But God's Presence also reminds the Israelites that God wants to establish a relationship with humans." Meier, Sam, *Eden-Tabernacle-Temple-Community*, Messianic Studies Institute Course Fall, 2022, Lesson 2 written summary received via e-mail November 3, 2022

LESSON 3:

FROM THE TABERNACLE OF MOSES TO DAVID'S TENT

 "So that [Yahweh] abandoned the dwelling place at Shiloh, the tent which He had pitched among men." Psalm 78:60

WE HAVE LEARNED that God desired a dwelling place among His people and the place He chose to rest was in a Tabernacle that had been built according to His very specific instruction. In fact, in Revelation we learn that John saw the heavenly original which had provided the pattern for this Tabernacle.[1]

Everything in the constructed Tabernacle was portable so that if the cloud by day/pillar of fire by night moved, all of Israel moved with it. The Ark of the Covenant carried by the priests on two poles would lead the way:

> Thus they set out from the mount of the LORD three days' journey, with the ark of the covenant of the LORD journeying in front of them for the three days, to seek out a resting place for them. The cloud of the LORD was over them by day when they set out from the camp. Then it came about when the ark set out that Moses said, "Rise up, O LORD! And let Your enemies be scattered, And let those who hate You flee before You." When it came to rest, he said, "Return, O Lord, *To* the myriad thousands of Israel." Numbers 10:33-36, italics in original

---

1   Revelation 15:5

Throughout the wilderness journey from Egypt to the land God had promised as Abraham's inheritance, the Ark had led Israel every step of the way. To be in the presence of the Ark of the Covenant was to be in God's Presence.

As Israel entered the Promised Land, it was the Ark carried by the priests that led the way across the flooded Jordan River.[2] It was the Ark that accompanied Israel as they marched around Jericho according to God's instruction and released a shout of victory when the walls of the city collapsed.[3] When the Promised Land had been sufficiently subdued by Israel, Joshua assembled the entire community at Shiloh.[4] God had chosen Shiloh as the first place He would dwell among them in that land.[5] As a result, Joshua set up the Tabernacle there. Shiloh, which was located between Bethel and Shechem in territory allotted to Ephraim,[6] became the center of Israel's government as well as her worship of Yahweh.[7]

---

2   Joshua 3
3   Joshua 6
4   Little is known with certainty about the Tabernacle between the time Israel entered the Promised Land and the documented fact that it was set up in Shiloh. *Easton's Bible Dictionary* is of the opinion that the Tabernacle housing the Ark was set up in Gilgal and remained in that location for seven years. Easton, Matthew George, *Easton's Bible Dictionary*, Third Edition (Thomas Nelson 1897) entry for *Tabernacle*. Retrieved from https://www.studylight.org/dictionaries/eng/ebd/t/tabernacle.html (last accessed November 24, 2022); *Unger's Bible Dictionary* reports that, "As long as Canaan remained unconquered and the people were still therefore an army, the Tabernacle was moved from place to place, wherever the host of Israel was for the time being encamped; it was finally placed at Shiloh (Josh. 18:1; 19:51)." Unger, Merrill F., *The New Unger's Bible Dictionary* (Moody Press 1988) entry for *Tabernacle of Is'rael* under *history*, p. 1239
5   Joshua 18:1; Jeremiah 7:12
6   *NIV Study Bible* (Zondervan Publishing 1995) study note Psalm 78:60, p. 862
7   Hilber, John W., "Psalms," in *Zondervan Illustrated Bible Backgrounds Commentary*, Vol. 5, edited by John H. Walton (Zondervan 2009) Tabernacle of Shiloh (Psalm 78:60) p. 385, citing Joshua 18:1; 1 Samuel 1:3; Balofsky, Ahuva, *Tabernacle Evidence Unearthed in Shiloh, Israel365News*, July 3, 2013. Retrieved from http://www.israel365news.com/tabernacle-evidence-unearthed-shilo (last accessed July 17, 2021)

My Dwelling Place 33

Archaeologists have been searching diligently for years for some kind of evidence that would point to the specific location of the Shiloh Tabernacle. In 2013, findings were presented at a conference of the Shiloh Association after archaeologists found holes hewn into stone that would have once anchored wooden poles. They were the very type of holes that would have been used for the posts of the portable Tabernacle. In addition, remains of several structures dating back to the times of Joshua and King David were found in that same area. These buildings contained items not commonly found in private residences of that time making it unlikely that they had served as family dwellings. Collectively, the archaeological evidence supports this dig site, just north of Tel Shiloh, as the likely location of the Shiloh Tabernacle during the time of the Judges.[8]

More recently three altar horns on stone blocks were discovered during excavations completed by Associates for Biblical Research at Shiloh, Israel. The Bible indicates that horns were an essential part of the altar and used in the Temple service. As a result, archeologists believe this to be additional credible evidence of the Shiloh Tabernacle.[9]

Shiloh was the location of the Tabernacle for 369 years[10] until the death of Eli who was both Judge and High Priest of Israel.[11] When the Philistines attacked Israel, the sons of Eli, Hophni and Phinehas (also Phineas), carried the Ark to the place of battle

---

8   Balofsky, Ahuva, *Tabernacle Evidence Unearthed in Shiloh*, Israel365News, July 3, 2013. Retrieved from http://www. israel365news.com/tabernacle-evidence-unearthed-shilo (last accessed July 17, 2021)

9   Berkowitz, Adam Eliyahu, *Horn of the Stone Altar Discovered at Shiloh*, Israel365News, November 1, 2019. Retrieved from https://www.israel-365news.com/139258/horn-of-the-stone-altar-discovered-at-shiloh/ (last accessed July 17, 2021)

10 Berkowitz, Adam Eliyahu, *Horn of the Stone Altar Discovered at Shiloh*, Israel365News, November 1, 2019. Retrieved from https://www.israel-365news.com/139258/horn-of-the-stone-altar-discovered-at-shiloh/ (last accessed July 17, 2021)

11 Eli immediately preceded Samuel as Judge. Samuel was the last of the Judges. He was succeeded by Saul, the first anointed King of Israel.

hoping to guarantee God's help. However, God was not pleased with Israel's sin and He had decreed defeat rather than victory. The Ark was never intended to be a type of good luck charm. Just as had been prophesied, Israel was defeated and Eli's sons were killed. The Ark was captured by the Philistines, Eli died when he heard the news and God's Presence departed from Shiloh.

The Psalmist captures this tragic moment in history in Psalm 78, which includes our Key Scripture for this lesson:

> So He brought them to His holy land, To this hill country which His right hand had gained. He also drove out the nations before them And apportioned them for an inheritance by measurement, And made the tribes of Israel dwell in their tents. Yet they tempted and rebelled against the Most High God And did not keep His testimonies, But turned back and acted treacherously like their fathers; They turned aside like a treacherous bow. For they provoked Him with their high places and aroused His jealousy with their graven images. When God heard, He was filled with wrath and greatly abhorred Israel; *So that He abandoned the dwelling place at Shiloh, the tent which He had pitched among men,* and gave up His strength to captivity and His glory into the hand of the adversary. He also delivered His people to the sword, and was filled with wrath at His inheritance. Fire devoured His young men, and His virgins had no wedding songs. His priests fell by the sword, and His widows could not weep. Psalm 78:54-64, italics added

The phrase, "And [Yahweh] gave up His strength to captivity And His glory into the hand of the adversary" refers to the capture of the Ark by the Philistines. Apparently, God also permitted the victorious Philistines to destroy Shiloh as well.[12] By the time of

---

12 *ESV Study Bible* (Crossway Books 2008) study note Psalm 78:56-64, p. 1036, citing Jeremiah 7:12-15. Unger, Merrill F., *The New Unger's Bible Dictionary* (Moody Press 1988) entry for *Shiloh*, p. 1183. In Jere-

My Dwelling Place	35

Jeremiah, it seemed to be a well-established fact that Shiloh was a deserted ancient site and no longer an authorized place for worshipping Yahweh.[13] Through the prophet Jeremiah God took credit for its destruction and left no doubt as to exactly why He permitted it to be destroyed. Even though Yahweh had spoken persistently to Israel, she would not listen. He called to her repeatedly and she did not respond to His voice by turning away from evil.[14]

Israel's election by Yahweh meant He had called them into "divine service."[15] As His priests on earth, Israel was accountable both individually and collectively for holiness (separation from the world).[16] Holiness is the only way to maintain a proper environment for Yahweh to dwell in close proximity to His Covenant people. Israel had signed on the dotted line agreeing to her responsibilities. By saying "yes" to her Covenant obligations, Israel agreed to three basic duties to assure that the proper environment was maintained for Yahweh to tabernacle among them:[17]

1. Individually and communally they agreed to diligently guard against even accidental "behavioral lapses that might result in polluting themselves, their land, or God's sanctuary."[18]

---

miah 7:12-15 the prophet speaks for Yahweh warning that if Israel does not repent and turn from her wicked ways, Solomon's temple in Jerusalem will endure the same destruction as Shiloh.
13   Thompson, J. A., *The Book of Jeremiah*, The New International Commentary on The Old Testament (Eerdmans 1980) Jeremiah 7:12, p. 281
14   Jeremiah 7:12-15
15   Kaminsky, Joel S., *Yet I Love Jacob: Reclaiming the Biblical Concept of Election* (Abington Press 2007) p. 97
16   Kaminsky, Joel S., *Yet I Love Jacob; Reclaiming the Biblical Concept of Election* (Abington Press 2007) p. 96
17   Kaminsky, Joel S., *Yet I Love Jacob; Reclaiming the Biblical Concept of Election* (Abington Press 2007) p. 97
18   Kaminsky, Joel S., *Yet I Love Jacob; Reclaiming the Biblical Concept of Election* (Abington Press 2007) p. 97

2. They had a responsibility, whenever a breach did occur, to determine what specific offense had been committed and where possible, identify the person who committed it.
3. When a breach was identified, it had to be atoned for exactly as prescribed by the Mosaic Law. That meant undertaking an obligation to ensure that the atonement was done the right way and with the right heart attitude.[19]

Israel did not faithfully fulfill what she had agreed to do. Behavioral lapses did occur for which there was no proper atonement. According to God's Law, without proper atonement, what is unclean ritually defiles what is set aside as holy. When that happens, God will no longer permit His Manifest-Presence to rest in that place. Ever since Mt. Sinai, the Ark had represented God's Dwelling-Presence and glory among His Covenant people. However, just as He could not dwell in the Garden with Adam after he chose Satan's plan over God's, God could not dwell among a people who refused to honor and serve Him as Lord.[20] Israel's failure to maintain the purity of Yahweh's chosen dwelling place in accordance with His holy standards resulted in Him abandoning the resting place He had chosen.

In spite of the fact that He abandoned His resting place, God continued to pursue His relationship with Israel so He could ultimately fulfill the desire of His heart to dwell among His creation. In His amazing grace God brought judgment against the Philistines as long as the Ark remained in their possession. In the hands of Israel, the Ark was a symbol of God's Dwelling-Presence among them. To the Philistines it became a symbol of God's intense jealousy for His Covenant people. After seven months

---

19 The required atonement might be "a sacrificial act, a fine, a confession, or some combination of these." If the breach was severe, the atonement could demand removing that individual from the community, either by excommunication or death. Kaminsky, Joel S., *Yet I Love Jacob; Reclaiming the Biblical Concept of Election* (Abington Press 2007) p. 97
20 1 Samuel 4:22; Jeremiah 7:12

of disaster and plague,[21] the Philistines decided to send the Ark back to the Israelites and it was transported to Beth-Shemesh, the nearest Israelite town.[22] When it arrived at Beth-Shemesh, God struck down 70 men[23] after they irreverently and impermissibly looked inside the Ark.[24] Remember the Ark of the Covenant had been designed for the most holy place inside the Tabernacle – the Holy of Holies. Only the High Priest was allowed to enter that sacred place to stand before the Ark in God's Presence. Even then, the High Priest was only permitted to enter once per year according to the exact instructions God had provided.

God never lowered His standards! Israel was obligated to handle the Ark exactly as Yahweh had specified. After all, because it signified the establishment of God's Kingdom on earth, it was the footstool of His throne on earth.[25] So, it was out of fear that the Ark was moved to Kirjath-Jearim[26] and placed in the house of Abinadab, a Levite.[27] Abinadab got it right. He understood the holy nature of the Ark and consecrated his son Eleazar to take

---

21 1 Samuel 6:1; It was commonplace for ancient people to assume that a plague was caused by an angry god, perhaps the god of their enemy. Long, V. Philips, "1 Samuel," in *Zondervan Illustrated Bible Backgrounds Commentary*, Vol. 2, edited by John H. Walton (Zondervan 2009) 1 Samuel 6:2, p. 299

22 1 Samuel 6:14

23 In biblical times the number 70 was indicative of a large number but not necessarily an exact number. Walton, Matthews, and Chavalas, *IVP Bible Background Commentary Old Testament* (InterVarsity Press 2000) 1 Samuel 6:19 under *putting seventy to death*, p. 289

24 1 Samuel 6:19

25 "The ark of the covenant signified the establishment of God's kingdom on earth; therefore, the ark became known as God's 'footstool.'" Longman III and Garland, general editors, *The Expositor's Bible Commentary: Psalms*, Vol. 5, Revised Edition (Zondervan 2008) Psalm 99:1-5, p. 738. See Lamentations 2:1; 1 Chronicles 28:2; Psalm 99:5; 132:7

26 Also known as Kiriath-arim (Ezra 2:25). "A Gibeonite town (Josh. 9:17), first assigned to Judah ([Joshua] 15:60 but after to Benjamin ([Joshua] 18:28))." Unger, Merrill F., *The New Unger's Bible Dictionary* (Moody Press 1988) entry for *Kirjath-Jearim*, p. 743

27 1 Samuel 7:1

proper care of it. He followed the pattern of the Lord who had set aside Aaron and his sons, consecrating them and making them holy for their tasks as priest which included care of the Ark.

The Ark remained under Eleazar's care throughout the judgeship of Samuel and the forty years that Saul reigned as king in Israel.[28] The next time Scripture records a location for the Tabernacle is when David visits the Tabernacle in Nob.[29] Nob was called the "city of priests (1 Samuel 22:19)" and was located in the territory of Benjamin.[30] Since at that time the Ark was in the house of Abinadab, under the care of his son, it would appear that the Tabernacle structure itself sat in Nob without either the Ark or God's Dwelling-Presence. After Saul completely destroyed Nob,[31] the Tabernacle was moved to Gibeon which was again in the land allotted to Benjamin.[32]

After David became King and made Jerusalem his capital city, he longed to establish a dwelling place for God in Jerusalem.[33] David, unlike Saul, understood that God was the true King of Israel and that His heart had always been to dwell among His people – resting among them as Sovereign Lord. While the Tabernacle structure was still in Gibeon[34] David set out to move the Ark from the house of Abinadab in Kirjath-Jearim to Jerusalem.[35]

---

28   2 Samuel 6:1-3
29   1 Samuel 21:1-6
30   Nob is described as a "town northeast of Jerusalem and south of Gibeah where the tabernacle was relocated after the destruction of Shiloh." *NIV Study Bible* (Zondervan Publishing 1995) study note 1 Samuel 21:1, p. 404, cites omitted
31   1 Samuel 22:14-19
32   Unger, Merrill F., *The New Unger's Bible Dictionary* (Moody Press 1988) entry for *Gibeon*, p. 472
33   Psalm 132:5
34   The Tabernacle was still located in Gibeon during the reign of Solomon and remained there until he built the first Temple. See: 2 Chronicles 1:3; 1 Kings 3:4
35   The Ark remained in Kiriath-Jearim until it was moved to Jerusalem by King David. Unger, Merrill F., *The New Unger's Bible Dictionary* (Moody

One of the great lessons we learn from David's life is that he consistently "inquired of the Lord" before going into battle.[36] His practice of doing so gave him great victory in battle. Tragically however, we don't read that David "inquired of the Lord" before attempting to move the Ark. What David failed to recognize in all his eagerness was that when the Ark was made, God established a very specific pattern for its proper transportation and those instructions had never changed.[37] Even though it had not been housed inside the Tabernacle for many years, that Ark still represented God's Dwelling-Presence and it was holy! It did not matter if David was Israel's anointed King or even that God considered him to be a man after His own heart.[38] God's rules still applied to David. Therefore, when David attempted to move the Ark using his own plan, rather than God's plan, Uzzah died because he touched the Ark. As a result, David experienced a dramatic and unforgettable life lesson in God's holiness!

After Uzzah's tragic death, David decided to abandon his current plan to move the Ark to Jerusalem and he placed the Ark in the home of Obed-Edom the Gittite. During that time, the house of Obed-Edom was greatly blessed! Three months later, after David had come to understand God's established pattern, he was able to successfully move the Ark to Jerusalem. That meant that the Ark had come to rest in David's city, the seat of his kingdom, in a Tent he had constructed for that purpose.

The Bible never explains why David did not move the Tabernacle itself to Jerusalem in order to house the Ark of the Cov-

---

Press 1988) entry for *Kiriath-Jearim*, p. 743, citing 2 Samuel 6:2-3,12; 1 Chronicles 15; Psalm 132
36 "Therefore David inquired of the Lord, saying, Shall I go and attack . . . (1 Samuel 23:2,4,10-12)?" "David inquired of the Lord, saying, 'Shall I pursue this band? Shall I overtake them?' (1 Samuel 30:8);" "Then David inquired of the Lord, saying, Shall I go up against the Philistines? (2 Samuel 5:19)."
37 Numbers 4
38 Acts 13:22

enant.³⁹ It is of note, however, that the entrance to the Tabernacle could only face east. That requirement automatically placed restriction on the options available for how it would be physically set up. The sheer size of the Tabernacle meant it would not physically fit in the City of David.⁴⁰ That practical reality may be the best explanation for why the Tabernacle structure remained at Gibeon and David set up a new Tent on Mt. Zion in Jerusalem to house the Ark.⁴¹ So, from the time David brought the Ark to Jerusalem until the completion of Solomon's Temple, the Tent of David and the Tabernacle co-existed. David appointed Levites to worship before the Lord in the Tent he constructed. He also appointed priests to perform the prescribed sacrifices in the Tabernacle of Moses even though the most Holy Place inside the Tabernacle no longer contained the Ark symbolizing God's Presence.⁴²

David understood that the Ark represented God's Dwelling-Presence on earth. Whether he had in mind that the Tent he set up was temporary or not, David used the occasion of the Ark's presence in Jerusalem to establish a pattern of worship in the earth that was remarkably different than that which took place in Moses' Tabernacle. From the time of his youth David was a

---

39 Dr. Sam Meier points to 1 Chronicles 21:28 – 2 Chronicles 22:1 for an explanation. He reads that biblical narrative as saying David was afraid of the angel of the Lord and therefore unilaterally decided to ignore the Tabernacle in Gibeon. He is also of the opinion that David selfishly wanted the blessing associated with the Ark (see 2 Samuel 6:11) to be near him in Jerusalem. Meier, Sam, Eden, *Tabernacle, Temple, Community: God's Changing Relationship to His People*, Messianic Studies Institute Course Fall, 2022, Lesson 3, November 7, 2022

40 Meier, Sam, Eden, *Tabernacle, Temple, Community: God's Changing Relationship to His People*, Messianic Studies Institute Course Fall, 2022, Lesson 5, November 21, 2022

41 1 Chronicles 15:1; The fact is that the standard practice of people groups at that time in history was to have the temple of the god next to the palace of the king, evidencing that divine authority was invested in the king. Meier, Sam, Eden, *Tabernacle, Temple, Community: God's Changing Relationship to His People*, Messianic Studies Institute Course Fall, 2022, Lesson 5, November 21, 2022

42 1 Chronicles 16:37-42

worshipper. His passion for offering sacrifices of praise to Yahweh no doubt influenced the establishment of continual praise and worship in the Tent which now housed the symbol of God's Dwelling-Presence among His people. It was David who proclaimed: "Yet You [God] are holy, O You who are enthroned upon the praises of Israel."[43] David understood that praise established a pathway to God's Presence; but more than that he understood that when God's people praise Him it invites God, as King, to establish His Sovereign rule over them. This is exactly what David wanted to accomplish!

Hear What The Spirit is Saying to the Church: _My people have understood so little about my desire to dwell among them. How different things would have been had they understood. As Sovereign King of the Universe I have desired to establish my Kingdom on earth as it is in Heaven. It has always been so, not just at the end of the age. But my holiness prevents me from establishing my Kingdom rule where the kingdom of darkness is invited among my people. Everything is about choice. I permit those that I created to choose which kingdom/Kingdom they will serve, but they must choose. They cannot live with one foot in the kingdom of darkness, serving the world and the world's ways and also live with the other foot in my Kingdom seeking my goodness and blessing. Adam's story should have provided clear instruction to my people that my holiness demands an "all or nothing" response. I will never "send" anyone to outer darkness, but I will honor the choice each person makes as to which kingdom/Kingdom they will serve. Choose today whom you will serve, but choose wisely and carefully because all of eternity hinges on your choice. And so it shall be forever and ever._

---

43 Psalm 22:3

LESSON 4:

FROM DAVID'S TENT TO SOLOMON'S TEMPLE

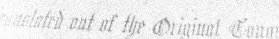

"Now therefore arise, O LORD God, to Your resting place, You and the ark of Your might; let Your priests, O LORD God, be clothed with salvation and let Your godly ones rejoice in what is good...." 2 Chronicles 6:41

IN OUR LAST lesson, we traced the movement of the Ark from the wilderness to a Tent in Jerusalem. We imagined that it was on David's heart from the outset to build a Temple for God's Dwelling-Presence and that the Tent was intended to be a temporary structure until a more permanent Temple could be built. As we will soon see, there was good reason that David would have had this intention. We know the story. When David announced his plans to Nathan the prophet, he received encouragement to do all that was in his heart to do.[1] That is, until Nathan received a word from the Lord and returned to David to deliver a very different instruction.

> But in the same night the word of the LORD came to Nathan, saying, "Go and say to My servant David, 'Thus says the LORD, "Are you the one who should build Me a house to dwell in? For I have not dwelt in a house since

---
1 Solomon later testified to the people, "Now it was in the heart of my father David to build a house for the name of the LORD, the God of Israel. But the LORD said to my father David, 'Because it was in your heart to build a house for My name, you did well that it was in your heart. Nevertheless you shall not build the house, but your son who will be born to you, he will build the house for My name.'" 1 Kings 8:17-19

the day I brought up the sons of Israel from Egypt, even to this day; but I have been moving about in a tent, even in a tabernacle. Wherever I have gone with all the sons of Israel, did I speak a word with one of the tribes of Israel, which I commanded to shepherd My people Israel, saying, Why have you not built Me a house of cedar?' Now therefore, thus you shall say to My servant David, 'Thus says the Lord of hosts, "I took you from the pasture, from following the sheep, to be ruler over My people Israel. I have been with you wherever you have gone and have cut off all your enemies from before you; and I will make you a great name, like the names of the great men who are on the earth. I will also appoint a place for My people Israel and will plant them, that they may live in their own place and not be disturbed again .... I will give you rest from all your enemies. The Lord also declares to you that the Lord will make a house for you. When your days are complete and you lie down with your fathers, I will raise up your descendant after you, who will come forth from you, and I will establish his kingdom. He shall build a house for My name, and I will establish the throne of his kingdom forever. I will be a father to him and he will be a son to Me ...." 2 Samuel 7:4-14

Let's supply some important background here. David had purposed in his heart to build "a house of rest" for Yahweh (1 Chronicles 28:2).[2] It was commonly understood in the ancient Near East that a king and the people he governed were responsible for providing "a place of rest" for the governing deity. Such "rest" was generally thought to be supplied by a temple. In fact, this

---

2 "Then King David rose to his feet and said, 'Listen to me, my brethren and my people; I *had* intended to build a permanent home [the Hebrew can literally be translated as "house of rest"] for the ark of the covenant of the Lord and for the footstool of our God ...." 1 Chronicles 28:2, italics in original. See NASB 1995 footnote 2 for literal translation of the phrase "permanent home."

responsibility to provide rest for the god (primarily in terms of shelter and food) was so crucial that it was considered "high treason" not to do so.[3] Nathan returned to David with a response that seems to challenge David's understanding of his kingly responsibility. It is a reminder that Yahweh is not like other gods. David is not like other kings and Israel is not like other ruled people. Rather than David and the people providing rest for Yahweh, it was always on His heart to provide rest for them![4]

Without explanation, David was given the plans for the Temple Solomon would build. While we don't know why God chose to give the plans to David, we do know that in those days it was generally understood in the ancient Near East that the "god" who planned to dwell in the temple was the only one who could authorize its construction. As a result, divine instruction (often delivered by a prophet) was deemed essential before a king would proceed with temple building preparation.[5] Perhaps it was in keeping with this cultural understanding that God supplied the specific details for the layout and design just as He had done with Moses hundreds of years earlier.[6]

> [11] David gave to his son Solomon the blueprints for the temple porch, its buildings, its treasuries, its upper areas, its inner rooms, and the room for atonement. [12] He gave him the blueprints of all he envisioned ["the pattern of all which was in the spirit with him"][7]

---

3   Long, V. Philips, "2 Samuel," in *Zondervan Illustrated Bible Backgrounds Commentary*, Vol. 2, edited by John H. Walton (Zondervan 2009) 2 Samuel 7:1, p. 442
4   Yahweh's plan for His created order is that His Covenant people would enter His rest with Him! See for example: Genesis 2:3; Exodus 20:8-11; Deuteronomy 5:12-14; Matthew 12:12; Hebrews 4
5   Walton, Matthews, and Chavalas, *The IVP Bible Background Commentary: Old Testament* (InterVarsity Press 2000) Haggai 1:7, p. 797
6   Ezekiel was also given detailed instruction by Yahweh for construction of a restored temple. See Ezekiel 40-48
7   *NET Bible Notes*, translator's note 19, 1 Chronicles 28:12. The source for this information is "*Net Notes*" however it will be descriptively cited as "*Net*

for the courts of the LORD's temple, all the surrounding rooms, the storehouses of God's temple, and the storehouses for the holy items. ¹³ He gave him the regulations for the divisions of priests and Levites, for all the assigned responsibilities within the LORD's temple, and for all the items used in the service of the LORD's temple. ¹⁴ He gave him the prescribed weight for all the gold items to be used in various types of service in the LORD's temple, for all the silver items to be used in various types of service, ¹⁵ for the gold lampstands and their gold lamps, including the weight of each lampstand and its lamps, for the silver lampstands, including the weight of each lampstand and its lamps, according to the prescribed use of each lampstand, ¹⁶ for the gold used in the display tables, including the amount to be used in each table, for the silver to be used in the silver tables, ¹⁷ for the pure gold used for the meat forks, bowls, and jars, for the small gold bowls, including the weight for each bowl, for the small silver bowls, including the weight for each bowl, ¹⁸ and for the refined gold of the incense altar. He gave him the blueprint for the seat of the gold cherubim that spread their wings and provide shelter for the ark of the LORD's covenant. ¹⁹ David said, "All this I put in writing as the LORD directed me and gave me insight regarding the details of the blueprints ["the whole in writing from the hand of the LORD upon me, he gave insight [for] all the workings of the plan."].⁸"
1 Chronicles 28:11-19 NET

A more literal translation of verse 19 from the Hebrew text is: "Everything in the writing (or document) [was] from YHWH's [Yahweh's] hand. On me [David] was [the task of] understanding/comprehending the workmanship of the pattern/model/rep-

---

Bible Notes" throughout the study.
8   *NET Bible Notes*, translator's note 27, 1 Chronicles 28:19

resentation."[9] Even though God had graciously given David the plan, God chose Solomon, David's son, to build the Temple.[10] David honored God's choice of Solomon and ordered all of Israel's leaders to assist his son in building the Sanctuary [*miqdash*] for Yahweh (1 Chronicles 22:19). (Refer back to Lesson 1 for a Word Study on the Hebrew term *miqdash*.)

Solomon completed the work on the Temple in 960 B.C.E.[11] The movement of the Ark from the Tent where David had housed the Ark to Solomon's Temple is documented for us in 2 Chronicles.

> Thus all the work that Solomon performed for the house of the LORD was finished. And Solomon brought in the things that David his father had dedicated, even the silver and the gold and all the utensils, *and* put *them* in the treasuries of the house of God. Then Solomon assembled to Jerusalem the elders of Israel and all the heads of the tribes, the leaders of the fathers' *households* of the sons of Israel, to bring up the ark of the covenant of the LORD out of the city of David, which is Zion. All the men of Israel assembled themselves to the king at the feast, that is *in* the seventh month. 2 Chronicles 5:1-3, italics in original

Solomon recognized that he had "surely built [God] a lofty house, a place for [His] dwelling forever (1 Kings 8:13)." Then Solomon prayed to dedicate the Temple and in so doing He acknowledged Israel's mission that "all the nations of the earth will recognize that the LORD is the only genuine God (1 Kings 8:60 NET)."

> When Solomon had finished praying … he arose from before the altar of the Lord …. And he stood and

---

9   Henry Neufeld, Email to Deborah Roeger November 16, 2022
10 2 Samuel 7; 1 Chronicles 17
11 Mabie, Frederick J., "2 Chronicles," in *Zondervan Illustrated Bible Backgrounds Commentary*, Vol. 3, edited by John H. Walton (Zondervan 2009) 2 Chronicles 2:1, p. 298

blessed all the assembly of Israel with a loud voice, saying: "Blessed be the LORD, who has given rest to His people Israel, according to all that He promised; not one word has failed of all His good promise, which He promised through Moses His servant. May the LORD our God be with us, as He was with our fathers; may He not leave us or forsake us, that He may incline our hearts to Himself, to walk in all His ways and to keep His commandments and His statutes and His ordinances, which He commanded our fathers. And may these words of mine, with which I have made supplication before the LORD, be near to the LORD our God day and night, that He may maintain the cause of His servant and the cause of His people Israel, as each day requires, **so that all the peoples of the earth may know that the LORD is God; there is no one else.**..." 1 Kings 8:54,56-60, bold added

The Temple was finished and the Ark was once again in its resting place in the Holy of Holies. Our Key Scripture for this lesson records the prayer of Solomon after the Ark was in place.

"Now therefore arise, O LORD God, to Your resting place, You and the ark of Your might; let Your priests, O LORD God, be clothed with salvation and let Your godly ones rejoice in what is good...." 2 Chronicles 6:41

Solomon's prayer requested God to come and inhabit the Temple he had built. It was an invitation for the Temple to become His new resting place among Israel. What happened next was reminiscent of what took place when Moses finished building the wilderness Tabernacle. In fact, a side-by-side comparison of these two events illustrates the remarkable similarity of God's powerful response when the work on each of these dwelling places was completed according to His instruction.

My Dwelling Place

Exodus 40:33b-35	2 Chronicles 7:1-2
Thus Moses finished the work. Then the cloud covered the tent of meeting, and the glory of the Lord filled the tabernacle. Moses was not able to enter the tent of meeting because the cloud had settled on it, and the glory of the Lord filled the tabernacle.	Now when Solomon had finished praying, fire came down from heaven and consumed the burnt offering and the sacrifices, and the glory of the Lord filled the house. The priests could not enter into the house of the Lord because the glory of the Lord filled the Lord's house.

So, we see that when the work was finished according to the pattern God had given, His glory came down and filled the place. As an initial matter we might ask, why did the glory have to fall in Solomon's Temple if it had already fallen in the wilderness Tabernacle? Remember the glory had departed from the Tabernacle during the time of Eli.

> Now a man of Benjamin ran from the battle line and came to Shiloh the same day with his clothes torn and dust on his head.... The man said to Eli, "I am the one who came from the battle line. Indeed, I escaped from the battle line today." And he said, "How did things go, my son?" Then the one who brought the news replied, "Israel has fled before the Philistines and there has also been a great slaughter among the people, and your two sons also, Hophni and Phinehas, are dead, and the ark of God has been taken." ... Now [Eli's] daughter-in-law, Phinehas's wife, was pregnant and ... she kneeled down and gave birth, for her pains came upon her.... And she called the boy Ichabod, saying, "The glory has departed from Israel" .... She said, "The glory has departed from Israel, for the ark of God was taken." 1 Samuel 4:12,16-22

It will be good for us to define this "glory" that can fall, can dwell in a place and can depart all at the will of God. To that end, a Word Study will be helpful.

Word Study

When we read that God's glory fell in the Tabernacle and the Temple, the Hebrew noun translated as **glory** *is kabod (also transliterated kavod) {kaw-bode'}. According to Dr. Merrill Unger kabod "refers to physical weight or 'quantity' of a thing – not meaning simply 'heavy,' but a heavy or imposing quantity."[12]*

When kabod is used in reference to God's glory it assumes an "unusual and distinctive meaning."[13] In those instances, "The glory is the Lord's presence (Ex. 16:10; 40:34f.); the Lord revealed in some specific act (Ex. 16:7; Nu. 14:22); his repute and character (Ps. 79:9); or is his exalted state ([Isaiah] 3:8; Je. 13:16)."[14] In sum, "his 'glory' involves revealing himself."[15] Mounce concludes that "The proper response to such revelation is to give Him 'honor' or 'glory.'"[16]

---

12 Hill, Gary, *The Discovery Bible*, HELPS Ministries, Inc., [H]13h [SN3519b] kāḇôḏ citing M. Unger, 187

13 Hillel, Vered, *The Wedding at Cana and the Glory of God*, Kesher Journal, Issue 39, Summer/Fall 2021. Retrieved from https://www.kesherjournal.com/article/the-wedding-at-cana-and-the-glory-of-god/ (last accessed October 17, 2023)

14 Motyer, J. Alec, *The Prophecy of Isaiah: An Introduction & Commentary* (InterVarsity Press 1993) Isaiah 40:5, p. 300

15 Keener, Craig S., *1 Peter: A Commentary* (Baker Academic 2021) 1 Peter 1:7, p. 79

16 Mounce, William D., editor, *Complete Expository Dictionary of Old & New Testament Words* (Zondervan 2006) entry for *glory*, under *Old Testament*, p. 289

Because this idea of God's glory is so important to our study, I think it is worthwhile to provide a rather lengthy quote from the entry for *kabod* found in the *Theological Wordbook of the Old Testament*.[17]

> The bulk of occurrences where God's glory is a visible manifestation have to do with the tabernacle[18] and with the temple in Ezekiel's vision of the exile and restoration.[19] These manifestations are directly related to God's self-disclosure and his intent to dwell among men. As such they are commonly associated with his holiness. God wishes to dwell with men, to have his reality and his splendor known to them. But this is only possible when they take account of the stunning quality of his holiness and set out in faith and obedience to let that character be manifested in them.[20]
>
> The several references which speak of God's glory filling the earth and/or becoming evident …. [are] not merely [speaking of] God's reputation which fills the earth, but it is the very reality of his presence. And his desire is that all persons gladly recognize and own this. His first step toward the achievement of these goals was to fill the tabernacle with his presence and then the temple.

So, what was the "glory" that fell in such great measure that no man, not even Moses or the first Temple priests, could stand in God's dwelling place? It was the weighty Manifest-Presence of Yahweh made visible in a way that men could perceive it. He had come as King to have complete dominion over His Covenant people. His Dwelling-Presence fell in a place that was uniquely prepared for Him to reside as Sovereign Ruler.

---

17 Harris, Archer, and Waltke, editors, *Theological Wordbook of the Old Testament* (Moody Press 1999) word # 943, p. 427
18 See for example: Exodus 16:10; 40:34
19 See for example: Ezekiel 9:3
20 Numbers 14:10; Isaiah 6:3; Ezra 10, 11

The ancient Hebrews understood the Ark to be the place where God's Presence dwelt. The Temple itself was conceived of as providing a link between heaven and earth.[21] In fact, it was understood that God's throne was in heaven and, as we noted in Lesson 3, the Ark represented His footstool on earth. In ancient times, the throne/footstool metaphor was a powerful picture in that a King's throne actually had a footstool to support the king's feet whenever he was seated on his throne.[22] Thus, the image of the Ark was one of God "sitting in state" on His throne and resting His feet on His footstool on earth. As long as the Temple stood in Jerusalem, the *Shekinah* glory was associated with the Ark in the Holy of Holies.

Why would His glory ever leave that place? Because simply stated, His Dwelling-Presence can only rest where He is enthroned as King – the absolute Sovereign. His Dwelling-Presence abides in a place He has chosen only when the people have made the choice to live under His Kingdom rule.

Hear What The Spirit is Saying to the Church: *So few people have truly understood the nature of my Dwelling-Presence. But I come now to make it known so that my Bride will understand what I am getting ready to do in the earth realm. I desire to be among my people; but my ability to dwell among my people is indeed limited to that place where I am able to rest as the enthroned King. I will not share my glory with another. I am either King of Kings and Lord of Lords or I am nothing to*

---

21 Beale, G. K., *The Book of Revelation*, The New International Greek Testament Commentary (Eerdmans 1999) p. 562, citing in part Terrien, *Omphalos Myth* pp. 317-318,323, and bibliography therein

22 The idea of the Ark being Yahweh's footstool is consistent with ancient Near Eastern thought. It was common that important documents, such as treaties which had been confirmed by oath, would be placed at the feet of the god. In the case of Israel, the Ark held the two stone tablets which Yahweh had written at Mt. Sinai. Those tablets contained the Covenant between Israel and Yahweh. Sherwin, Simon, "1 Chronicles," in in *Zondervan Illustrated Bible Backgrounds Commentary*, Vol. 3, edited by John H. Walton (Zondervan 2009) 1 Chronicles 28:2, p. 276

you. Because of who I am and who I have created you to be I have given you the choice. Choose this day who you will serve. If I am known as your Savior, then I must be evidenced in your life as your King. Your choice to make me King will advance my Kingdom rule on earth and I will come and dwell among those who are my people. It is the desire of my heart that it be so. What will your answer be?

Lesson 5:

From Solomon's Temple to Exile

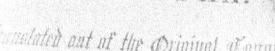

 "Then the glory of the LORD departed from the threshold of the temple and stood over the cherubim." Ezekiel 10:18

IN LESSON 4, we witnessed God's Dwelling-Presence at rest in Solomon's Temple. David had prayed that God would establish His dwelling place in Jerusalem (Psalm 132:5,7).[1] God's answer assured David He had chosen Jerusalem as His desired resting place.[2]

> For the LORD has **chosen** Zion [Jerusalem]; he has desired it for his dwelling place: "This is my resting place [*menuha*][3] forever; **here I will dwell**, for I have desired it...." Psalm 132:13-14 ESV, bold added

We looked briefly at these verses in Lesson 2. There we learned that *resting* place and *dwelling* place are synonyms. When God said "Here I will dwell" the word translated as "dwell" is the Hebrew word *yashab* {yaw-shab'}. Whereas the verbal root *škn* (as in *mishkan*, see Lesson 1) means to take up temporary residence, the verbal root *yšb* (as in *yashab*) signifies to take up a more long-

---

1 Longman III and Garland, general editors, *The Expositor's Bible Commentary: Psalms*, Vol. 5, Revised Edition (Zondervan 2008) Psalm 132:13-14, p. 930
2 See also Psalm 68:16
3 Refer to Word Study and discussion in Lesson 2

term, even permanent, residence.⁴ "When God is the subject of the root *yšb*, it is best to understand it as God's *enthronement* [as King] rather than his location .... He is free, for nothing can bind, restrict, or limit God. He may enter into time and space, but he is not bound to it."⁵

Because God designated Zion as His eternal resting place, Israel rested in the delusion that no matter what, God would *never* permit Jerusalem to be conquered or destroyed by another nation.⁶ However, the biblical truth is that God's "promised presence and attention occur only on [His] own terms."⁷ Because Israel's sin had violated God's non-negotiable terms associated with His continuing Presence, His glory left the Temple Solomon had built. The withdrawal of God's glory from the Temple before He permitted it to be destroyed by Babylon is narrated by the prophet Ezekiel. Step-by-step, the glory of God departed from what had been His dwelling place for almost four centuries.

The First Stage: Ezekiel 9:3

> Then the glory of the God of Israel went up from the cherub on which it had been, to the threshold of the temple.

---

4   Meier, Sam, *Eden-Tabernacle-Temple-Community*, Messianic Studies Institute Course Fall, 2022, Lesson 4 written summary received via e-mail November 17, 2022
5   Longman III and Garland, general editors, *The Expositor's Bible Commentary: Psalms*, Vol. 5, Revised Edition (Zondervan 2008) *Reflections: The Ark Of The Covenant And The Temple: Symbols Of Yahweh's Presence and Rule*, p. 931, italics in original
6   See for example: Jeremiah 7:3-12; Micah 3:11. *Holman Christian Standard Bible*, Study Bible edition (Holman Bible Publishers 2010) study note Psalm 132:13; Thompson, J. A., *The Book of Jeremiah*, The New International Commentary on The Old Testament (Eerdmans 1980) Jeremiah 7:4,5-6,7, pp. 277-279
7   Nelson, Richard D., *Deuteronomy*, The Old Testament Library (Westminster John Knox Press 2002) Moses As Intermediary under *Deuteronomy 5:8-10*, p. 81, citing for example: Deuteronomy 12:5,11,21; 15:9; 20:4; 24:15; 26:15

Next: Ezekiel 10:18-19 (our Key Scripture for this lesson)

> Then the glory of the LORD departed from the threshold of the temple and stood over the cherubim. When the cherubim departed, they lifted their wings and rose up from the earth in my sight with the wheels beside them; and they stood still at the entrance of the east gate of the LORD's house,[8] and the glory of the God of Israel hovered over them.

Finally: Ezekiel 11:22-24

> Then the cherubim lifted up their wings with the wheels beside them, and the glory of the God of Israel hovered over them. The glory of the LORD went up from the midst of the city and stood over the mountain which is east of the city. And the Spirit lifted me up and brought me in a vision by the Spirit of God to the exiles in Chaldea. So the vision that I had seen left me.

Just as Moses and Solomon each saw a physical manifestation of God's actual Presence, Ezekiel witnessed that manifestation, but rather than *entering* the Temple it was *exiting* the Temple! The last sight Ezekiel had of the departing divine glory was when "the glory of the LORD went up from the midst of the city, and stood upon the mountain which is on the east side of the city." The Babylonians destroyed Solomon's Temple in 586 B.C.E.

So, what happened? We saw that it was Israel's apostasy that led to the departure of God's glory from the Tabernacle during the time of Eli. Let's review Israel's history through the eyes of the prophet Isaiah during the time of Solomon's Temple, considered the "first Temple" period. The opening words of the book of Isaiah specify for us the time period during which Isaiah prophesied:

---

8   The east gate was the main entrance to the Temple area.

> The vision of Isaiah the son of Amoz concerning Judah and Jerusalem, which he saw during the reigns of Uzziah [probably beginning about 740 B.C.E.], Jotham, Ahaz *and* Hezekiah, kings of Judah. Isaiah 1:1

The kings listed in this verse ruled in Judah during the period of Israel's history known as the divided kingdom.[9] Isaiah was God's ordained messenger primarily to Judah, the southern kingdom. At Mt. Sinai God had stipulated a distinctive way of life for His Covenant people thereby separating them from all other nations. They were to keep the commandments God had given them so they would not profane their Covenant with Him and be exiled from the land of promise.[10] Like the prophets who preceded him, Isaiah condemned God's Covenant people for worship[11] that essentially amounted to nothing more than empty ritual. Isaiah also lamented over their growing idolatry which was akin to spiritual adultery.

Although lists of Israel's sins occur throughout the book of Isaiah, God summarizes her disobedience in Isaiah Chapter 5 with the following types of indictments: they call evil good and good evil (verse 20); they substitute darkness for light and light for darkness (verse 20); they are wise in their own opinion and clever in their own sight (verse 21); they have rejected the instruction of the Lord of Hosts, and they have despised the word of the Holy

---

9   The first three men to rule as Israel's King, Saul, David and Solomon, all ruled the descendants of Abraham as one united group of people. However, after King Solomon's death around 930 B.C.E., Israel split into two different people groups each ruled by their own king.

10 See for example: Leviticus 20:22-26; 26:14-39; Deuteronomy 28:15-68; 30:15-20

11 "The Hebrew verb *worship (hištahᵃwâ)* brings to mind a significant picture. The verb arises from a metaphor, namely, that of bowing down or prostrating oneself before someone whose high state is thereby acknowledged and to whom allegiance should be offered." Thompson, J. A., *The Book of Jeremiah*, The New International Commentary on The Old Testament (Eerdmans 1980) Jeremiah 7:1-2, p. 275

One of Israel (verse 24). Isaiah makes clear, however, that there is more behind the downfall of Judah than her idolatry and false worship – the monarchy in Judah will fall because King Ahaz, and later King Hezekiah, refuse to remain under the authority of God's Kingdom! No matter how capable a king might have been, he was required to rule as Yahweh's representative and to live in accordance with the revelation of His divine standards.[12]

As a part of his prophetic commission, Isaiah confronted King Ahaz at a very strategic point in his kingship. As we mentioned, at that time God's Covenant people were a divided people – the northern kingdom, known biblically as "Israel," and the southern kingdom, usually known in the Bible as "Judah."[13] Each kingdom had its own king. Israel (the northern kingdom) and Syria formed an alliance to combat the rising threat from Assyria. When Ahaz (king of Judah, the southern kingdom) refused to join this political alliance, Israel and Syria threatened to dethrone Ahaz and war resulted.[14] Ahaz was considering an alliance with Assyria to assist in Judah's defense against the coalition of Israel and Syria. God knew his thoughts! In response, God sent Isaiah to Ahaz with a strong message that his reliance should be in God alone not in foreign nations. Isaiah promised Ahaz that if he would be still and trust God in this matter, God would deliver Judah. Ahaz foolishly chose to put his trust in Assyria rather than God and his choice subjected Judah to the rule of Assyria, a pagan nation. As a result of this decision, Isaiah prophesied that God would use the very nation Ahaz sought as his protection to come against Judah and lay waste to the land.[15] Because of God's mercy, however, He would not permit the Assyrians to totally destroy Judah.

The Assyrian invasion Isaiah had prophesied took place during Hezekiah's reign[16] after Hezekiah stopped paying tribute to

---

12 Longman III and Garland, general editors, *The Expositor's Bible Commentary: Psalms*, Vol. 5, Revised Edition (Zondervan 2008) Psalm 72:1, p. 549
13 Although sometimes the Bible refers to the southern kingdom as "Israel."
14 734 B.C.E.
15 Isaiah 7:18-25
16 701 B.C.E.

Assyria. However, God used Isaiah once again as His messenger to King Hezekiah, the son of Ahaz. Isaiah boldly encouraged Hezekiah to stand still and watch the Lord fight the battle on behalf of Jerusalem. Unlike his father, Hezekiah believed God and refused to surrender to the Assyrian commander. In response to Hezekiah's faith and his submission to God's authority over Judah, God did exactly what He promised. He destroyed the Assyrian army[17] and Jerusalem was spared – for the time being.

However, there would be another test of faith for Hezekiah which he would fail miserably. When the King of Babylon sent letters and a gift to Hezekiah,[18] Hezekiah strangely showed the Babylonian representatives everything in the treasury and armory of Judah.[19] While the content of those Babylonian letters is not revealed in Isaiah's biblical account, scholars assume that through them Babylon was seeking a political alliance with Judah.[20] This conclusion is based in large part on two factors: 1) Hezekiah's friendly display of Judah's wealth which suggests that he was showing off what Judah would be able to contribute to such an alliance and 2) the fact that God was obviously not pleased – this was his father's mistake in instant replay! Like his father before him, Hezekiah was rejecting God's sovereign rule over Judah and placing his trust for safety and security in a foreign, pagan nation. The result was that Isaiah announced God's decision to permit Babylon to destroy Jerusalem and take some of Hezekiah's sons captive to Babylon.[21]

If you are even vaguely familiar with Old Testament history, it comes as no surprise that God disciplined His Covenant people because of their idolatry and their ethical and moral breaches

---

17 Isaiah 36:1-37:38
18 Isaiah 39:1
19 Isaiah 39:2
20 Motyer, J. Alec, *Isaiah*, Tyndale Old Testament Commentaries, Vol 20 (IVP Academic 1999) Isaiah 39:1-2, p. 270
21 Isaiah 39:5-8

of God's Covenant with them.[22] But did you know that God's displeasure with His Covenant people included their failure to depend on Him alone for their safety and security? "[D]efection to other gods could and often did imply subjugation to a political power associated with them."[23] That is to say, foreign gods were part of the package with a foreign political alliance.[24] When God's people rely on the nations around them for physical protection and prosperity God's role as sovereign King is usurped! Israel (both the northern and the southern kingdom) was in a Covenant relationship with Yahweh. It was designed to be an exclusive relationship. He was to be her husband – her sole provider and protector – her Shepherd, her King. He had promised on oath that He would always be faithful. He was to be Israel's unequivocal King and every earthly king was to function as His royal representative. To that end, a copy of God's Law was given to the Israelite King at his coronation. Conformity to God's divine Law was to distinguish his rule from the "human-centered rule of the nations" which surrounded them.[25] Israel's kings were to be servants and direct under-shepherds to Yahweh, ruling under *His* divine authority and direction.[26] Under no circumstances were

---

22 "The evil deeds in which Israel was involved were of two broad classes—the worship of false gods, and the perpetration of personal and social sins of an ethical and moral kind.... The ethical sins touched on matters of justice, honest, purity, etc. ([Jeremiah] 7:5,8)." Thompson, J. A., *The Book of Jeremiah*, The New International Commentary on The Old Testament (Eerdmans 1980) Jeremiah VI. The Message of Jeremiah under *A. The Message of Jeremiah To His Own Generation, 3. Sin and Repentance*, p. 111

23 McConville, J. G., *Deuteronomy*, Apollos Old Testament Commentary 5 (IVP Academic 2002) Deuteronomy 13:1-2 [2-3] under *Comment*, p. 236

24 "[R]eligous loyalties were often involved in a political alliance because the vassals of great kings were required to indicate at least a token acknowledgment of the deities of the overload (cf. 2 K. 16:10-16)." Thompson, J. A., *The Book of Jeremiah*, The New International Commentary on The Old Testament (Eerdmans 1980) Jeremiah 2:2, p. 163

25 Longman III and Garland, general editors, *The Expositor's Bible Commentary: Psalms*, Vol. 5, Revised Edition (Zondervan 2008) Psalm 72:1, p. 549

26 Block, Daniel I., *Beyond The River Chebar: Studies in Kingship and Eschatology in the Book of Ezekiel* (Cascade Books 2013) Zion Theology in the

they to ever substitute their own wisdom for His. The result of decisions to seek alliances with foreign nations rather than trust God's promises is that these kings ceased living under God's sovereign rule. They rejected God's Kingship in favor of being ruled by other earthly kingdoms which appeared stronger and safer and better able to provide for Israel's military defense. The end result is that those kings lost their crowns and their kingdom – the precise treasures they were trying to protect!

Individual rejection of God's ways and His right to govern them with His rules for their behavior (the Law of Moses), followed by national rejection of God's government (seeking provision and protection from pagan nations), resulted in God allowing them to suffer the consequences of the free will choices they had made! The very thing they trusted in guaranteed disaster.[27] This is the predictable result that is guaranteed when we trust the things of this world for our safety and security. Satan will inevitably twist what had appealed to us in our weakness and use that very thing to ultimately assure our bondage and our ultimate destruction.

After the decision Ahaz made to align with Assyria, the descendants of David who sat on Judah's throne were mere puppet kings – first to Assyria and then to Babylon. With the complete destruction of Jerusalem by Babylon in 586 B.C.E., both the crown and the independently sovereign kingdom of Israel ended.[28] This sad reality remained true even centuries later in the time of

---

Book of Ezekiel, p. 9. See for example: Psalm 2:6-9; 45:6; 72:1-4

27   Motyer, J. Alec, *Isaiah*, Tyndale Old Testament Commentaries, Vol 20 (IVP Academic 1999) Isaiah 7:18-8:8, p. 91

28   Baker, David W., "Isaiah," in *Zondervan Illustrated Bible Backgrounds Commentary: Old Testament*, Vol. 4, edited by John H. Walton (Zondervan 2009) Isaiah Introduction, pp. 3-7. Jehoiachin, king of Judah, was taken to Babylon in 597 B.C.E. He was the last direct heir of the Jewish line of kings. Jeremiah predicted that Jehoiachin would have no natural seed upon the throne (Jeremiah 22:30). Notably in Matthew 1:11 Jehoiachin (also known as Jeconiah) is listed in the genealogy of Jesus!

Christ. You may recall that at Christ's trial Israel's ruling leaders shouted they had no king but the Roman King called Caesar![29]

The kingdom of darkness, that which stands against God and His Kingdom, is empowered by lies and by human agreement with those lies. In fact, the first recorded sin (rebellion against God) in the Bible was the result of Eve coming into agreement with the lies of the serpent. To agree with Satan's plan gives him access to kill, steal and destroy.[30] "The only way to break an agreement with a lie is *repentance*."[31] Not surprisingly then, as we continue to explore the prophetic pattern in Isaiah, the prophet's repeated calls for *repentance* stand out. For example:

> People of Isra'el! **Return** to him to whom you have been so deeply disloyal! Isaiah 31:6 CJB, bold added

> I have swept away your transgressions like a cloud, and your sins like a mist. **Return** to Me, for I have redeemed you. Isaiah 44:22 HCSB, bold added

> Let the wicked one abandon his way, and the sinful one his thoughts; let him **return** to the Lord, so He may have compassion on him, and to our God, for He will freely forgive. Isaiah 55:7 HCSB, bold added

This is a place where a Word Study of the original Hebrew language will be very helpful and allow us to recapture what has been lost in translation. As we will see, there is a significant difference between the common English thought behind the word "repent" and the Hebraic understanding. In the English language, "repent" is a verb that means to feel or express sincere regret or remorse about one's sin or wrongdoing. Common synonyms

---

[29] John 19:15
[30] Johnson, Bill, *Strengthen Yourself in the Lord* (Destiny Image Publishers 2007) p. 67
[31] Johnson, Bill, *Strengthen Yourself in the Lord* (Destiny Image Publishers 2007) p. 69

include bewail, lament, regret and be sorry.[32] As we will see, repent is a word which has been lost in translation. The Hebraic understanding of "repent" goes well beyond merely feeling remorse or regret.

> ## WORD STUDY
>
> *The bolded word* **return** *in each of the quoted verses from Isaiah is the word shuwb {shoob} (also transliterated šûḇ or shub). It is the Hebrew word for repent and is the twelfth most frequently used verb in the entire Old Testament (used over 1000 times).*[33]
>
> *Shuwb is a verb of motion and properly refers to changing direction (condition, state, etc). The precise nature of change depends on the context, but generally shuwb can refer to: turning to, returning, restoring, turning away or turning back to.*[34] *When used metaphorically it refers to a radical change in lifestyle and behavior.*
>
> *There are two types of turning involved in true repentance: 1) to turn* **from** *evil and 2) to turn* **to** *the good.*[35] *In Jewish thought turning to God is the way to turn away from evil.*[36]

---

32 *Dictionary.com*, entry for *repent*. Retrieved from https://www.dictionary.com/browse/repent (last accessed July 10, 2021); *Thesaurus.com*, entry for *repent*. Retrieved from https://www.thesaurus.com/browse/repent (last accessed July 10, 2021)
33 Harris and Waltke, editors, *Theological Wordbook of the Old Testament* (Moody Press 1999) word #2340, p. 909
34 Hill, Gary, *The Discovery Bible*, HELPS Ministries, Inc., [H]39d (SN 7725) *shûḇ*
35 Harris and Waltke, editors, *Theological Wordbook of the Old Testament* (Moody Press 1999) word #2340, p. 909
36 Parsons, John J., *Thoughts on Repentance*, Hebrew 4 Christians. Retrieved from http://www.hebrew4christians.com/Holidays/Fall_Holidays/Elul/Teshuvah/teshuvah.html (last accessed July 10, 2021)

Notice that the Hebraic concept of repentance involves a change of action! The type of turning that God requires is turning to Him with all your heart, soul and strength (see 2 Kings 23:25). In other words, He requires our total allegiance. Notice also that repentance requires two actions: 1) the first step is to stop sinning and 2) the second step involves replacing the sinful behavior with what pleases God. That means repentance requires not only a confession with your mouth, it must be demonstrated by your actions.[37] What we see in the Bible is that God consistently rejects "the empty mouthing of [remorseful] phrases without true heart repentance" that is marked by a corresponding change of behavior.[38]

Isaiah called Judah to true biblical repentance, but Judah did not repent. As a result, in 586 B.C.E., about 90 - 100 years after Isaiah finished his prophetic commission, the Babylonians destroyed Jerusalem.[39] At that time most of the Hebrew people were taken to Babylon. The Babylonian captivity marks a low point in Israel's history. The nation had to face the full brunt of

---

37 To the prophet Isaiah, Israel's sin isn't simply missing the mark, it is considered to be direct rebellion against God. "The holiness of God is thus repudiated by a people whose entire life now reflects the exact opposite of character (cf. Psalm 78:40ff)." Childs, Brevard S., *Isaiah*, Old Testament Library Commentary (Westminster John Knox Press 2001) Isaiah 1:4-9, p. 18

38 Thompson, J. A., *The Book of Jeremiah*, The New International Commentary on The Old Testament (Eerdmans 1980) Jeremiah 3:19-20, p. 208

39 There were three different periods of deportation to Babylon. The first wave began with those who were taken to Babylon in 605 B.C.E. which included Daniel who was deported as a youth. (Daniel 1:1-6). In 597 B.C.E. Babylon captured Jerusalem and a second wave of deportation took place which included Ezekiel (2 Kings 24:15-17; Ezekiel 1). In 586 B.C.E. the Babylonians destroyed Jerusalem and the Temple, burning the city's walls and gates with fire (2 Kings 25; Jeremiah 39). All military, civil and religious leaders were either executed or taken into captivity. Only the poorest of the peasants of Judah were allowed to remain in the land which was by now a place of complete desolation. The southern kingdom of Judah ended and this marked the end of the First Temple Period.

the curses outlined in Deuteronomy as a result of their Covenant disobedience.

For a season they would be without a homeland of their own. Amazingly, even in their exile, God promised His Presence would go with them and He would provide for them a Sanctuary in the midst of their trial.

> Therefore say, "Thus says the Lord God, Though I had removed them far away among the nations and though I had scattered them among the countries, yet I was a **sanctuary** for them a little while in the countries where they had gone." Ezekiel 11:16, bold added

God, who had given up His dwelling place in the Sanctuary built for Him in Jerusalem, became a Sanctuary for the very people who rejected His Kingdom rule! Amazing. Incredible. Unbelievable. But that's our God! In the next lesson we will explore this mind-boggling idea of God Himself being a Sanctuary for His people.

Hear What The Spirit is Saying to the Church: *Oh that my people would believe what I say. I had warned through the mouth of my prophets – my sent ones – exactly what would take place if my Covenant people did not follow my ways and keep my commands. But they would not listen. In my great love for them I allowed the choices they made to bring the very results I had warned of. It is always so. I will force no man to choose me or choose my Kingdom rule over him. My Kingdom ways are not the ways of the world. No! Never do I force, never do I take captive. I am He who sets free and it is out of freedom that I rule and reign as King. Choice is the key. Choose wisely.*

LESSON 6:

GOD'S PRESENCE
DURING THE PERIOD
OF THE EXILE

 "... 'Thus says the Lord God, "Though I had removed them far away among the nations and though I had scattered them among the countries, **yet I was a sanctuary for them** a little while in the countries where they had gone."'
Ezekiel 11:16, bold added

AS WE HAVE seen, even after God's repeated warnings Judah did not repent. God kept His word and after three different deportations, all but the poorest of Judah's citizens had been removed from their homeland. In 586 B.C.E. Jerusalem was destroyed including the Temple Solomon had built.

Ezekiel was in the second group of Israelites who were deported to Babylon. While he was in Babylon he was given a vision that allowed him to see God's glorious Presence leaving Solomon's Temple. He was then commanded to tell the exiled Israelites what he had seen. God was no longer seated among the cherubim in the inner Sanctuary of Solomon's Temple.

All ancient people groups understood temples to be sacred spaces. As we noted in Lesson 4, they were thought to link heaven with earth. Therefore a temple provided an intersection between the human realm and the divine realm. Temples in the Near Eastern cultures of that day were always viewed as a means for divine Presence and blessing. In our present-day Western culture, we have grown accustomed to empty church buildings scattered indiscriminately throughout most of our cities. But to these ancient Hebrew people, the ramifications of God's glory leaving Solomon's Temple were unimaginable. In the surrounding cultures, the destruction or loss of a temple was viewed as disastrous for the community in which the temple had stood. Being defeated by an enemy who then destroyed your temple was generally thought to be the result of improper worship of the god associated with that temple.[1] The pattern found in the temple accounts of the ancient Near East is that a "patron deity of the city typically expressed its dedication to the local temple as long as the king, priesthood, and the people maintained the building and its rituals."[2] The Temple in Jerusalem had served as a "visible sign of Yahweh's presence among [His people] and as a symbol of their status as the people of Yahweh."[3] However, because a Sanctuary is "a place where God dwells in all his holiness,"[4] it can only ever be a true Sanctuary when it is filled with God's divine Presence. God wanted His Covenant people to know they had forfeited His Dwelling-Presence in their midst because of their own choices. Based on what we have learned so far, we now understand that His Dwelling-Presence was removed because He was no longer honored as King in the hearts of His Covenant people.

In the vision, Ezekiel watched as Yahweh's "throne-chariot convey[ed] [His] glory back to its real and eternal abode in the heavens."[5] God's Presence not only left the Temple in Jerusa-

---

1   The Persian King Cyrus who defeated the powerful Babylonians boasted that his success was "because the Babylonians had neglected the true worship of Marduk, their god." Baker, David W., "Isaiah," in *Zondervan Illustrated Bible Backgrounds Commentary*, Vol. 4, edited by John H. Walton (Zondervan 2009) Isaiah 8:8 under *Immanuel*, p. 48
2   Monson, John, "1 Kings," in *Zondervan Illustrated Bible Backgrounds Commentary*, Vol. 3, edited by John H. Walton (Zondervan 2009) 1 Kings 9:3, p. 42
3   Block, Daniel I., *The Book of Ezekiel: Chapters 1-24*, The New International Commentary on the Old Testament (Eerdmans 1997) Ezekiel 11:16, p. 350
4   Motyer, J. Alec, *The Prophecy of Isaiah: An Introduction & Commentary* (InterVarsity Press 1993) Isaiah 8:14-15, p. 95
5   Block, Daniel I., *The Book of Ezekiel: Chapters 1-24*, The New International Commentary on the Old Testament (Eerdmans 1997) Ezekiel 11:22-23,

My Dwelling Place 69

lem, the Ark of the Covenant, which had represented His Dwelling-Presence, literally disappeared from history. An explanation for its whereabouts is provided in 2 Maccabees 2:4-5 which is thought to be have been written about 150 B.C.E.[6] The author explains that Jeremiah had received a warning from God and he hid the Tabernacle and the Ark in a cave in Mt. Nebo.[7] As quoted below, the author concludes his account by indicating that this hiding place is not marked and will not be revealed until God is ready for it to be found.[8]

> … "The place shall be unknown until God gathers his people together again and shows his mercy. And then the Lord will disclose these things, and the glory of the

---

p. 358

6   The book of Second Maccabees was written in Greek for Jews living in the Greek speaking area in Egypt. The book provides a summary historical account of the persecution of the people of Judah while living under the reign of the Seleucids. Berthelot, Katell, *The Maccabean Victory Explained: Between 1 and 2 Maccabees*, The Torah.com. Retrieved from https://www.thetorah.com/article/the-maccabean-victory-explained-between-1-and-2-maccabees (last accessed October 22, 2023)

7   The mountain Moses ascended so he could see the Promised Land with his own eyes before he died.

8   On March 28, 2017 Breaking Israel News (now Israel365News) published an article written by Adam Eliyahu Berkowitz. The article originally titled, *Enigmatic Dead Sea 'Copper Scroll' Reveals True Locations of Lost Temple Treasures* discusses the efforts of Jim Barfield, working with Israel Antiquities Authority, to locate the hiding place of the "Temple vessels." Barfield is using directions provided on a copper scroll which was located in 1952 near Qumran on the shores of the Dead Sea. The scroll has been a mystery because while the other Dead Sea Scrolls contain religious and biblical works, the Copper Scroll is simply a list of 64 locations and corresponding amounts of gold and silver. Barfield believes this scroll identifies the location of the items hidden by Jeremiah as being in the area of Qumran. Note: The article has been retitled: *Secret Of Dead Sea Copper Scroll Unlocked: Revealing Location Of Lost Temple Treasures* and can be retrieved from https://www.israel365news.com/85762/enigmatic-dead-sea-copper-scroll-reveals-true-locations-lost-temple-treasures/#MqgodeeDtSEFeFCD.97 (last accessed July 10, 2021)

Lord and the cloud will appear, as they were shown in the case of Moses, and as Solomon asked that the place should be specially consecrated."[9]

We don't know with certainty that this account in 2 Maccabees is factually true. However, we do know that by choosing to enter into an alliance with Babylon for her protection, Judah had failed to put her trust in God alone. In response, God graciously gave Judah over to the choice she had made. This is a fundamental principle in all of Scripture. God has given us free will and He allows us to choose, but when we have not chosen wisely then He permits us to live with the consequences of our poor choice. Judah had chosen Babylon therefore, Babylon would be her ruler for a season!

Even so, Ezekiel informs us of something truly amazing. We concluded our last lesson with our Key Scripture for this lesson.

> Therefore say, "Thus says the Lord God, Though I had removed them far away among the nations and though I had scattered them among the countries, yet I was a **sanctuary** for them a little while in the countries where they had gone." Ezekiel 11:16, bold added

God takes full credit for Israel's present circumstances. The phrases, "Though *I* had removed them" and "though *I* had scattered them" indicates His Covenant people are precisely where *He* has put them. "Yet ...!" The word "yet" is a translation of the common Hebrew conjunction *waw*. Old Testament scholars Gleason Archer and Eugene Merrill assert that this Hebrew conjunction should never be ignored; every occurrence must be thoughtfully considered by the translator.[10] They point to the fact that such careful consideration is the only way to avoid separating thoughts that the author intended be joined together.[11] Here,

---
9   2 Maccabees 2:7-8 RSV
10 Hill, Gary, *The Discovery Bible*, HELPS Ministries, Inc., [H]9999 *waw*
11 Hill, Gary, *The Discovery Bible*, HELPS Ministries, Inc., [H]9999 *waw* under *Second Click, Illustrating "in plain English"*

My Dwelling Place

God's ownership for the fact that His Covenant people find themselves in Babylon is qualified by the astounding revelation that He has not parked them there and then forgotten about them. He went with them into their captivity! "For a little while" He became a Sanctuary for them in a foreign land. The phrase, *for a little while* can have several meanings. I am going to suggest that in this context it primarily refers to duration – a short amount of time.[12] We will come back to this phrase in our last lesson when we address the fact that the apostle John saw no physical Temple/Sanctuary in New Jerusalem because "the Lord God the Almighty and the Lamb are its temple/sanctuary."[13]

During the Babylonian exile, relationship with Yahweh is possible in some new way without the Temple.[14] Scholar J. Alec Motyer understands this announcement as a promise of God's "purely spiritual presence; the Immanuel-presence with the true, believing remnant" of Israel.[15] The idea of Holy Spirit[16] being present in the Old Testament is not a novel idea. Every memory Israel recorded about her exodus experience includes the appearance of God's Presence, although as we pointed out in Lesson 1, it

---

12 Scholar Daniel Block points out that there are several different ways in which the phrase "in a little while" could be understood. For example, it could refer to "a little sanctuary" or it could be a reference to a short time as in "a little while" or even a qualitative reference such as "to a limited extent." Block submits that the ambiguity is intentional in order to indicate, "that the presence of Yahweh would be experienced neither to the same degree nor on as permanent a basis as it had been heretofore." Block, Daniel I., *The Book of Ezekiel: Chapters 1-24*, The New International Commentary on the Old Testament (Eerdmans 1997) Ezekiel 11:16, p. 350
13 Revelation 21:22. In that verse the Greek word commonly translated as "temple" can also be properly translated as "sanctuary."
14 Block, Daniel I., *The Book of Ezekiel: Chapters 1-24*, The New International Commentary on the Old Testament (Eerdmans 1997) Ezekiel 11:16, p. 350
15 Motyer, J. Alec, *Isaiah*, Tyndale Old Testament Commentaries (IVP Academic 1999) Isaiah 8:13-14a, p. 97
16 As noted in the Preface, at times in this study I will refer to "the Holy Spirit" (His title) simply as "Holy Spirit" (His name) emphasizing His personal nature. Refer to Preface for additional explanation.

was often manifest through divine agents such as the cloud pillar, the fire pillar, the angel of the Yahweh or a dense cloud.[17] More recent scholarship reads prophetic texts in both Isaiah and Haggai as reflecting Israel's eventual understanding that these divine agents of the exodus were actually God's Spirit at work on their behalf.[18] If God's Spirit could lead Israel out of Egypt and through the wilderness, then His Spirit could certainly be with them as a Sanctuary (Hebrew *miqdash* {mik-dawsh'}) in exile.

We have seen the noun *miqdash* twice before in our study. In our first lesson we learned it was the word God used when He instructed Moses to build the Tabernacle in the wilderness (Exodus 25:8). In Lesson 4, King David used the same word when he gave instruction to build the first Temple (1 Chronicles 22:17-19). In our *miqdash* Word Study (see Lesson 1) we discovered it refers to a set apart place where God dwells in holiness among His people. It denotes the place of His Presence and it is often translated as "Sanctuary."[19]

A physical area devoted to the worship of God is considered sacred because of God's Presence.[20] However, Scripture has already made perfectly clear that God does not need a physical building in order to draw near. Consider, for example, the narrative relating the encounter Moses had with Yahweh at the site of the burning bush. In that instance, God instructed Moses that he was to remove his sandals because he was standing on *holy* (Hebrew *qodesh* {ko'-desh}) ground (Exodus 3:5). We have already learned

---

17   Levison, John R., *The Holy Spirit Before Christianity* (Baylor University Press 2019) pp. 7-8
18   Levison, John R., *The Holy Spirit Before Christianity* (Baylor University Press 2019). See for example: p. 74, pp. 110-111, among others. The specific prophetic texts Levison analyzes to reach his conclusion are Isaiah 63:7-14 and Haggai 2:4-5. Both texts are thought to be written following the Babylonian exile.
19   Harris, Archer, and Waltke, editors, *Theological Wordbook of the Old Testament* (Moody Press 1999) word # 1990f, p. 789 *under miqdash*
20   Block, Daniel I., *The Book of Ezekiel: Chapters 1-24*, The New International Commentary on the Old Testament (Eerdmans 1997) Ezekiel 11:16, p. 349

My Dwelling Place   73

that what made that particular dirt different than all the surrounding desert dirt is God's Presence.[21] In another example, God manifested His Presence on the top of Mt. Sinai for all of Israel to see and hear. However, He instructed Moses to set strict boundaries around the base of the mountain because His Presence caused the entire mountain to become holy ground (Exodus 19).

God planned to use Israel's exile to Babylon as a means of resetting their relationship with Him. The Temple, and the Tabernacle before it, was considered to be a special place of God's Presence. Those physical structures had symbolized His Ruling-Presence and protection. As we've noted, His holiness was associated with those meeting places.[22] Now the people themselves will need to provide the sacred space for His Presence to be among them while they are in exile.[23] Captivity is real, but it is not the only reality, nor is it to be the dispositive reality for Israel. Israel is to see herself as a people living in a foreign land whose God is among them. They are called to live in *that* reality which will demand that they be a holy, set-apart people.

Daniel and his three Hebrew friends understood their holiness requirement as exiles in Babylon. The book of Daniel details experiences of Daniel while he is in Babylonian captivity. A number of instances are recorded which highlight Yahweh's safety and protection. He manifested His Presence as protector and provider

---

21 "God's presence is what makes any place, anything, or anyone holy (Ex 3:5)." Baker and Carpenter, *The Complete WordStudy Dictionary of the Old Testament* (AMG Publishers 2003) word #6944, p. 982

22 Both the Hebrew verb *qadash*, meaning to consecrate or sanctify, and the noun *qodesh*, denoting apartness, holiness or sacredness, are related to the word *miqdash*. Harris, Archer, and Waltke, editors, *Theological Wordbook of the Old Testament* (Moody Press 1999) word #1990, 1990a, 1990f, p. 786

23 Scholar Daniel Block asserts "Here Yahweh promises to be for the exiles what the temple has heretofore been for them in Jerusalem. On the other hand, he changes the locus of worship, promising to be with the exiles on foreign soil, the unclean land (cf. [Ezekiel] 4:13) to which they have been banished." Block, Daniel I., *The Book of Ezekiel: Chapters 1-24*, The New International Commentary on the Old Testament (Eerdmans 1997) Ezekiel 11:16, p. 349

whenever Daniel and/or his friends chose to maintain their distinctive set apart identity rather than worship the king of their captors (Daniel 1,6). In one of those instances, Yahweh made His Protective-Presence known in the midst of a burning hot furnace as the Babylonian King looked on (Daniel 3)!

The idea that the Temple would be destroyed and replaced by God Himself was beyond revolutionary. It was most likely shocking and bewildering. Ezekiel, the son of a priest and a priest himself (Ezekiel 1:3), undoubtedly understood more than most the significance of what God had announced. The priests were the ones God had assigned the responsibility for maintaining the holiness of the Temple to assure His continued Dwelling-Presence. The prevailing view of the Israelites before the exile was that the very fact a Temple stood in Jerusalem was itself an iron-clad guarantee that Jerusalem could never be destroyed by a foreign power. In fact, it was mistakenly thought that, "Yahweh was obligated to defend his land and his people, and to prevent the divorce of the two."[24] The prophets worked hard to discredit Israel's unfounded trust in her land, her Temple and her earthly king as unconditional warranties of security. Jeremiah, in particular, stressed that while the Temple and the Ark of the Covenant were vitally important, as was circumcision, keeping the sabbath and engaging in proper sacrifices, all of these externals were "at best . . . only pointers to spiritual realities. Where men rested content with externals these became worthless, and in fact, dangerous."[25] The prophets understood that the very things God had provided in order to aid Israel in her relationship with Him had actually become "a hindrance to the attainment of true spiritual worship."[26] The people

---

24 Block, Daniel I., *The Book of Ezekiel: Chapters 25-48*, The New International Commentary on the Old Testament (Eerdmans 1998) Ezekiel 36:20-21, p. 347

25 Thompson, J. A., *The Book of Jeremiah*, The New International Commentary on The Old Testament (Eerdmans 1980) Introduction under *Some Important Issues for Exegesis* under *D. Jeremiah and The Cultus*, p. 67

26 Thompson, J. A., *The Book of Jeremiah*, The New International Commentary on The Old Testament (Eerdmans 1980) Introduction under *Some*

My Dwelling Place 75

would not listen. In fact, there were times when they called the prophets traitors and accused them of treason because of the truth they preached. In the end, Israel chose to ignore God's corrective instruction. Yahweh was left with no choice but to lovingly impose upon them the Covenant curses He had promised (Leviticus 26; Deuteronomy 28).

God knew the discouragement of the exiles and understood how easy it would be for hopelessness and despair to overtake them. He wanted them to know He had not abandoned them in spite of their exile. As a result, He went with them into captivity by becoming a Sanctuary Himself! In our first lesson we learned of God's intense desire for fellowship with His creation – especially those in Covenant relationship with Him. The announcement of God's Sanctuary-Presence is an excellent reminder of this continuing desire. While God's Dwelling- Presence was no longer among His people, His desire for fellowship with them was so strong that in spite of their rejection of Him as King, God drew near them in their captivity![27] To His Covenant people living in a foreign land this was nothing short of ground-breaking in their relationship with Yahweh. At that time in the ancient world "it was commonly thought that a deity could be worshipped [exclusively] on the soil of the nation to which he was bound."[28] In fact, pagan gods were generally considered to be first and foremost the god of a certain geographic territory and only secondarily the god of the people who lived in that land.[29] The exiles now living in

---

Important Issues for Exegesis under *D. Jeremiah and The Cultus*, p. 71

27 Scholar Daniel Block points out that the Bible never explains exactly how God's Covenant people in exile might have experienced His Presence. However, the fact that He was present is evidenced by the visions God provides to Ezekiel while he is in Babylon. Block, Daniel I., *The Book of Ezekiel: Chapters 1-24*, The New International Commentary on the Old Testament (Eerdmans 1997) Ezekiel 11:16, p. 350

28 *NIV Study Bible* (Zondervan 1995) study note 2 Kings 5:17, p. 527

29 Block, Daniel I., *The Book of Ezekiel: Chapters 1-24*, The New International Commentary on the Old Testament (Eerdmans 1997) Ezekiel 11:19-20, p. 354

Babylon had thought the land Yahweh was uniquely associated with was the Promised Land – the land from which they have been removed. To conceive of Him as a God of the *people* of Israel separate and apart from the Promised Land must have been an absolutely mind-boggling paradigm change.

Not only did God *promise* His Presence, as we saw in Daniel's experiences, He fulfilled that promise. The dreams and visions God gave to Daniel in his captivity provided additional evidence of His Presence in Babylon. Like Daniel, Ezekiel was also given multiple visions while in Babylon. We considered one of those visions at the beginning of this lesson. After receiving his inaugural vision by the Chebar canal in Babylon, Ezekiel concluded he had seen "the appearance of the likeness of the glory of the Lord."[30] In other words, He had seen a manifestation of Yahweh Himself! Ezekiel was so certain he was in the Presence of Yahweh that he fell face down in reverence and worship. In the visions they received, both Daniel and Ezekiel saw wheels on Yahweh's chariot-like throne.[31] Those wheels reveal the mobility of God's throne providing certainty that He is without boundaries. Unlike the pagan gods, Yahweh is not bound to a particular location or to any one specific structure. His throne is a moveable chariot that can go wherever He wants to go! He is God over *all* of His creation. He is carried along by cherubim and His Manifest-Presence moves in the earth as He wills. As scholar Daniel Block observes:[32]

> ... Yahweh's sudden appearance [to Daniel and] to Ezekiel among the deportees shatters the widespread myth that the influence of patron deities was localized in the territory over which they were understood to have jurisdiction, and that a person's access to the divinity depended on one's physical presence in the god's land.

---

30 Ezekiel 1:28 ESV
31 Daniel 7:9; Ezekiel 1:16
32 Block, Daniel I., *The Book of Ezekiel Chapters 1-24*, The New International Commentary on the Old Testament (Eerdmans 1997) Ezekiel 1:1, pp. 83-84, text of footnote 30 omitted

Yahweh could appear whenever and wherever he chose even in a foreign land, which was generally considered to be unclean (Amos 7:17; Ezek. 4:13).

We know this Presence of Yahweh in Babylon was different than His Dwelling-Presence that had been with Israel since the time of the exodus. After all, during exile they were living on foreign soil and ruled by the Babylonians (and later by the Persians). God was no longer their King in the natural. He had no such symbolic Dwelling-Presence in their midst. So, what does it mean that He was a "Sanctuary" for them during their exile? As we have learned, Sanctuary is the place where God dwells in his holiness. For Him to be a *Sanctuary* among them conveys the vitally important message that they are to be a holy, set-apart people while living in exile. While this holiness requirement is implied in God's Sanctuary-Presence revelation to Ezekiel, it is clearly expressed in His similar announcement through the prophet Isaiah.

> "Then He shall be a sanctuary [*miqdash*] [a sacred, indestructible shelter for those who fear and trust Him]; But to both the houses of Israel [both the northern and southern kingdoms—Israel and Judah, He will be] a stone on which to stumble and a rock on which to trip, A trap and a snare for the inhabitants of Jerusalem...."
> Isaiah 8:14 AMP

The Theological Wordbook of the Old Testament views *miqdash* in Isaiah 8:14 as a figurative reference to a place of refuge.[33] Isaiah's message clarified God's Presence among the exiles would be either a protective refuge or an entrapping snare. The sole determining factor would be contingent upon how His Covenant people respond to His holiness.[34] We have already learned that the word *miqdash* (Sanctuary) was the word commonly used for the Taber-

---

33 Harris, Archer, and Waltke, editors, *Theological Wordbook of the Old Testament* (Moody Press 1999) word #1990f under *miqdash*, p. 789

34 The pattern of the Bible is that "when people turn away from [God] with sufficient stubbornness, he turns away from them (Ro 9:17-21&NN)."

nacle or Temple. New Testament scholar Gregory Beale refers to God's Sanctuary-Presence during exile as "the replacement of the temple by the Lord himself."[35] The real Sanctuary was never the physical Temple, it was God Himself.[36] Israel's Covenant obligation had not changed. Because Yahweh is holy they were to live as a holy, set-apart people.[37] Those who did would find themselves in a spiritually protected refuge. On the other hand, those who chose not to would find that His holiness had become a snare for them.

> He who dwells in the shelter of the Most High Will abide in the shadow of the Almighty. I will say to the LORD, "My refuge and my fortress, My God, in whom I trust!" For it is He who delivers you from the snare of the trapper And from the deadly pestilence. He will cover you with His pinions, And under His wings you may seek refuge; His faithfulness is a shield and bulwark. Psalm 91:1-4

God's Presence in exile assured His availability to Israel in their captivity even absent a physical Temple structure. He wanted them to know He was never far from them. He had not left them on their own. While they might be experiencing the disastrous consequences of their choices, His goal was fellowship and provision that would result in knowing Him by experience. Ultimately that personal knowledge was intended to lead to repentance.

While writing this lesson I pondered at length the difference between His *Dwelling*-Presence and the *Sanctuary*-Presence during exile until finally I heard a new phrase. I knew immediately it was God's revelation. It was very early morning and I was walking

---

Stern, David, H., *Jewish New Testament Commentary* (Jewish New Testament Publications 1992) Hebrews 8:9, p. 691

35 Beale and Carson, editors, *Commentary on the New Testament Use of the Old Testament* (Baker Academic 2007) Romans 9:30-33, p. 651

36 *ESV Study Bible* (Crossway Books 2008) study note Ezekiel 11:14-21, p. 1514

37 Leviticus 11:44; 19:2; 20:7

My Dwelling Place 79

laps around Deck 5 of an Alaska-bound cruise ship. Once again, I was meditating on the concept of God being a Sanctuary for the exiles. Suddenly Holy Spirit simply whispered to my heart, "His Presence-of-Provision." My thoughts quickly turned to the way in which God had masterfully provided for the Hebrew children in the wilderness after He had led them out of their Egyptian captivity. They did not yet know Him as King. Their only experience had been to witness His mighty deliverance from their bondage of slavery. The wilderness made the perfect classroom setting for Him to teach them by experience "His Presence-of-Provision." He provided food, He provided water, He provided safety and He provided daily guidance. Each provision was according to His timetable, His plan and His purpose. Each provision was a carefully calculated lesson that He could be trusted, that He was a God who knew their need, that He was a caring God and that He would faithfully provide for those who chose to trust and obey Him. His provision was so much more than an impersonal relationship between a *provider-god* and people. At Mt. Sinai they had entered into a Covenant relationship with Him – one that was akin to an ancient marriage ceremony. He betrothed Himself to them and they responded in one accord as a wife to her husband.[38] God provided for Israel in the wilderness the way a husband provides for His wife!

Israel's exile period is in many ways thought to be a new exodus type of experience. For example, Israel's crossing of the Red Sea provides the backdrop for Isaiah 11:15 and 43:2,16-17.[39] Jer-

---

38 In ancient times a betrothed woman was considered "married" except that she did not begin to live with her "husband" until sometime later when the marriage ceremony actually took place.
39 *NIV Study Bible* (Zondervan Publishing 1995) Introduction to Isaiah, p. 1009 also points to other exodus allusions in Isaiah 4:5-6; 31:5 and 37:36. Scholar Bernard Anderson presents a list of passages in Isaiah 40-55 (40:3-5; 41:17-20; 42:14-16; 43:1-3,14-21; 48:20-21; 49:8-12; 51:9-11; 52:11-12; 55:12-13) in which he believes "the theme of the new exodus is the specific subject" of the passage. Anderson, Bernard W., *Exodus Typology in Second Isaiah*, Chapter XII of B. Anderson & W. Harrelson, eds.,

emiah 31:2 describes the captivity of Israel "as a new wandering in the wilderness."[40] Like Israel's exodus wilderness experience, God promised to provide the exiles with the type of sanctuary a husband provides for his wife – one with food, clothing, shelter, comfort and companionship. He wanted to leave no doubt that it was *not* a foreign king nor the gods of their captors who was providing for their needs. Just as He had done in the post-exodus wilderness experience, He would supply all of their need in exile! God wanted to woo Israel back to Himself. His desire was for her to recognize that *He* was all she needed and then one day – when the fullness of time had come – they would once again choose Him to be their Sovereign King.

In fact, the story of God's continuing Kingdom rule is a pattern which emerged during the first biblical account of God's Kingship in Genesis and does not conclude until the closing chapters of the book of Revelation. It is easy to overlook the continuity of the Kingship theme and its expression through Temple symbolism because the shape or form of the "Temple" changes in order to translate its function into the historical circumstances. Let's do a very quick review of biblical history and you'll see what I mean.

As we noted in our first lesson, the Garden of Eden is viewed by some scholars as God's first Temple on earth. God created the perfect paradise for His Kingdom rule on earth and then set man in the garden with Him. God walked in the Garden-Temple with man. However, when Adam sinned, not only was he cast out of the Garden-Sanctuary, but thereafter God's throne is always seen as being in heaven. After Adam's sin, the only earthly representa-

---

Israel's Prophetic Heritage: Essays in Honor of James Mullenburg (Harper & Brothers 1962) pp. 177-195 at p. 181. Retrieved from https://jbburnett.com/resources/anderson_isrprophet12-typol.pdf (last accessed October 3, 2023). J. R. Levison notes that Anderson's list is not accepted by all scholars. Levison, John R., *The Holy Spirit Before Christianity* (Baylor University Press 2019) Excursus 11, p. 147

40 Thompson, J. A., *The Book of Jeremiah*, The New International Commentary on The Old Testament (Eerdmans 1980) Jeremiah 31:2, p. 566

tion of God's Ruling-Presence among man is found in symbolic form.

During the wilderness journey from Egypt to the Promised Land, the symbol of God's dwelling Ruling-Presence was the Ark of the Covenant. As King, God was at that time ruling over a nomadic people and His Sanctuary accommodated that reality. As a result, the Ark was housed in a portable Tent structure that could move when the people moved.

At home in the Promised Land, before the land had rest from war, the Ark remained in a portable Tent structure. The Ark of the Covenant was the symbolic footstool of God's heavenly throne. Not until the end of David's reign as king did this symbol of God's Ruling-Presence among His people began to dwell in a permanent structure. David's success as a warrior king had established the physical boundaries of Israel's territory. Typical of ancient Near Eastern kings, David's son Solomon built the first Temple after he became Israel's king. For the first time in Israel's history Solomon's Temple provided a permanent structure to symbolize God's Kingdom reign among His Covenant people.

As we have seen in this lesson, after the destruction of this Temple by the Babylonians, God Himself became a Sanctuary-Presence inside the physical borders of another kingdom. Yahweh continued to choose symbolism of His Kingship which best fit the circumstances and He became "a veritable invisible temple" during exile.[41] Once again, God had translated the concept of His Kingship into Israel's present circumstances. The new format was a significant paradigm shift and a pivotal point in Israel's history. This new translation of "Temple" invites the possibility of a relationship with His Covenant people apart from the physical Tabernacle/Temple which had symbolized His Kingdom rule since the time of the exodus story. With this change of Temple format, the door is opened to a different expression of His

---

41 Beale, G. K., *The Temple and the Church's Mission: A Biblical Theology of The Dwelling Place of God*, New Studies in Biblical Theology 17 (Intervarsity Press 2004) p. 110

Kingship – sovereignly ruling His "Kingdom within the physical borders of another kingdom."[42] His rule and authority transcends every geographic boundary established by an earthly ruler!

Let me stop here to define the terms I am using. As previously noted, when I employ the term "Kingdom," I am referring to the spiritual Kingdom ruled by God from His heavenly throne which will continue to advance on the earth until the end of the age. On the other hand, throughout this study, I am using the term "kingdom" to define a distinctive people group who live under the authority of a human government without regard to the form of government. Throughout the remainder of this study I will continue to use the phrase "Kingdom within a kingdom" (God's Kingship present within the geographic borders of a ruling government of the world) or sometimes "Kingdom within other kingdoms" (God's Kingship honored within the geographic borders of more than one ruling government on the earth).[43] Because of my continued use of these phrases, it will be beneficial to add some additional explanation. To do so, we will turn to the recurring biblical metaphor of light and darkness which provides an excellent visual aid to understand the concept of a *Kingdom within a kingdom(s)*.

The New Testament uses light as a synonym for God's Kingdom.[44] The present earth is divided into distinct human kingdoms

---

42   About 18 months after I wrote this phrase "Kingdom within another kingdom" or "Kingdom inside a kingdom" in this lesson – a phrase I had never heard anyone use before, I heard Perry Stone describe Christ-followers in America by saying, "We are a Kingdom in a nation." By that he meant that within the nation of the United States, those who follow Christ are "in" [and therefore represent] the "Kingdom of God." I share the phrase Perry Stone used in the event it provides clearer understanding of the terminology God has led me to use in this study.

43   There is only one Kingdom of God, but there are as many kingdoms of the world as there are separate and distinct world governments. Unless those world governments have bowed to the authority of King Jesus, they are ruling on behalf of the kingdom of darkness.

44   See for example: John 8:12; 2 Corinthians 4:6; Revelation 21:23; 22:5. MacArthur, John, *The MacArthur Study Bible* (Thomas Nelson 2006) study

and is biblically pictured as being engulfed by spiritual darkness.[45] The principle way darkness manifests on earth is by way of sin.[46] Those who are depicted as remaining in darkness are ruled by Satan. They functionally do his work and belong to his kingdom. In direct contrast, God is Light and no darkness is found in Him (1 John 1:5). In fact, "he removed darkness from those who came to the light by forgiving sin ...."[47] Salvation is metaphorically described as turning from darkness to come into the Light (Acts 26:18; Ephesians 5:8).[48] Those who have transferred from the kingdom of darkness into God's Light (Colossians 1:13) are called *lights of the world* – a city on a hill that cannot be hidden (Matthew 5:14). They are transformed and become those who are "inwardly charged with new, outshining life."[49] Allowing God's Light to shine through them is their ultimate task in the present age.[50] Using the light-darkness motif Paul advised Christ-followers to walk in the ways of Christ so they would shine "like bright lights in a [dark] world full of crooked and perverse people (Philippians 2:15 NLT)." All over the world there are *lights shining among the darkness*. They are citizens of heaven living among the various distinct kingdoms on the earth. They are presently in a united

---

note Colossians 1:12 under *in Light*, p. 1801
45   See for example: Isaiah 60:1-2
46   Brown, Raymond E., *The Epistles of John: A New Translation With Introduction and Commentary By Raymond E. Brown*, The Anchor Yale Bible, Volume 30 (Yale University Press 1982) 1 John 1:5 – 2:2 under *Comment A. God is Light Without Darkness* (1 John 1:5) p. 230
47   Brown, Raymond E., *The Epistles of John: A New Translation With Introduction and Commentary By Raymond E. Brown*, The Anchor Yale Bible, Volume 30 (Yale University Press 1982) 1 John 1:5 – 2:2 under *Comment A. God is Light Without Darkness* (1 John 1:5) p. 230. To say "'God is light' is not an abstract definition but [like other 'God is ... formulas' it] portrays God's identity revealed in terms of function." Ibid, p. 229
48   Jesus is the Light sent into the world by the Father. John 8:12; 12:46
49   Motyer, J. Alec, *The Prophecy of Isaiah: An Introduction & Commentary* (InterVarsity Press 1993) Isaiah 60:1-5, p. 494
50   Barth, Markus, *Ephesians Translation and Commentary on Chapters 1-3*, The Anchor Bible Vol 34 (Doubleday 1974) Ephesians 3:1-13 under *Comment IV The Servant Church*, p. 364

spiritual Kingdom although physically located in the various geographic kingdoms of this world. Wherever they are gathered together Jesus promised to be among them (Matthew 18:20) and they function as an outpost of God's heavenly Kingdom.[51] The day will come when all those in the spiritual *Kingdom of Light* will live forever in the "unrestricted presence of God and the Lamb."[52] The goal of God's heart to dwell among His people will be fulfilled. Whereas everyone who chose to remain in the darkness (all the other citizens of the various geographic kingdoms of the earth) will go to their eternal doom.

With that explanation, let's continue on in our study. We have learned that over time the initial symbol of God's divine rule as King, the Garden of Eden, gave way to various structures some moveable, some more permanent, until the symbol of His Presence is no longer a physical structure and *He* becomes an actual "invisible Temple." As our study continues to unfold, we will see that this paradigm shift of a *Kingdom inside a kingdom* is the essence of the promised New Covenant. New Testament writers understood that the early Church lived on earth as a colony of Christ-followers who were citizens of another Kingdom. Regardless of Rome's earthly rule, God was their true King. They were taught to think of themselves as resident aliens living temporarily in a foreign country while their real home was elsewhere. It was a paradigm shift that began in the period of the exile and continued right up to the closing scenes of Revelation.

---

51 The church was never intended to be "an end in itself, [it is called to be] a functional outpost of God's kingdom." Barth, Markus, *Ephesians Translation and Commentary on Chapters 1-3*, The Anchor Bible Vol 34 (Doubleday 1974) Ephesians 3:1-13 under *Comment IV The Servant Church*, p. 364. An outpost is "a small military camp or position at some distance from the main force; a remote part of a country or empire." *Microsoft Bing Dictionary*. Retrieved from https://www.bing.com/search?q=what+is+an+outpost&form=ANSNB1&refig=f934a724402b4d3f8df0aafe3c4ee3ba&pc=U531 (last accessed October 14, 2023).

52 Bauckham, Richard, *The Theology of the Book of Revelation* (Cambridge University Press 1993) p. 140

We've seen that the corrective discipline of exile wasn't the last of God's Word to Judah. Exile was not a sign of God's unfaithfulness, "but rather the 'strict adherence to [the covenant's] fine print. Israel has brought on itself the covenant curses by trampling underfoot the covenant grace of Yahweh.'"[53] Yet in God's grace, restoration is always the purpose and the intended result of divine discipline which is purposefully designed to lead to repentance. His promised restoration of Israel will be the subject of our next lesson.

Hear What The Spirit is Saying to the Church: *Everything I do is for my Name's sake. I set my protective hand over my Covenant people as I sent them into exile. Oh, that they would have obeyed my warning when spoken through my prophets – my sent ones. But indeed I gave them over to the choices they had made. Yet was I with them to lead them, to guide them, to protect them as a Father protects and provides for his children … as a husband protects and provides for his wife. So, I was with them. My desire was indeed for their repentance, for them to come to know me as their only protector and provider. My desire was for continuing fellowship with them so they would know me. No longer would I depend on their outward obedience to my commands. No longer would I depend on their choice of me as their King. So I had my prophet deliver the message announcing the paradigm change I had ordained. I would replace their heart of stone with a heart of flesh. I would put my commands in their hearts so that once again I might dwell among them not only as protector and provider, not only as the one who provides salvation in time of need, but as King. My Kingdom rule would be set up in their midst when once again they choose me over the ways of the world. And indeed we are moving toward the fullness of*

---

53 Ezekiel 16:15-43; Peterson, Brian Neil, *Ezekiel in Context: Ezekiel's Message Understood in Its Historical Setting of Covenant Curses and Ancient Near Eastern Mythological Motifs* (Pickwick Publications 2012) p. 73, citing Ezekiel 16:15-43

that time on my Kingdom calendar when once again my Dwelling- Presence will rest among them – not in a Temple made by human hands, but in a Temple I have created to serve just such a purpose. And so it shall be.

LESSON 7:

PROMISED RETURN OF
GOD'S PRESENCE

"Then [the one guiding me] led me to the gate, the gate facing toward the east; and behold, The glory of the God of Israel was coming from the way of the east. And His voice was like the sound of many waters; and the earth shone with His glory. And it *was* like the appearance of the vision which I saw ... when He came to destroy the city. And the visions *were* like the vision which I saw by the river Chebar; and I fell on my face. And the glory of the LORD came into the house [*bayith*] by the way of the gate facing toward the east. And the Spirit lifted me up and brought me into the inner court; and behold, the glory of the LORD filled the house [*bayith*]." Ezekiel 43:1-5, italics in original

AS WE HAVE said, exile is not the last chapter for Yahweh's Covenant people. In fact, exile was actually designed by God to be a new beginning! I mentioned in our last lesson that God had chosen to give Israel a *reset*. We'll begin this lesson by considering the nature of the reset God had in mind. As we've learned, Israel had become more dependent on Solomon's Temple, the Promised Land and their earthly king than their heavenly King. God decided it was time to remove all the props and return to a time when His relationship with Israel was simply that – a connection between the two of them absent everything else. He would figuratively return them to a period in their history when they had come out of Egyptian bondage into the wilderness to learn about Him. From the wilderness they were to enter the Promised Land with that experienced-based knowledge and live as His Covenant people. Similarly, in exile, stripped of everything else, they were free once again to focus on Him alone. When the captivity was over they were to return to the land with that newly gained experience-based knowledge. Then they could live the life of obedience and holiness He desired.

The wilderness period following their Egyptian captivity was a pattern that could be repeated. That wilderness experience in Israel's history laid the foundation for Israel individually and collectively to be in right relationship with Yahweh. God ordained that their initial relationship would be governed by the Covenant He made with them at Mt. Sinai. In the exile period, the prophets had spoken of a New Covenant relationship Israel would have with God. The exile period would lay a new foundation for Israel individually and collectively to be in a different type of relationship with Yahweh. The new would be markedly different from the former because the former Covenant required that *the people* build the meeting place for God (the Tabernacle). It required *the people* to consecrate their own hearts for total loyalty, submission and obedience to Yahweh. The former Covenant required *the people* to fully love God out of their own spirits. The New Covenant, on the other hand, would shift responsibility to God and He Himself would initiate all of those elements. *He* would build the Temple, *He* would give them a new heart to love Him and *He* would put a new Spirit in them to obey all of His commands. The period of the exile set the stage for the promised New Covenant relationship.

Our Key Scripture for this lesson contains another vision Ezekiel experienced while in Babylon. In this vision, Ezekiel saw the same glory that had departed from Solomon's Temple. However, this time the *Shekinah* glory was returning to God's *house* and filling His *house* once again with His glory. His *Shekinah* glory

My Dwelling Place

had filled the wilderness Tabernacle and later Solomon's Temple.[1] When Isaiah was commissioned by God to be His prophetic voice, Isaiah saw this same glory filling the heavenly Temple.[2]

Ezekiel states twice that this glory, which is associated with God's Presence, filled the "house." As noted in our Key Scripture, the Hebrew word is *bayith* {bah'-yith} which can refer to a dwelling habitation such as a house, Temple, or palace.[3] In fact, some translator's use the word "Temple" instead of "house" in our Key Scripture.[4] However, *bayith* can also refer to a household. It is used to denote a collective family unit such as a clan, dynasty or a family of descendants.[5] As we will soon see, this new Dwelling-Presence does not fill the same type of material Temple that formerly hosted God's glory. *Bayith* as used in our Key Scripture refers to people – the family of God, not a physical building. How can that be? In our last lesson, we took note that God's Sanctuary-Presence among the exiles was a new form of Temple. In the fullness of time on God's Kingdom calendar, He introduced a new type of the Temple-form which met the needs of that new circumstance and laid the foundation for the New Covenant.

Ancient Israel, as was generally true of other nations of the day, regarded certain conditions to be essential to their well-being. These included: 1) a sovereign nation-state, 2) a king, 3) an army,

---

1 Exodus 40:34-35; 1 Kings 8:10–11
2 Isaiah 6:4
3 *The NAS Old Testament Hebrew Lexicon*, entry for *Bayith*. Retrieved from https://www.biblestudytools.com/lexicons/hebrew/nas/bayith.html (last accessed August 26, 2022)
4 See for example: "The glory of the LORD entered the temple by way of the gate that faced east. Then the Spirit lifted me up and brought me to the inner court, and the glory of the LORD filled the temple." Ezekiel 43:4-5 HCSB
5 Baker and Carpenter, *The Complete WordStudy Dictionary of the Old Testament* (AMG Publishers 2003) word #1004, p. 131; Harris, Archer, and Waltke, editors, *Theological Wordbook of the Old Testament* (Moody Press 1999) word # 241, p. 105

4) national borders and 5) a Temple.⁶ Not one of these conditions remained intact when Yahweh sent His Covenant people into exile. Without these false props, however, Israel was rightly positioned to receive new perspectives and new understanding. What they were now well-situated to learn is that obedience to Yahweh is the essential ingredient of their well-being, with obedience defined exclusively by their Covenant relationship with Him.⁷

The fact that Ezekiel was called and ministered as a prophet of Yahweh *in* Babylon "debunked the theological misconception that Yahweh could only operate and be worshipped *in* Jerusalem and Judah."⁸ God's people needed to revise their limited understanding of who He is. He is not confined (as other gods were thought to be) to a specific building or even to the borders of a specific nation. "Yahweh is not '*in* the sanctuary; he *is* their sanctuary.'"⁹

As we are learning, Yahweh's Sanctuary provision in Babylon provided the genesis of the New Covenant. In our next lesson, we will see how God continues to theologically re-educate His people regarding His sovereignty and His holiness. In this regard, we will see how the New Covenant-Presence continues to unfold in history even after a new physical Temple is constructed in Jerusalem. In subsequent lessons we will trace the unfolding Covenant to Christ and then to His devoted followers as they pursue their world-wide mission.

---

6   Thompson, J. A., *The Book of Jeremiah*, The New International Commentary on The Old Testament (Eerdmans 1980) Jeremiah 29:7, p. 546
7   Thompson, J. A., *The Book of Jeremiah*, The New International Commentary on The Old Testament (Eerdmans 1980) Jeremiah 3:13, p. 201
8   Peterson, Brian Neil, *Ezekiel in Context: Ezekiel's Message Understood in Its Historical Setting of Covenant Curses and Ancient Near Eastern Mythological Motifs* (Pickwick Publications 2012) p. 334, italics added
9   Peterson, Brian Neil, *Ezekiel in Context: Ezekiel's Message Understood in Its Historical Setting of Covenant Curses and Ancient Near Eastern Mythological Motifs* (Pickwick Publications 2012) p. 114, italics added, citing Kutsko, *Between Heaven and Earth*, pp. 2-3 and Rendtorff, *Concept of Revelation*, p. 37

Our focus in this lesson will be on the Old Testament announcements of the New Covenant. The New Covenant prophecies were given as a part of God's promised plan to restore to Israel after her period of exile. It is *this* Covenant which followers of Christ typically identify and celebrate as the *New* Covenant Jesus instituted. As a result, we have an important incentive for understanding this *New* Covenant which has sadly and unfortunately been largely lost in translation.

Let's begin with the only direct reference to "a New Covenant" in the entirety of the Old Testament.[10]

> "Behold, days are coming," declares the Lord, "when I will make a new [*chadash*] covenant with the house of Israel and with the house of Judah, not like the covenant which I made with their fathers in the day I took them by the hand to bring them out of the land of Egypt, My covenant which they broke, although I was a husband to them," declares the Lord. "But this is the covenant which I will make with the house of Israel after those days," declares the Lord, "I will put My law within them and on their heart I will write it; and I will be their God, and they shall be My people. They will not teach again, each man his neighbor and each man his brother, saying, 'Know the Lord,' for they will all know Me, from the least of them to the greatest of them," declares the Lord, "for I will forgive their iniquity, and their sin I will remember no more." Jeremiah 31:31-34

The prophet Ezekiel was Jeremiah's contemporary. God used him to provide additional insight about Jeremiah's New Covenant announcement.[11]

---

10 Thompson, J. A., *The Book of Jeremiah*, The New International Commentary on the Old Testament (Eerdmans 1980) Jeremiah 31:31, p. 579

11 Guthrie, George H., *2 Corinthians*, Baker Exegetical Commentary On The New Testament (Baker Academic 2015) 2 Corinthians 3:3, p. 192

And I will give you a new [*chadash*] heart, and a new [*chadash*] spirit I will put within you. And I will remove the heart of stone from your flesh and give you a heart of flesh. And I will put my Spirit within you, and cause you to walk in my statutes and be careful to obey my rules. Ezekiel 36:26-27 ESV[12]

Now that we have read the primary biblical prophecies of the promised *New* Covenant, a helpful starting place for our discussion will be a Word Study to discover what God meant by "new." Once we understand this word in its proper context, we will be well on our way to understanding what we commonly call the New Covenant.

WORD STUDY

When Jeremiah 31 and Ezekiel 11 employ the word **new** *(as in New Covenant, new heart and new spirit) the Hebrew adjective is chadash {khaw-dawsh'}. It refers to that which is new, renewed or fresh.*[13]

Its' verbal root is used biblically in the sense of restoring the Temple (2 Chronicles 24:4,12), repairing its altar (2 Chronicles 15:8), renewing the kingdom (1 Samuel 11:14) or rebuilding cities (Isaiah 61:4).[14] *The Greek equivalent is kainos {kahee-nos'} which refers not only to the New Covenant (Luke 22:20) but also to the new man (Ephesians 2:15) and the new creation (2 Corinthians 5:17).*

---

12   See also: Ezekiel 11:19-20
13   Baker and Carpenter, *The Complete WordStudy Dictionary of the Old Testament* (AMG Publishers 2003) word #2319, p. 317
14   Harris, Archer, and Waltke, editors, *Theological Wordbook of the Old Testament* (Moody Press 1999) word # 613, p. 265

My Dwelling Place 93

Scholar Markus Barth views the biblical use of the word *new* as an eschatological term that refers to "a final fulfillment of God's will and work."[15] Because the verb form of *chadash* means to make new, to restore, to repair, to renovate or reconstruct, scholars suggest that is the underlying meaning of a *New* Covenant. As a result, the phrase "New Covenant" could properly be translated as "renewed Covenant."[16] We find a relevant biblical example of this meaning of *chadash* in Job 29:20 when Job said:

My strength will be refreshed [*chadash*] within me, and my bow will be renewed in my hand. Job 29:20 HCSB[17]

Recall that Job experienced intense suffering at the hands of the adversary when God granted Satan permission to "test" Job. In the opening verses of Chapter 29, Job recalls the days of his former glory – the days *before* his suffering began. In those days God had blessed him and made him successful. He was honored and respected in his community. When Job asked for his strength to be refreshed [*chadash*] within him, he was expressing the longing of his heart in the midst of his present suffering. He yearned for the time when his glory was "fresh" in him.[18] The desire of his heart was to be "a 'new man' with youthful strength."[19]

---

15 Barth, Markus, *Ephesians Translation and Commentary on Chapters 1-3*, The Anchor Bible Vol 34 (Doubleday 1974) Ephesians 2:11-22 Comment VI The Fruit of Peace: the New Man and the House of God under *A. One New Man*, p. 309

16 See for example: Keener, Craig S., *The IVP Bible Background Commentary: New Testament* (Intervarsity Press 1993) Hebrews 8:8-9, p. 665. "[I]n a very real way the New Covenant renews the Old Covenant." Stern, David, H., *Jewish New Testament Commentary* (Jewish New Testament Publications 1992) Messianic Jews (Hebrews) 8:8b-12, p. 690

17 "My glory is *ever* new [*chadash*] with me, And my bow is renewed in my hand." Job 29:20, italics in original

18 Harris, Archer, and Waltke, editors, *Theological Wordbook of the Old Testament* (Moody Press 1999) word # 613a, p. 266

19 Walton, Matthews, and Chavalas, *The IVP Bible Background Commentary Old Testament* (InterVarsity Press 2000) Job 29:20, p. 507

The context of Job's longing is very similar to the context in which God promised the *New* Covenant to Israel. What is front and center in both of these circumstances – Job's suffering and the suffering of the exiles – is genuine concern about what happens *after* the present trial concludes. Will there be hope after suffering? Biblical hope is not mere wishful thinking, it is confident expectation! Can there be confident expectation of restoration following suffering? Is God trustworthy in His goodness?

In the case of Job, as well as that of the exiles, the hope is for a return to the former glory (referring to the magnificence or greatness previously experienced). The desire is for a renewal of the glory that had once been experienced but had faded during the period of suffering. The hope was for a fresh glory to come after suffering.

Chadash can imply returning something to its original condition. When God refers to the promised New Covenant as *chadash*, He is focusing on restoration and renewal of the former Covenant – making it like new again. Look again at the promise as spoken through Ezekiel, this time I'll quote from Chapter 11.

> And I will give them one heart, and put a new [*chadash*] spirit within them. And I will take the heart of stone out of their flesh and give them a heart of flesh, that they may walk in My statutes and keep My ordinances and do them. Then they will be My people, and I shall be their God. Ezekiel 11:19-20

God said, "I will take the heart of *stone* out of their flesh." In ancient Jewish literature, the rabbis associated a "stone" with an evil inclination. God will remove from His people their "stubborn and unresponsive" hearts that are inclined towards evil.[20] In place of their stony hearts which are insensitive to His commands

---

20 *NET Bible Notes*, study note a, Ezekiel 36:26. Source: *Bible Gateway*. Retrieved from https://www.biblegateway.com/passage/?search=ezek+36%3A26-27&version=NET (last accessed September 7, 2023)

My Dwelling Place 95

and incorrigible,[21] God will give His people a new "heart of flesh" meaning one that sets its will to be responsive and obedient to Him.[22] In addition to their supernatural *heart transplant*, He promises to put His own Spirit in them.[23] As illustrated in Ezekiel 37:1-14, His Spirit animates and breathes new life into those who receive it.[24] The result is that He will cause His people to be obedient to Him.[25] Even under the former Covenant the people

---

21 Block, Daniel I., *The Book of Ezekiel: Chapters 25-48*, The New International Commentary on the Old Testament (Eerdmans 1998) Ezekiel 36:26-27, p. 355 noting that "stone ... speaks of coldness, insensitivity, incorrigibility, and even lifelessness."
22 *Net Bible Notes*, study note b, Ezekiel 36:26. Source: *Bible Gateway*. Retrieved from https://www.biblegateway.com/passage/?search=ezek+36%3A26-27&version=NET (last accessed September 7, 2023). The term "flesh" is used here differently than it is often used in the New Testament. Its New Testament use by Paul, for example, typically refers to what a person values and how he acts without the aid of the Holy Spirit. *Holman Christian Standard Bible*, Study Bible edition (Holman Bible Publishers 2010) study note Philippians 3:3 under *do not put confidence in the flesh*, p. 2046
23 Block, Daniel I., *The Book of Ezekiel: Chapters 25-48*, The New International Commentary on the Old Testament (Eerdmans 1998) Ezekiel 36:26-27, p. 356. *NET Bible Notes* suggests an alternative read as God promising to put His Spirit in the midst of them. *NET Bible Notes*, translator's note c, Ezekiel 36:27. Source: *Bible Gateway*. Retrieved from https://www.biblegateway.com/passage/?search=ezek+36%3A26-27&version=NET (last accessed September 7, 2023). God gave frequent assurance to Israel that He was in their midst. See for example: Exodus 29:45-46; Deuteronomy 7:21; 23:14
24 Block, Daniel I., *The Book of Ezekiel: Chapters 25-48*, The New International Commentary on the Old Testament (Eerdmans 1998) Ezekiel 36:26-27, p. 356
25 Scholars view the exhortations of Jesus that His disciples "abide in Him" and His promise to "abide in them" (John 15) as a reference back to Old Testament covenant theology including the prophetic texts which promised a future new covenant. Beale and Carson, editors, *Commentary on the New Testament Use of the Old Testament* (Baker Academic 2007) The Book of Glory ([John] 13:1-20:31) under *Jesus the True Vine and the Disciples' Need to Remain in Him (John) 15:1-17)* p. 492; *ESV Study Bible* (Crossway Books 2008) study note John 15:4, p. 2054

of God were identified as those who had His instruction in their hearts (Isaiah 51:7). God has always required true devotion to be evident in the heart and not just in outward actions.[26] Those who have cultivated that heart condition are the ones who are said to "know" Him.

When God says, *"Then they will be My people, and I shall be their God"* He is referring to proper Covenant relationship. The phrase is borrowed from ancient marriage language and custom.[27] It is used throughout the Old Testament to supply a unifying thread from the Abrahamic Covenant all the way to the closing scenes of Revelation with its vision of the new heaven and new earth.[28] At issue in both Jeremiah and Ezekiel is God's Kingship and the hope of His Ruling-Presence dwelling once again among the people who are faithful to His Covenant. As we have seen, that type of relationship between God and His people is commonly expressed in terms of a husband and wife relationship.

The restoration of God's Name and the re-establishment of His Kingship are the very purpose of His promise of renewal.[29]

---

26 *Holman Christian Standard Bible*, Study Bible edition (Holman Bible Publishers 2010) study note Psalm 37:31, p. 918. "The first covenant was meant to be written on people's hearts (Deut 30:11-14), and the righteous actually had it there (Ps 37:31; 40:8; 119:11; Is 51:7); but according to Jeremiah, most of Israel did *not* have it in their hearts (cf. e.g., Deut 5:29)." Keener, Craig S., *The IVP Bible Background Commentary: New Testament* (Intervarsity Press 1993) Hebrews 8:8-9, p. 665

27 Block, Daniel I., *The Book of Ezekiel: Chapters 1-24*, The New International Commentary on the Old Testament (Eerdmans 1997) Ezekiel 11:19-20, p. 354

28 "God's announcement, 'I will be their God and they will be my people' ... was made first to Moses (Exodus 6:7, Leviticus 26:12), then to the Prophets (Jeremiah 32:38; Ezekiel 11:20; 37:27), and last to the New Testament writers, where it applies both to the present ([Hebrews 8:8], 2C 6:16) and to the future (Rv 21:3&N)." Stern, David, H., *Jewish New Testament Commentary* (Jewish New Testament Publications 1992) Hebrews 8:8b-12, p. 690

29 "I am not doing *this* for your sake," declares the Lord God, 'let it be known to you. Be ashamed and confounded for your ways, O house of Israel!' ... Then the nations that are left round about you will know that I, the Lord, have rebuilt the ruined places *and* planted that which was desolate; I, the Lord, have spoken and will do it." Ezekiel 36:32,36, italics in original

My Dwelling Place

His promise extends well beyond returning the people to the land. He promised to breathe new life into His relationship with Israel. The crux of the New Covenant promise is a transplanted heart empowered by God's own indwelling Spirit.[30] His Spirit would invite them, enable them and equip them to walk in daily fellowship with Him. The result will be the type of relationship that not only enables obedience but continually urges a heartfelt desire for obedience! The heart that desires the things God desires creates the *ideal* dwelling place for Him. As He dwells in that heart, He will faithfully and fully accomplish His perfect will without hindrance.[31]

David, who was called a "man after God's own heart," cried out for a clean heart and a renewed spirit after the prophet Nathan had confronted him about his sin with Bathsheba.[32] He understood that the heart is naturally sinful and that only God can provide the solution.[33] This was a lesson God sought to teach Israel through their exile experience. It is characteristic of God that exile was not merely the consequences of disobedience. He designed it to be a life-size classroom experience! God was giving His people a practical life lesson that even without the physical Temple in their midst they would be able to worship Him. Even without their own land they could live a life of worship and walk out their true calling to be a light to the nations. Even without the physical Temple He could keep them safe and be their provision. Even without their earthly king He would be their King.

He had removed all the things they thought gave them their identity and brought them their security. What remained was *Him – He* was the constant thread in their personal and national

---

30 Scholar Daniel Block points out that God promises to *give* His Covenant people a new heart, but the spirit He promises will be placed *within* them. Block, Daniel I., *The Book of Ezekiel: Chapters 25-48*, The New International Commentary on the Old Testament (Eerdmans 1998) Ezekiel 36:26-27, p. 356

31 Personal Journal June 29, 2019

32 Psalm 51:10

33 "The heart is more deceitful than anything else, and incurable—who can understand it?" Jeremiah 17:9 HCSB

life and identity! He would follow them into exile. He would not cease being their God. In the circumstance of exile, they were to intercede for their enemy – the very ones who had destroyed all they had known and now held them captive. In *this* way they would learn true worship and what it was to be the people of Yahweh who could be used as a light to the nations.

God's intent was full restoration of an obedient people living under His Kingdom rule in the land He had promised to them as an inheritance. Ultimately, deliverance and restoration will be the result of Yahweh's own direct intervention on their behalf and will require "the establishment of an entirely new order."[34] This "new order" will begin in a very real way during exile.

Now against this backdrop of the New Covenant promise, let's return to our Key Scripture where Ezekiel watches the glory of King Yahweh once again fill His house. As we have already established, Ezekiel saw a new Temple or House of Yahweh. The glory he observes is the visible manifestation of Yahweh's Presence. This vision confirms that Yahweh will once again take up residence in Jerusalem in the midst of His Covenant people.

What Ezekiel saw is actually a new form of Temple represented by those who are in Covenant with Yahweh – the collective members of God's household. Clearly Ezekiel's vision is a part of God's promised restoration to His then exiled people. When put in a larger biblical context, especially that provided by Isaiah, we begin to understand that God's restorative plans involve a bigger picture than just returning Israel to the Land. The end of the exile will signal the beginning of the fulfillment of God's redemptive plans for the nations. (An important part of Abraham's promised blessing was that all the nations on earth would be blessed through him. Genesis 18:18-19)

This New Covenant order would begin with Israel living as a *Kingdom within a kingdom*. Israel's return to the Promised Land

---

34 Block, Daniel I., *The Book of Ezekiel Chapters 1-24*, The New International Commentary on the Old Testament (Eerdmans 1997) Ezekiel 11:17-20, p. 351

would not result in a return of self-governance in the world's eyes. As we have previously noted, the Persians had appointed a governor for the returning exiles so that even when physically back in their own land they remained under the rule of the Persian Empire. As ancient history records, after exile Israel remained a poor and insignificant province of first Persia, then Greece, then Rome.[35] Even so, there is a consistent picture of an expanding Kingdom – a growing number of people choosing to be ruled by God as their King, living among pagan nations. That reality necessitates the changed Temple form and results in the promised heart transformation of the New Covenant.

Let me explain. Under the New Covenant, the ones who receive "a heart of flesh" through God's supernatural heart transplant process are the ones who make a choice to live under Yahweh's Kingdom rule. It is clear that possessing the Law of God is no guarantee of right relationship with Him.[36] That Law must be obeyed whole-heartedly with exclusive devotion to Yahweh. The new heart is both sensitive and responsive. It represents, in essence, an internalized law that transforms the way of life. Internalization of God's Law is evidence of an intimate relationship between the King and His faithful subjects. Each one delights in willing obedience of the King's commands. In short, the Kingdom of God is found wherever God is whole-heartedly obeyed as King. It is a spiritual Kingdom that has no physical borders.

Formerly, under the Mt. Sinai Covenant, Israel received God's Law and then lived together as one nation in their own land, segregated as it were from the rest of the nations. They were self-governed by a king. That king was Yahweh's co-regent and ideally represented Yahweh's rule over the people as they followed God's divine Law handed down at Mt. Sinai. A paradigm

---

35 At the close of biblical history, the Roman Empire was ruling the land of Israel. Various groups continued to rule the land until Israel at last became an independent state in 1947.

36 Block, Daniel I., *The Book of Ezekiel: Chapters 1-24*, The New International Commentary on the Old Testament (Eerdmans 1997) Ezekiel 11:19-20, p. 353

change must occur, however, when God's Kingdom rule expands to include all of the other nations. Expanding His rule to other nations creates a practical problem. When all of God's Covenant people live in one place (the Promised Land) and the only law of that land is God's Law, then an external law code is easy to communicate and administer. However, as His Kingdom rule extends over an ever-increasing number of people who physically reside within the physical boundary lines of other nations, each with their own governing law in the natural,[37] an internalized Law has a distinctive advantage. Under those conditions, internalization becomes a very practical way to administer the Law of God and assure obedience.

God's promise of restoration and redemption involves a new heart, a new spirit, a New Covenant and a new glory in an ever-expanding Kingdom ruled by the only true King. His perfect plan involves Temple-form changes which permit His Kingdom to be effectively translated into a newly ordered world. That has always been God's plan. In our remaining lessons we will continue to explore His redemptive blueprint and watch His unfolding plan whereby His dwelling place returns to earth.

Hear What The Spirit is Saying to the Church*: Are you seeing how my plan has been lost in translation? It is time to set the record straight. Understanding my plan of redemption which does indeed establish my dwelling place on earth for all of eternity is vital in the coming days. I have always desired that my people know of my plans. I desire nothing to be by surprise – no, that is the way of my adversary. So, open your eyes, open your heart, open your ears to hear what the Spirit is saying to the church. Then come out from her my people – be cleansed and set apart that I may indeed give you a new heart and put my Spirit in you. Then will I be your God and you will be my people. Then will my plan of redemption be fulfilled. And so it shall be. Amen.*

---

37 In other words, a "Kingdom living among other kingdoms."

LESSON 8:

A REBUILT TEMPLE
WITHOUT
A DWELLING PRESENCE

 "Then the word of the LORD came by Haggai the prophet, saying, 'Is it time for you yourselves to dwell in your paneled houses while this house *lies* desolate?' Now therefore, thus says the LORD of hosts, 'Consider your ways!'" Haggai 1:3-5, italics in original

IN LESSON 6, we discussed God's Sanctuary-Presence which was with the exiles in Babylon. We also considered the difference between His new form Presence-of-Provision and His former Ruling-Presence which had been symbolized by the Ark of the Covenant. In true prophetic fashion, Isaiah, Jeremiah and Ezekiel, each in his own way, brought forth the warning of the impending exile followed closely by a strong message of comfort and restoration. The essence of God's message of hope, the *New Covenant*, was the subject of our last lesson. Haggai and Zechariah then came on the scene as God's mouthpiece in the post-exile era. In this lesson we will explore their messages to the weary community who had been permitted to return to their homeland from Babylon, albeit under the rule of the new Persian government. The former exiles arrived in Jerusalem to find it in shambles and their beloved Temple left in ruins by the Babylonians.

Let's set the context for our lesson by enumerating a few facts from the biblical record:

1. Jeremiah had prophesied that at the completion of seventy years of captivity God would remember His people and would restore them to their land (Jeremiah 29:10).
2. Isaiah had prophesied that God would use a leader named Cyrus to facilitate His divine plan allowing those who had been taken captive by Nebuchadnezzar to be restored to the land from which they were taken (Isaiah 44-45).
3. The king who issued the decree to build a Temple in Jerusalem was Cyrus, a Persian ruler (539 B.C.E.). The dimensions and principles of construction were prescribed in decrees of the Persian kings (Ezra 6:3–4). They also provided the materials from Sidon (Ezra 3:7; 6:4, 8).
4. Judah no longer had a self-governing king. The former kingdom of Judah was now under the dominion of the King of Persia and as a vassal-territory of the Persian Empire it was ruled by a Persian appointed governor (Haggai 1:1).
5. The first exiles to return to Judah with Zerubbabel (537 B.C.E.) began Temple construction by building an altar to offer burnt offerings according to the Law of Moses. It was built on the same ground where it had previously stood. Then the people observed the Feast of Tabernacles which celebrates God's glory and His Dwelling-Presence (Ezra 3:1-5).
6. In the second month of the second year after their return they began to lay the foundation for the new Temple (536 B.C.E.) (Ezra 3:8).
7. Temple construction stopped after they celebrated the completion of the foundation. Scholars and commentators suggest various explanations for why construction did not continue at this time. Haggai makes clear that the people had become discouraged and had turned to building their own homes thinking it was not time to build the Temple (Haggai 1). Notably the *Jewish Study Bible* and reputable scholars suggest the people did not view this

Temple construction as being legitimate because there was no king on the throne in Judah to approve and support this project.[1]

8. Sixteen years had lapsed since the beginning of Temple construction when the Lord commissioned Haggai to chastise the people's lack of diligence and misplaced priorities.[2] God made it clear that the presence of the Temple was a necessary condition for the prosperity of the land and the people. Temple construction began again in 520 B.C.E. (Haggai 1). (The Old Testament books of Haggai and Zechariah are set during this time period).

9. As the people obeyed and resumed construction God promised that He would be with them (Haggai 1:13).

10. When there was mourning and complaint that this Temple paled in comparison to Solomon's Temple, God encouraged continued construction and promised that a time would come when the glory of this latter Temple would be greater than the former one (Haggai 2:9). Most scholars suggest that the glory of this Temple was in fact greater for at least two reasons: 1) Herod remodeled this Second Temple into something greater than Solomon's Temple and 2) 500 years later Jesus – the King of Glory – physically entered the Second Temple (Luke 2:22,46; 19:45).

---

1 Meyers and Meyers, *Haggai, Zechariah 1-8: A New Translation with Introduction and Commentary*, The Anchor Bible Vol 25B (Doubleday 1987) Zechariah 3:9 under *this stone*, p. 206; Zechariah 4:10 under *such a day of small things*, p. 252; Berlin and Brettle, editors, *The Jewish Study Bible: Featuring The Jewish Publication Society Tanakh Translation* (Oxford University Press 2004) Haggai 1.1-15a,2; 1.15b-2.9, pp. 1244-1246

2 Merrill, Eugene, *An Historical Survey of the Old Testament*, 2nd edition (Baker Academic 1991) p. 292. Haggai's reference to their houses being "paneled" (Haggai 1:4) informs the reader that these were not houses in the process of being built, they were "fully appointed." Walton, Matthews, and Chavalas, *The IVP Bible Background Commentary: Old Testament* (InterVarsity Press 2000) Haggai 1:4, p. 797

11. In 516 B.C.E. construction was completed on the Second Temple under the leadership of Zerubbabel.[3] This was 70 years after the destruction of Solomon's Temple by the Babylonians which had occurred in 586 B.C.E.
12. The gold and silver articles that had been taken by Nebuchadnezzar from Solomon's Temple were placed in the new Temple (Ezra 5:14; 6:5). However, the Temple lacked the Ark of the Covenant. This new Temple was dedicated in 515 B.C.E. with great joy (Ezra 6:14-16).

Scholars debate how best to calculate the 70 years[4] of exile prophesied by Jeremiah and recognized by Daniel.[5] Indeed there are several historical dates that could be used to trigger the beginning and ending dates for the exiles. For example, the clock could begin with the first deportation of Jews to Babylon (which as noted in Lesson 6 included Daniel) and end with the date the first Jews returned to Jerusalem. For our purposes, however, in tracing God's Dwelling-Presence, it is instructive that 70 years lapsed between Nebuchadnezzar's destruction of the first Temple in 586 and the completion of the second Temple by Zerubbabel. Could

---

3   This is why the Temple is sometimes known as Zerubbabel's Temple. It is also known as The Second Temple.

4   As an initial matter it is important to recognize that: "Biblical numbers are not always intended to be taken at their face value. They are often used indefinitely – as round figures – or rhetorically, for emphasis or in a hyperbolic sense.... Many numbers [such as 70] are noteworthy for their symbolic nuances.... Seventy (the product of two sacred numbers, seven times ten) is used as a round figure, with symbolic or sacred nuances." *Numbers, Typical and Important*, Jewish Virtual Library. Retrieved from http://www.jewishvirtuallibrary.org/jsource/judaica (webpage no longer available). A similar article containing this quote can be found at Encyclopedia.com, *Numbers, Typical and Important*. Retrieved from https://www.encyclopedia.com/religion/encyclopedias-almanacs-transcripts-and-maps/numbers-typical-and-important#:~:text=Biblical%20numbers%20are%20not%20always%20intended%20to%20be,rhetorically%2C%20for%20emphasis%20or%20in%20a%20hyperbolic%20sense (last accessed October 24, 2023)

5   Daniel 9

God's word through Jeremiah have been a specific reference to the time period when He would give Judah over to her choice to be ruled by a foreign nation – the 70 years during which there was no Temple in Jerusalem to stand as a sign of Yahweh's Kingship?

Support for such an understanding can easily be found if we put ancient temple building practice in its historical context. In the days of the Old Testament, society was typically organized into kingdoms and people groups were generally organized as king (rulers) and people living under the authority of the king (the ruled).[6] "[P]ractically without exception, where there were cites, there were kings.... Each kingdom had its own domestic, foreign and religious policies."[7] In fact, as we previously noted in Lesson 7, this reality set the stage for internalized rule of God under the terms of the New Covenant!

In the ancient Near East, temple building was uniquely the privilege and responsibility of kings.[8] Simply put, in those days building a temple had to be approved and supported by the king who ruled over that territory.[9] As a matter of fact, constructing a new temple "was an important task for a new king, and preparations for the project would begin soon after the monarch's

---

6 Berthelot, Katell, *Jews and Their Roman Rivals: Pagan Rome's Challenge to Israel* (Princeton University Press 2021) p. 368
7 Power, Cian, *Kingship in the Hebrew Bible*, Teaching the Bible: An e-newsletter for public school teachers by Society of Bible Literature. Retrieved from https://docplayer.net/21752444-Kingship-in-the-hebrew-bible-by-cian-power.html (last accessed December 31, 2022)
8 Scholar Brevard Childs notes Scripture provides "classic example[s] of how the Hebrew Bible appropriated ancient Near Eastern tradition for its own purpose in a demythologized [reinterpreted so as to be free of mythical elements] form." Childs, Brevard S., *Isaiah*, Old Testament Library Commentary (Westminster John Knox Press 2001) p. 403
9 Berlin and Brettle, editors, *The Jewish Study Bible: Featuring The Jewish Publication Society Tanakh Translation* (Oxford University Press 2004) study note to Haggai 1.1-15a, p. 1245. At the same time, the gods were viewed as the ultimate builders of their own temples. Hilber, John W., "Psalms," in *Zondervan Illustrated Bible Backgrounds Commentary*, Vol. 5, edited by John H. Walton (Zondervan 2009) Psalm 78:69, p. 386

enthronement."¹⁰ In that era a temple was much more than a place of worship as we know it today. The temple in the ancient Near East was a central element in establishing the administration of the new king.¹¹ "Erecting a temple in an administrative center [of his kingdom] was an integral part of the process of establishing the authority of the [new] political regime."¹² At that time in history temples were built by a king to legitimize his "dynastic claims."¹³ That is to say a temple was an important way to express his expectation that a succession of powerful leaders from his own family line would rule in this territory for generations to come.

It is easy and convenient, and even somewhat accurate, to view Zerubbabel's Temple as having been constructed by decree of the Persian Kings – initiated by Cyrus and then later supported by Darius. However, a closer look at Haggai and Zechariah make clear the Temple was completed at the divine instruction of Yahweh, the true King of Israel, and it is in this context that we will find our Key Scripture for this lesson. Our foundational text is Haggai 1:

> In the second year of Darius the king, on the first day of the sixth month, the word of the LORD came by the prophet Haggai to Zerubbabel ... governor of Judah, and to Joshua ... the high priest, saying, "Thus says the LORD of hosts, 'This people says, "The time has not come, even the time for the house of the LORD to be

---

10 Mabie, Frederick J., "2 Chronicles," in *Zondervan Illustrated Bible Backgrounds Commentary*, Vol. 3, edited by John H. Walton (Zondervan 2009) 2 Chronicles 2:1, p. 297
11 Meyers and Meyers, *Haggai, Zechariah 1-8: A New Translation with Introduction and Commentary*, The Anchor Bible Vol 25B (Doubleday 1987) Haggai 2:1-23 under *Comment*, p. 73
12 Meyers and Meyers, *Haggai, Zechariah 1-8: A New Translation with Introduction and Commentary*, The Anchor Bible Vol 25B (Doubleday 1987) Haggai 1:2 under *to be built* , p. 22
13 Meyers and Meyers, *Haggai, Zechariah 1-8: A New Translation with Introduction and Commentary*, The Anchor Bible Vol 25B (Doubleday 1987) Zechariah 3:9, p. 206

rebuilt." Then the word of the Lord came by Haggai the prophet, saying, "Is it time for you yourselves to dwell in your paneled houses while this house *lies* desolate?" Now therefore, thus says the Lord of hosts, "Consider your ways! ... Then Zerubbabel ... and Joshua ... with all the remnant of the people, obeyed the voice of the Lord their God and the words of Haggai the prophet, as the Lord their God had sent him. And the people showed reverence for the Lord. Then Haggai, the messenger of the Lord, spoke by the commission of the Lord to the people saying, "'I am with you,' declares the Lord." So the Lord stirred up the spirit of Zerubbabel ... and the spirit of Joshua ... and the spirit of all the remnant of the people; and they came and worked on the house of the Lord of hosts, their God, on the twenty-fourth day of the sixth month in the second year of Darius the king Haggai 1:1-5,12-15, italics in original

Let's also consider a portion of related text from Zechariah Chapter 1:

... On the twenty-fourth day of the eleventh month ... in the second year of Darius, the word of the Lord came to Zechariah the prophet .... Then the angel of the Lord said, "O Lord of hosts, how long will You have no compassion for Jerusalem and the cities of Judah, with which You have been indignant these seventy years?" The Lord answered the angel .... So the angel ... said to me, "Proclaim, saying, 'Thus says the Lord of hosts, "I am exceedingly jealous for Jerusalem and Zion.... **I will return to Jerusalem with compassion; My house will be built in it," declares the Lord of hosts,** "and a measuring line will be stretched over Jerusalem."' Zechariah 1:7,12-14,16, bold added

Both Haggai and Zechariah make clear that God's "house," the Second Temple in Jerusalem,[14] is to be built according to God's command. As we have seen, only a king had the ability to build a temple. However, as we have previously noted, for the king to proceed he had to have authorization from the god who would be worshipped in that temple. Temple building was that king's political announcement that 1) he was the ruling authority in that territory and 2) he expected his family line to continue ruling after him. What Haggai and Zechariah make clear is that God is the deity who is authorizing the Temple and by doing so He is establishing His Kingship among Judah once again. But there's a problem – Judah is no longer a self-governing kingdom. Political oversight in Judah is now provided by a Persian-appointed governor who rules the territory under the authority of the Persian King. Nonetheless, it is undeniable that Yahweh is undertaking action which at that time was uniquely and exclusively reserved for the rightful territorial king.

The question arises then as to "Who is the legitimate *king* of Judah. Is it the Persian King or is it Yahweh?" Not surprisingly, that's the question asked by the angel of the Lord.

> Then the angel of the LORD said, "O LORD of hosts, how long will You have no compassion for **Jerusalem and the cities of Judah**, with which You have been indignant these seventy years?" Zechariah 1:12, bold added

The reference to *Jerusalem and the cities of Judah* "is a [blatant] political designation for the realm of the Davidic ruler."[15] That

---

14 In both Haggai and Zechariah, the Hebrew word translated as house is the word *bayith* {bah'-yith} which can also be properly translated as "Temple." In Lesson 7 we learned that, depending on context, *bayith* can also refer to the family or household itself. The context in the quoted passages from Haggai and Zechariah suggest the physical Temple to be the best understanding of the word.

15 In other words, this is a reference to the king who rules Israel in the line of King David.

said, the angel's question seems to be more concerned with the political identity of these people than with their welfare. "Their autonomy had been severely curtailed by the events of the past generation. Now ... work on the rebuilding of the temple had begun. The question of the monarchy, an associated expression of Judean autonomy, was thereby reopened."[16] The angel was asking when God planned to re-establish Israel under its own sovereign rule.

The answer to our question about the legitimate king of Israel reveals the paradigm shift that occurred at the time of the exile. The people would decide for themselves. For the first time ever in Israel's history as a nation, God was now offering His Covenant people the opportunity to *choose* the kingdom/Kingdom to which they will be subject without changing their physical location and without open rebellion. Where you have a true King and people who obey Him, you have the beginning of a Kingdom![17] The people of Israel can choose to remain exclusive subjects of the Persian King or they can choose to come under Yahweh's sovereign rule and be citizens of His *Kingdom within a kingdom*.[18] Those who chose Yahweh as King would physically live in the territory belonging to the Persian Empire but their hearts would be ruled by Yahweh. They would be subjects of the spiritual Kingdom He ruled while they were living within a physical nation ruled by Persia. In essence they would bring back to the Promised Land the type of relationship they had with Him while in exile.

Jesus recognized this type of dual citizenship responsibility when He was asked about whether it was lawful to give a poll-tax to Caesar.[19] His carefully crafted answer struck a God-honoring balance between the two rulers. Jesus made clear that being a Kingdom citizen within an earthly kingdom allows for the pay-

---

16 Meyers and Meyers, *Haggai, Zechariah 1-8: A New Translation with Introduction and Commentary*, The Anchor Bible Vol 25B (Doubleday 1987) Zechariah 1:12 under *Jerusalem and the cities of Judah*, p. 116
17 Wright, N. T., *Simply Jesus* (HarperOne 2011) p. 116
18 A spiritual Kingdom within a physical nation.
19 Matthew 22:17

ment of what is *due* to the human ruler and to God. He acknowledged that the people can be both a dutiful citizen of a kingdom on earth and a loyal servant of Yahweh. In the first century His answer would have been surprising in that there was an assumed incompatibility between being loyal to the governing authority and loyalty to God. The answer Jesus gave suggests that commonly held presumption was incorrect.[20]

The Temple that publicly re-asserted God's Kingdom rule over His Covenant people was finally completed and dedicated. Most assuredly the people must have waited with great expectation for the glory to fall. However, there is no biblical record of the *Shekinah* glory of God ever coming to dwell in this new Temple. In fact, according to ancient Jewish writings the second Temple lacked not only the Ark of the Covenant, but also the glory that had been previously experienced in both the Tabernacle and the first Temple.[21]

None of this should have come as a surprise to Israel. God had used His prophets to lay a foundation for a new understanding. The Ark may have symbolized Yahweh's Presence among His people, but He would not cease to faithfully fulfill His Covenant promises simply because the Ark was not present in the Temple.[22] In fact, a Temple without an Ark was not without precedent. In Lesson 3 we took note of the fact that from the time David brought the Ark to Jerusalem until the completion of Solomon's Temple, the Tent of David and the Tabernacle co-existed. David appointed Levites to worship before the Lord in the Tent he constructed. He also appointed priests to perform the prescribed

---

20 France, R. T., *The Gospel of Matthew*, New International Commentary on the New Testament (Eerdmans 2007) Matthew 22:15-22, p. 830
21 Barton, George A., *Temple, The Second*, Jewish Encylopedia.com, citing the *Babylonian Talmud* (Yoma 22b). Retrieved from http://www.jewishencyclopedia.com/articles/14309-temple-the-second (last accessed July 10, 2021)
22 Thompson, J. A., *The Book of Jeremiah*, The New International Commentary on The Old Testament (Eerdmans 1980) Introduction under *IV. Some Important Issues for Exergesis, D. Jeremiah and the Cultus*, p. 69

sacrifices in the Tabernacle of Moses even though the most Holy Place inside the Tabernacle no longer contained the Ark symbolizing God's Presence.[23]

The prophets knew that what the people needed all along was to return to their proper relationship with Yahweh. The new Temple in Jerusalem was rightly the center of sacrifice and would remain so from the post exile period until Jesus became the once for all sacrifice! God had provided a way for Israel, once again, to keep her Covenant commitments to Him. However, His primary call to His people was for them to love Him (obey Him) with all of their heart. "At no time in Israel's history was sacrifice, divorced from the obedience demanded by the covenant, regarded as something acceptable to Yahweh."[24]

Isaiah had anticipated that there would be a divine mandate to rebuild a temple after exile (Isaiah 44:28). However, he also understood that God would not be limited to the Temple in Jerusalem. "He is still the transcendent God, filling all heaven, touching earth with his foot."[25] Isaiah had prophesied He was not exclusively Israel's God (Isaiah 56:1-8). Exile proved He was a God on the move! His plan of restoration had always included the Gentile nations. God never intended His Dwelling-Presence to return to the localized Temple in Jerusalem in the way Israel had experienced His Ruling-Presence before the exile. However, He was King nonetheless – King not only of Israel but a world-wide God of a distinctive set apart people. J. Alec Motyer points out that "if the people of God lose distinctiveness there is nothing for anyone to join nor any good reason for seeking to do so!"[26]

---

23   1 Chronicles 16:37-42
24   Thompson, J. A., *The Book of Jeremiah*, The New International Commentary on The Old Testament (Eerdmans 1980) Introduction under *IV. Some Important Issues for Exergesis, D. Jeremiah and the Cultus*, p. 68
25   Motyer, J. Alec, *The Prophecy of Isaiah: An Introduction & Commentary* (InterVarsity Press 1993) Isaiah 66:1, p. 533
26   Motyer, J. Alec, *The Prophecy of Isaiah: An Introduction & Commentary* (InterVarsity Press 1993) Isaiah 56:3-7, p. 466

This then is the paradigm shift that occurred at the time of the exile. In fact, it was prophesied even before the exile, but only understood in hindsight. In the next lesson we will continue to explore this paradigm shift of His Presence in the aftermath of the exile.

Hear What The Spirit is Saying to the Church: *My Dwelling-Presence was for a season among my people when I was able to rest among them as Lord, not only as Savior. After I left Solomon's Temple I have not yet rested again and it will not be so until the new heaven and new earth is fully created. Then will I rest again in new form as the Temple. By my Spirit and by my might nations join my "Kingdom within a kingdom" until such time as all have chosen their king. Then will I honor each one's choice and I will say to those who have chosen me that they are my chosen people and I will forever be their King. Then will I say to the others, depart from me you who practice lawlessness.*

LESSON 9:

A NEW COVENANT
TYPE OF PRESENCE
AMONG GOD'S PEOPLE

"Then [the angel] said to [Zechariah], 'This is the word of the LORD to Zerubbabel saying, "Not by might nor by power, but by My Spirit," says the LORD of hosts.'" Zechariah 4:6

AS PREVIOUSLY NOTED, the Babylonian captivity was a low point in Israel's history. Covenantal disobedience meant they had to face the full brunt of the curses outlined in Deuteronomy and for a season they were without a homeland of their own. However, in our last lesson we learned that it was Yahweh who provided Kingly instruction to Israel to build a new House for Him in Jerusalem. In this lesson we will continue to explore His Presence among His Covenant people who had returned to the Promised Land and begun to rebuild their lives and His Kingdom in that place. We begin with our Key Scripture for this lesson.

Zechariah 4:6 is likely a familiar verse. However, this Scripture is often quoted out of context. The message it contains is first and foremost best understood in terms of the political reality of Zechariah's day and as such its message fits right into our study. A closer look at the words "might" and "power" will enlighten our understanding of God's message.

WORD STUDY

The word **might** *is the Hebrew word chayil {khah'-yil} and its primary meaning is strength. As a result, chayil is used more than 100 times in the Bible to denote an "army," "host," or "forces."*[1]

The word **power** *is the Hebrew word koach {ko'-akh} which is a general term referring to power or strength in a variety of contexts.*[2] *Figuratively, it conveys the "general ability to cope with situations."*[3] *Koach also references a capacity to act. In this sense it "refers to all kinds of social, political, and economic forces; or general physical and intellectual capacity and determination."*[4]

"The combination of 'power' and 'might' is to be understood as 'military might' or 'powerful armies,' either of which would signify political autonomy since the presence of an army is the distinguishing mark of an independent state."[5]

---

1. Harris, Archer, and Waltke, editors, *Theological Wordbook of the Old Testament* (Moody Press 1999) word # 625a, p. 272; "Hebrew *hyl* ("might") often means an army or military force." Meyers and Meyers, *Haggai, Zechariah 1-8: A New Translation with Introduction and Commentary*, The Anchor Bible Vol 25B (Doubleday 1987) Zechariah 4:6, p. 244
2. Baker and Carpenter, *The Complete WordStudy Dictionary of the Old Testament* (AMG Publishers 2003) word #3581, p. 502
3. Harris, Archer, and Waltke, editors, *Theological Wordbook of the Old Testament* (Moody Press 1999) word #973a, p. 437
4. Harris, Archer, and Waltke, editors, *Theological Wordbook of the Old Testament* (Moody Press 1999) word #973a, p. 437; Baker and Carpenter, *The Complete WordStudy Dictionary of the Old Testament* (AMG Publishers 2003) word #3581, p. 502
5. Meyers and Meyers, *Haggai, Zechariah 1-8: A New Translation with Introduction and Commentary*, The Anchor Bible Vol 25B (Doubleday 1987) Zechariah 4:6, p. 244

My Dwelling Place   115

As we see from our Word Study, the phrase "power and might" refers to a human army. At this time in Israel's history, she was not fully autonomous and she no longer had the army which had previously conquered the Promised Land against foes who were much larger and more powerful. In fact, as a province of Persia, Israel had no army whatsoever. The *powerful army* referred to here is the army of the Persian Empire – which indeed in that day would have been seen as the most powerful army in the known world. They had conquered the mighty Babylonians to become the new rulers of a vast empire. But they would *not* be the ones to build a new Temple in Jerusalem!

The compound name which identifies Yahweh in our Key Scripture is "LORD of hosts." This title is biblically associated with God's Kingship and it is used to affirm His sovereign rule "that encompasses every force or army, heavenly, cosmic and earthly."[6] The Hebrew term for "host" is *tsaba'* {tsaw-baw'} and most of its Old Testament uses have something to do with warfare, armies, or fighting.[7] The title *LORD of hosts* highlights "God's role in leading the heavenly hosts in battle."[8] In other words, this is an explicit reference to the fact that Yahweh has an army! As pointed out in our Word Study, in the ancient Near East an army was virtually synonymous with a kingdom since it was a very visible "mark of a sovereign state."[9] In those days, the presence of an army assured political independence. In Zechariah 4:6, God is distinguishing between two armies and two kingdoms. The first is the Persian

---

6   Harris, Archer, and Waltke, editors, *Theological Wordbook of the Old Testament* (Moody Press 1999) word # 1865b, pp. 750-751
7   *Jehovah Sabaoth - LORD of Hosts*, Precept Austin. Retrieved from http://www.preceptaustin.org/jehovah_sabaoth_-_lord_of_hosts (last accessed July 10, 2021)
8   Berlin and Brettle, editors, *The Jewish Study Bible: Featuring The Jewish Publication Society Tanakh Translation* (Oxford University Press 2004) study note Psalm 24:10, p. 1309
9   Meyers and Meyers, *Haggai, Zechariah 1-8: A New Translation with Introduction and Commentary*, The Anchor Bible Vol 25B (Doubleday 1987) Oracular Insertion: Zerubbabel and the Temple, 4:6b-10a, p. 269

kingdom symbolized by its might-and-power-human army and the second is Yahweh's Kingdom symbolized by His title as Commander-in-Chief of His army of hosts. L ORD *of hosts* "asserts the fact of Yahweh's return to Zion and the reestablishment of his mighty power."[10]

As we continue to unpack our Key Scripture, the Hebrew word for spirit is *ruah* or *ruwach* {roo'-akh}. "God's 'spirit' is his involvement in and control over human events."[11] Whenever we see a reference to the Presence of His Spirit, "life-giving divine activity is either already in progress or not far behind."[12] Here His *ruah* is a sign that God is present and active in rebuilding the temple.[13] Zerubbabel was reminded that because Yahweh had ordained him to lead He would also equip and empower him to be "the vehicle for [God's] divine activity" so he could accomplish the mission God had given to do.[14] It was to be a relationship that was entirely dependent on *God's Spirit* to do the heavy lifting!

---

10 Meyers and Meyers, *Haggai, Zechariah 1-8: A New Translation with Introduction and Commentary*, The Anchor Bible Vol 25B (Doubleday 1987) Haggai 1:2 under *of Hosts*, p. 19

11 Meyers and Meyers, *Haggai, Zechariah 1-8: A New Translation with Introduction and Commentary*, The Anchor Bible Vol 25B (Doubleday 1987) Zechariah 4:6, p. 244

12 Hubbard, Robert L., Jr. "3. The Spirit and Creation" in *Presence Power And Promise: The Role of the Spirit of God in the Old Testament*, edited by Firth and Wegner (IVP Academic 2011) p. 91

13 Meyers and Meyers, *Haggai, Zechariah 1-8: A New Translation with Introduction and Commentary*, The Anchor Bible Vol 25B (Doubleday 1987) Zechariah 4:6, p. 244

14 "It is not so much that the *ruah* empowers the person, but that the person becomes the vehicle for the divine activity." Walton, John H., "2. The Ancient Near Eastern Background Of The Spirit Of The Lord In The Old Testament" in *Presence Power And Promise: The Role of the Spirit of God in the Old Testament*, edited by Firth and Wegner (IVP Academic 2011) p. 49. In this way Zerubbabel becomes Yahweh's instrument. See also: Block, Daniel I., "10. The View From The Top: The Holy Spirit in Prophecy," in *Presence Power And Promise: The Role of the Spirit of God in the Old Testament*, edited by Firth and Wegner (IVP Academic 2011) p. 188

My Dwelling Place 117

The message to Zerubbabel in Zechariah 4:6 is clear. The Temple will be built by God's Kingdom through the power of His Spirit.

We might wonder why there was a need for the Temple if there was no Ark to be placed in the Holy of Holies, no footstool for God's heavenly throne and no dwelling place between the cherubim. Interestingly, the Bible does not provide a clear and specific answer in any of the Temple-building instructions given to the post-exile community. Its notable absence suggests to us that no reason is articulated because it was clearly and inherently understood by those who received the instruction. In other words, no reason needed to be given to the ancient Hebrews who heard and obeyed God's command to build the Second Temple. In the culture of their day they understood what we have lost in translation over the centuries. The ancient Hebrews would have known from cultural experience that there were many varied reasons for an established Temple.

First and foremost, they knew by experience that "kingship in the ancient Near East is unthinkable outside of the institution of the temple.... [I]n each of the ancient Near Eastern traditions that we know anything about, all of the important royal and state functions are carried out [in the temple]."[15] As we noted in our last lesson, the temple in the ancient Near East was a central element in establishing the administration of the new king. Of particular note is that a temple expressed the commissioning king's expectation that a succession of powerful rulers from his own family line would govern this territory for generations to come. To the Jewish people who had just returned from exile, expectations of restoring an independent monarchy would naturally accompany temple

---

15 Lundquist, John Milton, *Studies On The Temple In The Ancient Near East*, Doctor of Philosophy Dissertation, University of Michigan (1983) pp. 193-194. Retrieved from http://bhporter.com/Porter%20PDF%20Files/Studies%20on%20the%20Temple%20in%20the%20ancient%20Near%20East.pdf (last accessed October 4, 2023)

reconstruction.[16] Where there was a restored Temple, there had to be a restored King and His Kingdom!

It has been universally understood throughout history that kings govern and rule – it's what they inherently do! In fact, the very idea of kingship implies that there are those who are loyal followers. In Israel's history the Temple was the primary place where the people who followed Yahweh demonstrated their obedience to His Kingship. As a noted in Lesson 6, in the ancient Near East it was universally understood that:

> The destruction or loss of the temple [was] seen as calamitous and fatal to the community in which the temple [had] stood. The destruction [was] viewed as the result of social and moral decadence and disobedience to God's word.... [That was true because] there [was] a close interrelationship between the temple and law in the ancient Near East. [Therefore] [t]he building or restoration of a temple is perceived as the moving force behind a restating or "codifying" of basic legal principles, and of the "righting" and organizing of proper social order. The building or refurbishing of temples is central to the covenant process.[17]

In ancient understanding, obedience to the king established his kingdom. Thus, a kingdom is where the king is obeyed. The exile and destruction of the former Temple evidenced the fact that God's Presence had been removed because He had in essence been

---

16 Meyers and Meyers, *Haggai, Zechariah 1-8; A New Translation with Introduction and Commentary*, The Anchor Bible Vol 25B (Doubleday 1987) Haggai 2:4 under *all you people of the land*, p. 51

17 Lundquist, John M. "The Common Temple Ideology of the Ancient Near East," in *The Temple in Antiquity: Ancient Records and Modern Perspectives*, ed. Truman G. Madsen (Religious Studies Center, Brigham Young University 1984) pp. 53–76 under *The Temple: A Preliminary Typology*, items #9b and 15. Retrieved from https://rsc.byu.edu/temple-antiquity/common-temple-ideology-ancient-near-east (last accessed October 21, 2023)

My Dwelling Place 119

"dethroned."[18] The restoration of the Temple by Yahweh of Hosts "asserts the fact of Yahweh's return to Zion and the reestablishment of His mighty power."[19] Moreover, Yahweh's command to rebuild His Temple was proof positive that He was not only reasserting His right to govern, but He was reinstituting His Covenant relationship with the remnant who had returned to the Land – the early stages of His *New* Covenant relationship as we noted in Lesson 7.

A careful read of Haggai Chapter 1 reveals not only that God commanded the former exiles to build His Temple but that He promised to respond to their obedience by providing for them as a King provides for His subjects. As we will see, His Kingly provision and His Presence were expressly conditioned upon their obedience to build His Temple.

> "... Thus says the LORD of hosts, 'Consider your ways! Go up to the mountains, bring wood and rebuild the temple, that I may be pleased with it and be glorified,' says the LORD.... Then Zerubbabel ... and Joshua ... with all the remnant of the people, obeyed the voice of the LORD their God and the words of Haggai the prophet, as the LORD their God had sent him. And the people showed reverence for the LORD. **Then** Haggai, the messenger of the LORD, spoke by the commission of the LORD to the people saying, 'I am with [*'eth*] you,' declares the LORD." Haggai 1:7-8,12-13, bold added

Haggai 1:13 helps us understand God's conditional Temple-Building-Presence. In context, the word "then" (placed in bold text) introduces the *I-am-with-you promise*. The word order

---

18 Meyers and Meyers, *Haggai, Zechariah 1-8: A New Translation with Introduction and Commentary*, The Anchor Bible Vol 25B (Doubleday 1987) Haggai 1:2 under *of Hosts*, p. 18
19 Meyers and Meyers, *Haggai, Zechariah 1-8: A New Translation with Introduction and Commentary*, The Anchor Bible Vol 25B (Doubleday 1987) Haggai 1:2 under *of Hosts*, p. 19

makes clear that God promised His Presence *after* the people agreed to build the Temple! God repeated His promised Presence in Haggai 2:4.

> On the twenty-first of the seventh month, the word of the LORD came by Haggai the prophet saying, 'Speak now to Zerubbabel … and to Joshua … and to the remnant of the people saying, "Who is left among you who saw this temple in its former glory? And how do you see it now? Does it not seem to you like nothing in comparison? But now take courage, Zerubbabel," declares the LORD, "take courage also, Joshua … and all you people of the land take courage," declares the LORD, "**and work [follow my command]; for I am with [*'eth*] you**,"' declares the LORD of hosts. Haggai 2:1-4, bold added

What does it mean that God is "with" them? The primary definition for "with" found in Dictionary.com is "accompanied by; accompanying" and that pretty well embodies our common understanding of its usage. However, by doing a Word Study of the original Hebrew word we're going to see an important connotation of this word which sheds new light on God's message through His appointed messenger, Haggai.

WORD STUDY

*The word **with** in Haggai 1:13 and 2:4 is the Hebrew word 'eth {ayth}. It is a term that can denote close proximity in location (being near or at a place) but it can also describe close personal connection meaning together within the context of relationship.*[20] *Genesis 5:22,24 uses the word 'eth highlighting Enoch's "special relationship*

---
20 Baker and Carpenter, *The Complete WordStudy Dictionary of the Old Testament* (AMG Publishers 2003) word #854, p. 111; *Brown-Driver-Briggs*

> with God."²¹ *The idea of "walking with God" expresses Enoch's "life spent in full accord with God's will and in closest intimacy with Him."²²*
>
> *Biblically the word 'eth is used to refer to "presence" and may indicate "companionship for the purpose of help." It specially denotes being in one's possession/keeping or in one's knowledge/memory.²³*

The biblical notion of "with" has the power of union and closeness. As one scholar explains, the phrase *with you* "denotes divine presence with its attendant power."²⁴ In our study we have been highlighting the fellowship aspect of God's Presence among His people which has been largely expressed through provision and protection. In fact, we could safely say that Scripture teaches that a basic principle in God's Kingdom is: God's Presence is about fellowship and from that fellowship provision and protection naturally flow.

We have noticed that God's promised Presence is conditional. In fact, after exile it is specifically conditioned upon Israel's obedience to build the Temple. Even though it is a *New* Covenant relationship, God does not leave it to their imagination to consider what this relationship looks like. As we continue our reading in

---

     entry for *'eth*. Retrieved from http://biblehub.com/hebrew/854.htm (last accessed July 10, 2021)
21 Alexander, T. Desmond, *Genesis: A Commentary By T. Desmond Alexander*, Genesis 5:6-32. Retrieved from https://www.thegospelcoalition.org/commentary/genesis/#section-11 (last accessed October 25, 2023)
22 Sarna, Nahum M., *The JPS Torah Commentary: Genesis*, The Traditional Hebrew Text with the New JPS Translation Commentary (The Jewish Publication Society 1989) Genesis 5:21-24 under *walked with God*, p. 43
23 *Brown-Driver-Briggs* entry for *'eth*. Retrieved from http://biblehub.com/hebrew/854.htm (last accessed July 10, 2021)
24 Meyers and Meyers, *Haggai, Zechariah 1-8: A New Translation with Introduction and Commentary*, The Anchor Bible Vol 25B (Doubleday 1987) Haggai 1:13 under *with you*, p. 35

Haggai 2, we can clearly see God purposefully refers them back to the time of their exodus from Egypt. Let's continue reading beginning again at verse 4:

> Yet now be strong, O Zerubbabel, declares the Lord. Be strong, O Joshua, son of Jehozadak, the high priest. Be strong, all you people of the land, declares the Lord. Work, for **I am with you**, declares the Lord of hosts, according to the covenant that I made with you when you came out of Egypt. My Spirit remains in your midst. Fear not. For thus says the Lord of hosts: Yet once more, in a little while, I will shake the heavens and the earth and the sea and the dry land. And I will shake all nations, so that the treasures of all nations shall come in, and I will fill this house with glory, says the Lord of hosts. Haggai 2:4-7 ESV, bold added

As we proceed with our discussion of Haggai 2, take note of the restated promised *I am with you*, which is in bold text. Our Word Study pointed out that *'eth* can denote "being in one's possession/keeping or in one's knowledge/ memory." We could accurately translate verse 4 then as follows: "do the work because I am keeping you in my remembrance." He commands them to be obedient because He is remembering. We find the parallel command in verse 5 for Israel to remember God!

Grammatically in the Hebrew text, the opening phrase of verse 5 "the Word that I covenanted with you" is somewhat unusual. According to *Barnes' Notes* the more exact idiom would be, "Remember, take to heart."[25] In the Bible a person's heart is the decision-making center which means the heart "is the source of

---

25 Barnes, Albert, *Barnes' Notes On The Old And New Testaments*, Haggai 2:5 under *The words which I covenanted*. Retrieved from https://www.studylight.org/commentaries/eng/bnb/haggai-2.html (last accessed October 25, 2023).

both rebellion and perseverance in obedience."[26] Yahweh exhorts them to remember, to take to heart, His Covenant with them. God says He was remembering the time of the exodus when He brought them out of Egypt and promised to be with them. He asked them to remember too. He speaks to these people who had returned from exile as if they were the ones who personally experienced the exodus promise because in Jewish thought whatever happened to their forefathers personally happened to them.[27]

Why does God announce that He is remembering and then instruct them to remember too? First let's be clear on what Hebraic remembrance is. In Jewish thought remembering is more than mentally recalling something. To remember "implies an action."[28] It recaptures "the past in a way that [leads] to action in the present."[29] In other words, it is like saying, "Do it again now!"

What was so important about the exodus that God wanted to *do it again now*? The exodus of Israel from Egypt is the formative story for Israel – how God took a group of former Egyptian slaves and made them into a mighty nation. As N. T. Wright points out, "The story of the exodus is the story of how 'God became king.'"[30] God's message during Israel's restoration period was essentially, "Remember how I formed you as a nation and became your King!

---

26 Cockerill, Gareth Lee, *The Epistle to the Hebrews*, New International Commentary on the New Testament (Eerdmans 2012) Hebrews 13:9, p. 695
27 This is a biblical pattern. See for example: Deuteronomy 1:6 where Moses speaks to the second generation of Israel as if God had spoken to them directly at Mt. Sinai. The author uses the phrase "to us" which links the present generation hearing His words to the Horeb (aka Sinai) generation. Nelson, Richard D., *Deuteronomy*, The Old Testament Library (Westminster John Knox Press 2002) Deuteronomy 1:6-8, p. 18. See also: Daniel's prayer in Daniel 9
28 Barth, Markus, *Ephesians: Introduction, Translation, and Commentary on Chapters 1-3*, The Anchor Bible Vol 34 (Doubleday 1974) Ephesians 1:16 under *mentioning you in my prayers*, p. 147
29 Thompson, J. A., *The Book of Jeremiah*, The New International Commentary on The Old Testament (Eerdmans 1980) Jeremiah 15:15, p. 395
30 Wright, N. T., *How God Became King: The Forgotten Story Of The Gospels* (Harper One 2012) p. 153

Remember when you stood before me at Mt. Sinai and I gave you my Law and you, in one voice, responded that you would obey." As we have previously pointed out, the Sinai kingship metaphor is also expressed in terms of an ancient marriage. God is saying to the people who have returned to the Promised Land, "Let's repeat our marriage vows, those vows which established My Kingdom rule and assured my Protection-and-Provision-Presence with you. Let's do it again!"

Like those former slaves of the exodus generation, the former exiles Haggai addressed were not yet a safe and secure community fully experiencing the benefits of Covenant relationship with Yahweh. These new citizens of a *Kingdom within a kingdom* would be identified by their obedience to King Yahweh. He promised them that in their obedience He would be for them exactly what He was for their forefathers in the wilderness between Egypt and the Promised Land. His With-Them-Presence was a promise related directly to building the Temple – the reestablishment of His Kingdom rule among them. In other words, His Presence could be *with them* in the community because of their obedience. By His Presence, He offered Himself, His guidance, His ways, *His* power and might. By their acceptance and their obedience, they would establish His Kingdom rule and His Abiding-Presence would dwell in their hearts. The *Kingdom within a kingdom* that is established by their choice is a Kingdom where hearts are ruled by God regardless of the geographic boundaries of the physical kingdom where they live!

We have here the unanticipated foundation for the *New* Covenant! Jeremiah and Ezekiel had both prophesied it – we have long thought that it didn't begin until the time of Christ. However, when rightly understood and no longer lost in translation we can see that God's *New* Covenant is a Covenant with Israel that actually begins to take shape during the post-exile restoration period in Judah's history.

The *Shekinah* glory never returned to that Temple made by men's hands because it was not God's plan for His glory to be confined to a material Temple again. For the time being His true dwelling place remained in heaven. However, His Spirit, which had provided a Sanctuary for them in exile, would now abide in their midst in the Promised Land (Haggai 2:5) as they faithfully walked out their Covenant relationship with Him. The stage is now set for Emmanuel – God with us – Jesus who is the Christ, the promised Messiah! We'll meet Him in our next lesson.

***Hear What The Spirit is Saying to the Church**: I am establishing the truth of My Kingdom. It has indeed been lost in translation over the centuries; but I have never forgotten my purpose and my plan. I have never forgotten my Covenant relationship with my people Israel. Though she strayed from my ways, she was never out of sight. My plan has always been to bless her and to redeem her and bring her to myself. To do so required me to change the way in which I met her and provided for her in order to best meet her where she was. I have always reached out to her even when she did not reach out to me. And so it shall be until the fullness of my plan has been reached. Now will my Temple move forth in a new way and yet as a King I will have an established Temple that will host my Presence in ways not yet seen or understood. Prepare for my coming glory. For it will come in a new and unexpected way and will be more powerful than ever experienced in past days. My Temple, My Rule, My Kingdom these are inseparable and testify of me and my power. But they also establish the truth of my grace and my glory. Hear what the Spirit is saying to the Church. Hear and respond, become citizens of my Kingdom which at present is within a kingdom, but will not forever be so.*

LESSON 10:

CHRIST AS KING AND TEMPLE

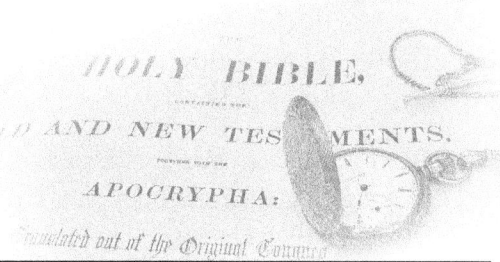

 "And the Word became flesh, and dwelt among us, and we saw His glory, glory as of the only begotten from the Father, full of grace and truth." John 1:14

IN OUR LAST lesson, we considered the words of Haggai as it related to God's post-exile Temple-building instruction. We took note that God's promise to "be with" the people was expressly conditioned upon their obedience to build the new Temple. What God desired more than a material Temple was a people whose heart longed to obey His word.[1] His Presence could be *with them* in the community because they were obedient. Their prior rejection of Him as their King had resulted in His glory leaving Solomon's Temple. Their post-exile obedience demonstrated the re-establishment of His Kingdom rule among them.

Our Key Scripture declares an amazing truth, "the Word became flesh and dwelt among us and we saw His glory." John informs us the Word is Jesus. Ezekiel had seen a vision of God's glory returning. Through the prophet Haggai Yahweh had promised a greater glory than the returning exiles had yet experienced.

> "This is the promise I made to you when you came out of Egypt, and My Spirit is present among you; don't be afraid." For the LORD of hosts says this: "Once more, in a little while, I am going to shake the heavens and the

---

1 Motyer, J. Alec, *The Prophecy of Isaiah: An Introduction & Commentary* (InterVarsity Press 1993) Isaiah 66:1-24, p. 533

earth, the sea and the land. I will shake all the nations … I will fill this house with glory, says the LORD of Hosts.… The final glory of this house will be greater than the first, says the LORD of Hosts.…" Haggai 2:5-6,9a HCSB

As we learned in our last lesson, "LORD of Hosts" is a reference to Yahweh as Commander-in-Chief of His armies providing solid evidence that He rules a Kingdom. The Psalmist identifies the LORD of Hosts as the *King of Glory*![2] In the portion of Haggai 2 just quoted, God continues His remembrance of the exodus from Egypt and promises to "shake once more" His creation. In the ancient Near East, the image of shaking typically referred to a manifestation of the god.[3]

One of the most familiar biblical accounts of such a shaking occurred at Mt. Sinai when the entire mountain trembled because Yahweh had descended upon it.[4] Haggai 2 draws a deliberate parallel between God's shaking by which He revealed Himself to all of Israel at Sinai and what God promises to do for Israel after their exile.[5] As we shall see, the manifestation of deity God promises is none other than King Jesus – "the most stupendous descension of God in history: the incarnation of the Son of God."[6] This reconstructed Temple will manifest in the Physical-Presence of Jesus. This "shaking" will usher in a new type of glorious Temple!

If we were to conduct a survey among self-identified Christians world-wide and ask the questions, "What was the mission of Jesus? Why did the Father send Him?" answers would no doubt

---

2 Psalm 24:10
3 Hoglund, Kenneth G., "Haggai," in *Zondervan Illustrated Bible Backgrounds Commentary*, Vol. 5, edited by John H. Walton (Zondervan 2009) Haggai 2:6, p. 197
4 Exodus 19:17-18
5 Hoglund, Kenneth G., "Haggai," in *Zondervan Illustrated Bible Backgrounds Commentary*, Vol. 5, edited by John H. Walton (Zondervan 2009) Haggai 2:6, p. 197
6 Barrett, Michael P. V., *Haggai: A Commentary By Michael P. V. Barrett*, Haggai 2:6-9. Retrieved from https://www.thegospelcoalition.org/commentary/haggai/#section-13 (last accessed October 26, 2023)

vary. Even so, for most, especially those in America, an immediate answer would likely sound something like: *"He came to die on the cross to take away our sins so that we can go to heaven."* Or they might state the future in terms of *"having eternal life."*

This is not a wrong answer; it is simply a woefully incomplete answer. To get right to the point, we will see just how clearly Scripture records the message of the gospel as announcing that Jesus has come as the promised King and as a new form of Temple! The Father sent His Son to usher in His rightful rule – the Kingdom of God. Jesus, as the legitimate King, followed the kingly pattern of the times by establishing a Temple. By doing so He fulfilled the Word of the Lord spoken through Haggai which promised to fill this house/Temple with a glory such that this *final* [could also be translated as *future* or *latter*] glory will be greater than the first.[7]

While much could be written about the Kingship of Jesus, our goal here can be achieved by taking a fresh look at the gospels. In them we will find the most straight-forward witness which points directly to the Kingship of Jesus. For example:

1. Matthew's opening chapter identifies Jesus as "the son of David" and traces His claim to the throne through Joseph. This documented lineage established Jesus was the promised Davidic descendent who was born as the new Davidic *King* (Matthew 1:1-16).
2. Shortly after the birth of Jesus, "[The wise men from the east] said, 'Where is the one born destined to be *king* of the Jews' (Matthew 2:2 MIT)?"
3. Shortly before His death, Jesus fulfilled a prophecy that He would ride into Jerusalem on the colt of a donkey as *"King"* (Mark 11:1-10). Matthew informs us that this event fulfilled the prophecy found in Zechariah 9:9.[8]

---

7 Haggai 2:7,9a
8 "Rejoice greatly, Daughter Zion! Shout in triumph, Daughter Jerusalem! Look, your King is coming to you; He is righteous and victorious, humble and riding on a donkey, on a colt, the foal of a donkey." Zechariah 9:9 HCSB

4. At His trial Jesus confirmed His Kingship when "Pilate asked Him, saying, 'Are You the *King* of the Jews?' And He answered him and said, 'It is as you say' (Luke 23:3)."
5. The cross Jesus hung on bore His rightful title. "Pilate also wrote an inscription and put it on the cross. It was written, 'JESUS THE NAZARENE, THE KING OF THE JEWS' (John 19:19)."

Luke provides the most detailed account in all of the New Testament regarding the commencement of Jesus' public ministry.[9] Luke 4:16-31 summarily reveals the entire ministry of Jesus by means of an Old Testament quote which comes largely from the first two verses of Isaiah 61.[10] In the fullness of His Father's time, Jesus stood up in the Nazareth synagogue and read from the scroll of Isaiah:

> The Spirit of the Lord God is upon me, Because the LORD has anointed me To bring good news to the afflicted; He has sent me to bind up the brokenhearted, To proclaim liberty to captives And freedom to prisoners; To proclaim the favorable year of the LORD. Isaiah 61:1-2a

Background images of kingship weave themselves in and out of this mission statement text. However, a clear understanding of this proof of His Kingship will require us to place the biblical text in the prevailing cultural context of the times in which it was written. As a side note, this is *always* a good practice for sound Bible interpretation. In fact, failure to take the time to understand cultural context all too often results in the meaning of the text being either confused or completely lost in translation.

The text Jesus read at the outset of His ministry opens with the words, "THE SPIRIT OF THE LORD IS UPON ME, BECAUSE HE

---

9   Bailey, Kenneth E., *Jesus Through Middle Eastern Eyes: Cultural Studies In the Gospels* (IVP Academic 2008) p. 147

10 Luke's account of the Nazareth scroll reading of Isaiah 61:1-2a may also include a phrase from Isaiah 58:6.

ANOINTED ME...."[11] When placed in light of ancient cultural custom, it becomes easy to recognize the reference to kingship. The Bible uses the phrase "anointed one" thirty-nine times.[12] Not surprisingly, thirty-one of those biblical uses refer to Israel's king. In biblical times it was common to anoint kings with oil. We see evidence of this practice, for example, in 1 Samuel 16:13 when Samuel anointed David. The practice of a Suzerain (more powerful) king anointing his vassal kings (kings who ruled subject to the Suzerain king) was also known in both the Egyptian and Hittite kingdoms.[13] When Israel anointed a man as king, he took on the title "the LORD's anointed" indicating his "vassal status as the Lord's earthly representative and his consecration to and authorization for divine service .... The king's status as 'the anointed' implied his divine enabling and his inviolability."[14] The one anointed was to represent God's power and His divine intervention as he performed the duties of the kingly office to which he was anointed.[15]

The remainder of the text Jesus read from Isaiah's scroll revealed His mission statement: "TO PREACH THE GOSPEL TO THE

---

11 Luke 4:18a, uppercase text in original
12 Within the Old Testament, anointing "conveyed authority and life from the spirit [of God]." Walton, John H., "2. The Ancient Near Eastern Background Of the Spirit Of the Lord In The Old Testament," in *Presence Power And Promise The Role of the Spirit of God in the Old Testament*, edited by Firth and Wegner (IVP Academic 2011) p. 49
13 Long, V. Philips, "1 Samuel," in *Zondervan Illustrated Bible Backgrounds Commentary*, Vol. 2, edited by John H. Walton (Zondervan 2009) 1 Samuel 2:10, pp. 278-279
14 Long, V. Philips, "1 Samuel," in *Zondervan Illustrated Bible Backgrounds Commentary*, Vol. 2, edited by John H. Walton (Zondervan 2009) 1 Samuel 2:10, p. 279
15 Jesus came as a "vassal king" under His Father. "Therefore Jesus answered and was saying to them, 'Truly, truly, I say to you, the Son can do nothing of Himself, unless it is something He sees the Father doing; for whatever the Father does, these things the Son also does in like manner (John 5:19).'" "For I did not speak on My own initiative, but the Father Himself who sent Me has given Me a commandment as to what to say and what to speak (John 12:49)."

POOR. HE HAS SENT ME TO PROCLAIM RELEASE TO THE CAPTIVES, AND RECOVERY OF SIGHT TO THE BLIND, TO SET FREE THOSE WHO ARE OPPRESSED, TO PROCLAIM THE FAVORABLE YEAR OF THE LORD."[16] As we will see, His words conform to what was widely known as a kingly "clean slate" decree.[17]

Let's consider some additional background information. God had commanded Israel to celebrate Jubilee every 50 years.[18] Jubilee significantly impacted two primary areas of life in Israel: 1) provisions for setting Hebrew slaves free and 2) land provisions which included a Sabbath rest for the land as well as a reversion of all land back to the original owner. Behind both of these provisions is the premise that all debt has been satisfied because it is treated as being paid in full. Scholars recognize that Isaiah 61 was a Jubilee promise. Therefore, when Jesus used Isaiah 61 as His mission statement, He was initiating Jubilee.[19] In fact, the mission of Jesus has been summarized by one scholar as the appointed one

---

16 Luke 4:18-19, uppercase text in original
17 "A growing number of scholars are convinced that the Gospel of Luke and the Book of Acts are Jubilee 'proclamations,' as it were …. In other words, the Kingdom of God in Luke is understood as God's eschatological and final Jubilee proclamation." Sanders, James A., *Jubilee in the Bible*, Biblical Theology Bulletin: Journal of Bible and Culture, Vol. 50, Issue 1 pp. 4-6 (2020) https://doi.org/10.1177/0146107919892838. Abstract retrieved from https://journals.sagepub.com/doi/full/10.1177/0146107919892838 (last accessed October 26, 2023)
18 Leviticus 25
19 Herod the Great died in 4 B.C.E. when Jesus was a young child (Matthew 2:19). Assuming then that Jesus was born in 7/6 B.C.E. and was baptized when he was about 30 years old (Luke 3:23), He began His ministry during a Jubilee season. Even if Jubilee was not actually celebrated during the time of Jesus' ministry, scholars seem to agree that at the very least Jubilee was recognized as a way to measure time and date events in the second Temple period. Barker, Margaret, *The Time Is Fulfilled, Jesus and the Jubilee*, 1999, p. 3. Retrieved from http://www.margaretbarker.com/Papers/JesusAndTheJubilee.pdf last accessed July 10, 2021). Margaret Barker is a British biblical scholar.

My Dwelling Place

"who was to implement the final jubilee, a once-for-all, exile-ending release for the poor."[20]

Let's add to that background one additional fact. There is a wealth of ancient history which clearly documents that new kings in the ancient Near East commonly issued a Jubilee-like decree to cancel debts shortly after becoming enthroned.[21] These so-called royal "clean slate" proclamations typically cancelled personal debts, freed citizens who had been enslaved for debt and restored traditional family landholdings.[22] In other words, these types of kingly decrees essentially accomplished the same goals as Jubilee. By doing so, they sought to remove tangible evidence which could otherwise linger as a reminder of the previous king's rule.[23] As kingly proclamations these clean-slate decrees were:

> ... the central aspects of that boundary-moment when allegiances are shifted to the new king, when the [new] sovereign's power authorizes the cancellation of policies and penalties imposed by the ruler(s) whose reign is ending, and when the slate is cleared so that the agenda of the new sovereign can be unveiled.[24]

In fact, this idea of a royal clean slate decree is an appropriate way to understand what Cyrus, as the new Persian King, did when he released the captive Jews to return to their homeland! We find

---

20 Perrin, Nicholas, *Jesus the Temple* (Baker Academic 2012) p. 14
21 Perrin, Nicholas, *Jesus the Temple* (Baker Academic 2012) p. 149
22 Hudson, Michael, *The Lost Tradition of Biblical Debt Cancellations* (1993) p. 76. Retrieved from https://michael-hudson.com/wp-content/uploads/2010/03/HudsonLostTradition.pdf (last accessed October 26, 2023). This paper was based on research done as a Research Fellow at Harvard University's Peabody Museum in Babylonian economic history. It was originally published by the Henry George School of Social Science (New York City).
23 Ringe, Sharon H., *Luke 4:16-44 – A Portrait of Jesus as Herald of God's Jubilee*, p. 76
24 Ringe, Sharon Hilda, Doctoral Dissertation: *The Jubilee proclamation in the ministry and teaching of Jesus: a tradition-critical study in the Synoptic Gospels and Acts* (1981) p. 125

that story in the book of Ezra. When set against proper historical context, we learn that Cyrus was doing exactly what kings of that day did when they became king! He was establishing himself as the new king who now deserved allegiance. He would be aided in his goal by cancelling policies and penalties which had been imposed on the Jewish captives by the Babylonian kings.

So, these ancient *release* edicts appear to establish a noticeable border or distinct boundary between the old and the new. They help mark a visible sign for the beginning enthronement of a new king.[25] Jesus did exactly what new kings at that time would often do. He proclaimed a "clean slate" decree to define His new Kingdom. When He stood in the Nazareth synagogue and read the words from Isaiah 61, Jesus was most certainly announcing His mission was that which Isaiah had prophesied for the coming Messiah. However, He was also standing up among His own people to deliver His inaugural Kingly address and issue a conventional clean-slate decree.[26]

When Jesus announced that *the Kingdom of Heaven is here*,[27] He was saying "God's promised reign is beginning" – "God is now taking control."[28] The citizens of this Kingdom of God form a *Kingdom within a kingdom* because their hearts have chosen to align with God's sovereign rule. Their choice has established them as members of God's household.[29] Their true citizenship is in heaven.[30] N. T. Wright asserts that when rightly understood "the 'kingdom of heaven' is not about people going to heaven. It is

---

25 Ringe, Sharon Hilda, Doctoral Dissertation: *The Jubilee proclamation in the ministry and teaching of Jesus: a tradition-critical study in the Synoptic Gospels and Acts* (1981) p. 72

26 Sloan, Robert B., Jr., *The Favorable Year of the Lord: A Study of Jubilary Theology in the Gospel of Luke*. A dissertation presented to the faculty of Theology of the University of Basel, Switzerland, for the Degree of Doctor of Theology (Schola Press 1977) p. 54

27 Matthew 4:17; Mark 1:15

28 France, R. T., *The Gospel of Matthew*, New International Commentary on the New Testament (Eerdmans 2007) Matthew 3:2, p. 102

29 Ephesians 2:19

30 Philippians 3:20

My Dwelling Place

about the will of heaven coming to earth.... God's rule becoming a reality on this earth."[31] That is exactly what we see unfolding in the gospels. Time and time again, Jesus healed people, set them free from demonic possession and raised the dead. In so doing, He is announcing, "The rightful King of the world had come, and all that stood in the way of the establishment of his [K]ingdom—sin, death, hell, Satan—was being decisively overcome."[32]

As we have previously noted, in the ancient Near East a new ruling king had the right to build a temple which had been authorized by the god. So, if Jesus is really proclaiming to be the new victorious King, we would expect Him to build a new temple. That is exactly what He announces to His Jerusalem audience!

> ... "Destroy this temple, and in three days I will raise it up." John 2:19

In the original Greek text, John 2:19 is in the form of an imperative which actually reads more like, "Go ahead and [destroy this temple] and see what happens."[33] John informs us that Jesus used the word "temple" as a means of referring to His physical body.[34] In His Physical-Presence on earth, Jesus is in fact the Temple because the fullness of God was dwelling in Him (Colossians 2:9). Jesus came as Immanuel – God with us. During His earthly ministry the *Shekinah* glory rested on Him in a greater way than it had ever been present in any man-made Temple/Tabernacle.[35] He was sent to be "the unique place on earth where God's revelatory

---

31 Wright, N. T., *How God Became King: The Forgotten Story Of The Gospels* (Harper One 2012) p. 43
32 Gilbert, Greg, *What is the Gos·pel?* (Crossway 2010) p. 89
33 *NET Bible Notes*, translator's note 43, John 2:19
34 "The Jews then said, 'It took forty-six years to build this temple, and will You raise it up in three days?' But He was speaking of the temple of His body." John 2:20-21
35 Beale, G. K., *The Temple and the Church's Mission: A Biblical Theology of The Dwelling Place of God* (InterVarsity Press 2004) p. 178

presence is located."³⁶ He was the earthly "Temple-place" where God's sovereign Ruling-Presence was able to dwell unhindered.

"[B]y offering his life for all as the atoning and covenant-establishing sacrifice," His death and resurrection became the climax of His temple-building role.³⁷ When the physical body of Jesus was resurrected, a new Spirit-indwelt Temple began to take shape. "It is through his resurrection that Jesus fulfills the role of the eschatological temple-builder and indeed becomes the [new] temple, the source of life, light, and truth – God's glory."³⁸ This new Temple was "inaugurated through the Spirit"³⁹ when Jesus became the cornerstone and it will be completed by His followers who are spiritual building stones (1 Peter 2:2-10). When Jesus announced His cornerstone role in this new Temple it was in the context of defending His authority to cleanse the Jerusalem Temple.⁴⁰

> Jesus said to [the chief priests and elders who questioned Him], "Have you never read in the Scriptures: 'The stone that the builders rejected has become the cornerstone; this was the Lord's doing, and it is marvelous in our eyes'? ..." Matthew 21:42 ESV

Jesus was asking a rhetorical question. He wasn't looking for an answer, He was making a dramatic point. Of course, the chief priests and elders would have read the Scriptures. The implication is that *because* they had read the Scriptures they should understand

---

36 Beale, G. K., *The Temple and the Church's Mission: A Biblical Theology of The Dwelling Place of God* (InterVarsity Press 2004) p. 178
37 Beale, G. K., *The Temple and the Church's Mission: A Biblical Theology of The Dwelling Place of God* (InterVarsity Press 2004) p.180, quoting Kim, Seyoon, "Jesus—The Son of God, the Stone, the Son of Man, and the Servant: The Role of Zechariah in the Self-Identification of Jesus," in *Tradition and Interpretation in the New Testament: Essays in Honor of E. Earle Ellis for His 60th Birthday*, editor Gerald F. Hawthorne and Otto Betz (Eerdmans; Mohr Siebeck 1987) pp. 134-148 at p. 143 while noting that Kim's entire article supports this notion
38 Perrin, Nicholas, *Jesus the Temple* (Baker Academic 2012) p. 55
39 Perrin, Nicholas, *Jesus the Temple* (Baker Academic 2012) p. 55
40 See: Matthew 21:12-13,23

My Dwelling Place   137

what He was saying to them.[41] We will first look at the imagery presented by the cornerstone[42] metaphor and then address what Jesus was saying to the religious leaders of His day.

When constructing a new temple in ancient times, the very first step was to lay the cornerstone as the foundational stone which would then serve to stabilize the rest of the stones. This first stone was vitally important since it was not only "the focal point of a building, [it was] the thing on which [the building] most depends for its structural integrity."[43] The cornerstone not only bore the weight of the building, it also served as a standard to level the rest of the building.[44] Jesus announced that He is *that* Stone! He is the new focal point of the Temple. He is what the new Temple depends on for its structural integrity.

Jesus was quoting the Greek translation of Psalm 118:22-23. These verses in Psalm 118 refer to a righteous suffer (likely a king in Israel's history, perhaps even King David) who is delivered from

---

41 Gundry, Robert H., *Commentary on the New Testament* (Hendrickson Publishers 2010) Matthew 21:42-44, p. 95
42 Some scholars, like Robert Gundry, believe the reference to this stone points to the cornerstone because it was the first stone laid in a foundation and all other stones were laid out in alignment with that first stone. Gundry, Robert H., *Commentary on the New Testament* (Hendrickson Publishers 2010) Mark 12:8-11, p. 194. Others, such as R. T. France, believe the stone refers to the "highest stone in a corner of the wall" because he views that stone as a more direct translation of the ancient Greek text from which Jesus quoted. France, R. T., *The Gospel of Matthew*, New International Commentary on the New Testament (Eerdmans 2007) Matthew 21:42, p. 815. In his commentary on the Psalms, scholar John W. Hilber notes that the original text of Psalm 118:22 could refer either to a foundation stone or a capstone noting that both were particularly important to the building. Hilber, John W., "Psalms," in *Zondervan Illustrated Bible Backgrounds Commentary*, Vol. 5, edited by John H. Walton (Zondervan 2009) Psalm 118:22, p. 422
43 Ryken, Wilhoit, and Longman III, editors, *Dictionary of Biblical Imagery* (Intervarsity Press 1998) entry for *Cornerstone*, p. 166
44 *Holman Christian Standard Bible*, Study Bible edition (Holman Bible Publishers 2010) Psalm 118:22, p. 996

his oppressors.[45] The verses rely on construction imagery to praise Yahweh for His wonderful deeds – just like a cornerstone in a building, Yahweh has given His suffering servant prominence.[46] "In sum, the LORD, as the master builder, takes a stone thrown away by the builders and places it as a very important and conspicuous stone in his building 'to the surprise and astonishment of those who … have seen the whole thing.'"[47] The chief priests and elders may have rejected Him as the cornerstone, but Jesus wanted them to know that He was divinely chosen and put in place by the Father!

Now that we understand Jesus' use of the cornerstone metaphor, let's add some contextual background so we can understand why He provided this as an important part of His defense for cleansing the Temple. Nicholas Perrin views the temple cleansing act of Jesus as being for a two-fold purpose: 1) a symbolic act of cleansing a temple which had been profaned by corruption and 2) an eschatological act signaling "God's sovereign and decisive in-breaking into temple affairs."[48]

> The historical evidence indicates that the temple regime of Jesus' day had made a practice out of dipping into temple funds, extorting from lower-level priests, soliciting bribes, neglecting tithes, and grossly overcharging faithful Jews requiring temple service.… [E]ach of the activities would have undoubtedly been regarded as different counts of one overriding crime: stealing from

---

45 Beale, G. K., *The Temple and the Church's Mission: A Biblical Theology of The Dwelling Place of God* (InterVarsity Press 2004) p. 184
46 Longman III and Garland, general editors, *The Expositor's Bible Commentary: Psalms*, Vol. 5, Revised Edition (Zondervan 2008) Psalm 118:22-23, p. 857
47 Waltke, Bruce, *Psalms 107–150: A Commentary By Bruce K. Waltke*, Psalm 118:22-24, quoting Hossfeld and Zenger, *Psalms 3*, p. 241. Retrieved from https://www.thegospelcoalition.org/commentary/psalm-107-psalm-150/ (last accessed November 1, 2023)
48 Perrin, Nicholas, *Jesus the Temple* (Baker Academic 2012) p. 89

the temple (*ma'al*). In Jewish thought, to steal from the temple was to profane the temple.[49]

Despite the fact that the Ark was no longer in the Holy of Holies and that no one ever recorded the descent of God's *Shekinah* glory falling on the Second Temple, it was still highly regarded. The Second Temple was treated as if it were in fact the dwelling place of God on earth. For centuries the Jewish people brought their sacrifices to this Temple and celebrated their annual feasts here. When it was desecrated by the Seleucid ruler Antiochus IV Epiphanes and later dedicated by him to the pagan god Zeus, it gave rise to a Jewish war for independence. Jesus respected the Second Temple as His Father's house and condemned those who would steal from it through their greedy dishonesty. Paul testified that he had committed no crime against this Temple.[50] Even so, it seems as if God designed the Second Temple to be a transitional Temple as He waited for the fullness of time to send His Son. The coming of His Son ushered in an entirely new Temple form. "Not made by 'human hands', this temple [will] continue to be built up until the day of redemption, the temple's completion, and the climax of history."[51] This heaven-sent Temple will ultimately give way to the New Jerusalem Temple vision John records in Revelation 21:22 which we will consider in our last lesson.

Now that we understand the mission of Jesus as King and Temple we can accurately examine the mission Jesus gave the church which was initiated in the first century. That will be the subject of our next lesson.

Hear What The Spirit is Saying to the Church:
Regardless of whether people understand or agree, my Cove-

---

49 Perrin, Nicholas, *Jesus the Temple* (Baker Academic 2012) pp. 98-99, citing Milgrom, J., *The Concept of Ma'al in the Bible and the Ancient Near East*, JAOS 96 pp. 236-247 at pp. 236-237, 245-247 for the statement that stealing from the Temple profaned it.
50 Acts 25:8
51 Perrin, Nicholas, *Jesus the Temple* (Baker Academic 2012) p. 75

nant plan marches forward to find its true fulfillment. And so it will be. In the coming days my Temple will be complete. Then will my Glory fall in a new way such as has never been known before. Truly eye has not seen nor has ear heard of what I'm about to do. Be faithful above all else to build my Temple in these days. Accept my Son as the true Cornerstone for that is the reason He was sent. But I say again, so few understand. Yet my Word will not return to me void. It will indeed accomplish all that I have sent it forth to accomplish. My church will marvel and I will be well pleased that it is so.

LESSON 11:

BUILDING GOD'S TEMPLE,
THE MISSION
OF THE CHURCH

"So then you are no longer strangers and aliens, but you are fellow citizens with the saints, and are of God's household, having been built on the foundation of the apostles and prophets, Christ Jesus Himself being the corner *stone*, in whom the whole building, being fitted together, is growing into a holy temple in the Lord, in whom you also are being built together into a dwelling of God in the Spirit."
Ephesians 2:19-22, italics in original

IN LESSON 10, we learned that Jesus was both King and Temple and that His mission statement was in the form of a clean-slate decree such as was typical of new kings. We concluded with His declaration that He was the cornerstone selected by God which gave notice that He was beginning to build a new Temple. In this lesson we will look at the mission He gave His disciples then and now – a mission which when fulfilled will unveil the new heaven and new earth.

As we have seen from our study thus far, God has the sovereignty to dwell where He desires. The fact that He chooses to dwell among His chosen people demonstrates His faithful commitment to them. Yet, as we have learned, He maintains His independence and liberty to dwell where He wills. He alone chooses where and how to manifest His Dwelling-Presence. We have also learned that when God chooses a dwelling place, His choice is best understood through the lens of His enthronement as King.[1] That is to say, His Presence only chooses to dwell where He is permitted to rule as King! Neither the Tabernacle in Shiloh, nor the Temple in Jerusalem, would retain His glory in the midst of a stubbornly rebellious people who rejected His sovereign rule.

Throughout history the Temple is the structure God has consistently chosen as a symbol of His Kingly rule.[2] We have been tracing how God has changed that Temple structure, the House where He dwells, over time to provide the best fit for the circumstances surrounding His Covenant people. We have followed His Presence from the Ark of the Covenant in the wilderness Tabernacle, to Solomon's Temple. We observed His Presence become a gracious Sanctuary-Presence among the exiles and then the With-Them-Presence in response to their Temple-building obedience when they returned from Babylon. Finally, in our last lesson we saw the Ruling-Presence of God manifested in Jesus who walked among God's Covenant people as the promised Messiah!

After His resurrection and before His ascension to sit at the right hand of His Father,[3] Jesus gave His small group of disci-

---

1   Longman III and Garland, general editors, *The Expositor's Bible Commentary: Psalms*, Vol. 5, Revised Edition (Zondervan 2008) *Reflections: The Ark of the Covenant and the Temple Symbols of Yahweh's Presence and Rule*, pp. 931-934
2   Temples were something ancient peoples understood. They were built as a house for their local deity. It was customary for pagan temples to have statutes that were believed to be a representation of the god for whom the temple was built. Hundley, Michael, *Near Eastern Temples*, Biblical Studies, Oxford Bibliographies. Retrieved from https://www.oxfordbibliographies.com/display/document/obo-9780195393361/obo-9780195393361-0243.xml (last accessed October 21, 2023). Yahweh on the other hand prohibited His Covenant people from making anything that represented His likeness.
3   "Sitting at the right hand" is "a metaphor of privileged relationship and [being] a legal heir." Hilber, John W., "Psalms," in *Zondervan Illustrated Bible Backgrounds Commentary*, Vol. 5, edited by John H. Walton (Zondervan 2009) Psalm 110:1 under *Sit at my right hand*, p. 418. Right hand indicates derived authority and power. In other words, it indicates Jesus is sharing His Father's Kingly throne.

ples what we commonly refer to as the "great commission." Let's read it together. We are so familiar with these verses that I am intentionally choosing a translation with less familiarity to most of us. We will read the text from the *Complete Jewish Bible* (CJB). I have inserted in brackets the more commonly used English words where CJB uses Hebrew words.

> Yeshua [Jesus] came and talked with them. He said, "All authority in heaven and on earth has been given to me. Therefore, go and make people from all nations into talmidim [disciples], immersing them into the reality of the Father, the Son and the Ruach HaKodesh [Holy Spirit], and teaching them to obey everything that I have commanded you. And remember! **I will be with you always, yes, even until the end of the age.**" Matthew 28:18-20 CJB, bold added

As an initial matter, did you catch the promised With-You-Presence until the end of the age? This is the same With-You-Presence God promised in response to Israel's obedience to build the Temple! The Greek word *meta* {met-ah'}, which is translated as "with" in Matthew 28:20, has the same meaning as the Hebrew word *'eth* we looked at in Lesson 9. Both words promise Presence that denotes "companionship for the purpose of help."[4] In this promised *meta / 'eth* Presence is a Kingdom principle worth noting. The difference between those in Covenant relationship with Yahweh and those who choose otherwise is *not* the incidence or absence of trial, suffering or even illness. It is that God's Presence is *with* His Covenant people in the midst of every life hardship. His divine Presence supplies grace that is sufficient, wisdom that is vital and peace that passes understanding. The unrighteous (those who have rejected Him) must face their trials without this prom-

---

4   Refer to Lesson 9 Word Study for *'eth*. Greek word *meta* defined by Bromiley, Geoffrey W., *Theological Dictionary of the New Testament* (Eerdmans 1985) entry for *syn-meta* under B. *The Range of Meaning of syn and meta*, p. 1103. "*[M]eta* may also denote standing by someone, helping someone."

ised Presence! We will explore this notion of suffering more fully in our last lesson. However, for now let's continue with our consideration of the commission Jesus gave His disciples.

What we are going to see is that Jesus is essentially instructing them to, "Go build My new Temple." God's promised Presence in response to obedient temple-building has never changed. Obedience to build the Temple demonstrates choice to come under God's Kingdom rule as a matter of the heart. In spite of the fact that the inward decision God expects is a heart matter, notice He wasn't asking for some private mental acceptance of His rulership. He was asking for an outward demonstration – go and make *talmidim*. So, what are *talmidim*? To answer that question, I'm going to quote in large part from the Preface to this study (footnotes are omitted here).

> By the time of Jesus, discipleship was well-established within the Jewish culture. All the great sages, rabbis and teachers of Torah had *talmidim* (disciples). A *talmid* (a disciple) was on a pilgrimage that was far more than an intellectual pursuit. The *talmid*'s goal was to be like the rabbi – he wanted to assimilate the essence of who the rabbi was into his own life. This was radical discipleship – it was a complete re-making of the one who was being discipled so as to become like his rabbi in knowledge, wisdom and ethical behavior. In other words, a *talmid*'s deepest desire was to follow his rabbi so closely that he would start to think and act just like his rabbi. Jesus summed up the goal of discipleship this way: "every disciple fully trained will be like his teacher." A *talmid*'s behavior would be a reflection on their teacher's reputation – either positively or negatively. That means perseverance was a standard requirement for every *talmid*. Once a *talmid* was fully trained, he would become a teacher and he would disciple *talmidim* of his own. What Jesus had begun by making *talmidim* of His

first followers, the body of Christ now does as they make new *talmidim* of Jesus. We see the apostle Paul following this established rabbinic pattern when he says, "Imitate me, as I also imitate Christ. Now I praise you because you always remember me and keep the traditions just as I delivered them to you."

The commission is to go make disciples of Christ. When we understand disciple-making in its first-century context, most of us would have to admit that the intention Jesus had for making disciples is vastly different than many self-designated "Christians" today. The void that is left by our western interpretation of the great commission is no doubt due in part to the fact that we have all too often condensed that commission into a "salvation decision" rather than a "Lordship/Savior decision." Christianity was never designed to be a belief system, it was intended to be a lifestyle. The great commission is meant to create a distinct Kingdom culture – a "Kingdom-living culture."[5]

> The danger in seeing or preaching the gospel only as a [make-a-decision-for-Christ] transaction is that once the "deal" is done, the believer may have the sense that he or she has checked the box and is done with the gospel having procured the salvation and avoided hell. But ... this actually only represents the starting point for God's good news.[6]

The mission of the church goes much further than prompting a person to "make a decision for Christ." Jesus stated the mission in terms of making "disciples" – true *talmidim*. Discipleship as Jesus envisioned it is not a one-time decision. It begins with a choice that then demands continuous *action*. Said another way, the decision to make Jesus Lord and Savior of your life simply

---

5   McKnight, Scot, *The King Jesus Gospel: The Original Good News* (Zondervan 2011)

6   Bock, Darrell L., *Recovering The Real Lost Gospel: Reclaiming The Gospel As Good News* (B & H Academic 2010) p. 4

places your feet in the starter blocks. It is then a life-long race to the finish line to be continually growing and changing into the likeness of Christ. True discipleship is marked by a lifestyle of trusting belief evidenced by how one lives life. Scholar Christopher Zoccali refers to those who make this lifestyle choice "Christ allegiants."[7] We are called to live our faith out loud! In fact, discipleship without corresponding behavior which evidences that loyalty would have been untenable to Jesus and foreign to His first disciples.

So, what does "making *talmidim*" all over the world have to do with building a Temple? We can find the answer in the temple-building language used by both Paul and Peter. An example of Paul's use of the temple metaphor is found in our Key Scripture for this lesson.

> So then you are no longer strangers and aliens, but **you are fellow citizens with the saints**, and are of God's household, having been built on the foundation of the apostles and prophets, Christ Jesus Himself being the corner stone, in whom the whole building, being fitted together, is **growing into a holy temple in the Lord**, in whom you also are being built together into a dwelling of God in the Spirit. Ephesians 2:19-22, italics omitted, bold added

The image of Christ-followers being God's temple is found in two other places in Paul's writing, both in epistles to the church at Corinth.[8]

---

7   Zoccali, Christopher, *Reading Philippians After Supersessionism: Jews, Gentiles and Covenant Identity, The New Testament after Supersessionism* (Cascade Books 2017) pp. 75-76

8   "When we come to the apostle Paul, we find a corpus of literature permeated with temple imagery." Perrin, Nicholas, *Jesus The Temple* (Baker Academic 2012) p. 65. Scholar Nicholas Perrin argues that Paul employs Temple imagery frequently not as an incidental metaphor but in heavy reliance on his Jewish background and especially the expectation of an eschatological Temple.

My Dwelling Place

> Do you not know that **you [plural] are God's temple** and that God's Spirit dwells in you? 1 Corinthians 3:16 ESV, bold added

> What agreement has the temple of God with idols? For **we are the temple of the living God**; as God said, "I will make my dwelling among them and walk among them, and I will be their God, and they shall be my people...." 2 Corinthians 6:16 ESV, bold added

In all of these quotes Paul chose the Greek word *naos* {nah-os'} translated at "Temple" (in other translations "Sanctuary"). This is the term employed for the actual Sanctuary area of the Jerusalem Temple which historically symbolized both the place and the fact of God's dwelling among His people.[9] In fact, according to existing ancient literature, the term *naos* is only used to refer to "inorganic structures built for the worship of a deity who ... is 'frequently perceived to be using it as a dwelling.'"[10] Paul's point is that God's Spirit inhabits this new form of Temple and that's what makes it a Temple.[11] In other words, Jesus is the Temple

---

9 Fee, Gordon D., *The First Epistle To The Corinthians*, New International Commentary on the New Testament (Eerdmans 1987) 1 Corinthians 3:16, p. 146; Verbrugge, Verlyn D., "1 Corinthians," *The Expositor's Bible Commentary: Romans ~ Galatians*, Vol. 11, Revised Edition, edited by Longman III and Garland (Zondervan Academic 2006) 1 Corinthians 3:16, p. 286

10 Basham, David Anthony, *Paul, The Temple, And Building A Metaphor*, Dissertation submitted for the degree of Doctor of Philosophy in the School of Religious Studies at McGill University, December 15, 2022, quoting BDAG, "ναός," 665. Retrieved from file:///C:/Users/Deb/Downloads/ edecfbee-b2bf-4d05-a71c-d6690b599e2b.pdf (last accessed October 26, 2023)

11 In his second letter to the church at Corinth, Paul wrote, "For we are the temple of the living God; just as God said, 'I will dwell in them and walk among them; And I will be their God, and they shall be My people....'" According to *Net Bible Notes*, "The OT text that lies behind this passage (Lev 26:11–12) speaks of God dwelling in the midst of his people. The Greek preposition *en* in the phrase *en autois* ('in them') can also have that meaning ('among' or 'with'). However, Paul appears to be extending the

because God's fullness dwells in Him. Christ-followers are the Temple because God's Spirit dwells in us (1 Corinthians 6:19) Peter also refers to Christ-followers as God's temple.

> You are coming to Christ, who is the living cornerstone of God's temple. He was rejected by people, but he was chosen by God for great honor. And **you are living stones that God is building into his spiritual temple**. What's more, you are his holy priests. Through the mediation of Jesus Christ, you offer spiritual sacrifices that please God. 1 Peter 2:4-5 NLT, bold added

Peter employs the phrase *living stones* to identify those who share in the resurrected life of Christ and therefore are able to function like Him.[12] It is this new form of Temple which now hosts God's glory.[13] The first living stones to be put in place after the death of Christ were the disciples who were obediently waiting in Jerusalem according to the instruction they received before they watched Christ ascend. We find the account in familiar text from the book of Acts:

> In the first book, O Theophilus, I have dealt with all that Jesus began to do and teach, until the day when he was taken up, after he had given commands through the Holy Spirit to the apostles whom he had chosen. He presented himself alive to them after his suffering by many proofs, appearing to them during forty days and speaking about the kingdom of God. And while staying with

---

imagery here to involve God (as the Spirit) dwelling *in* his people, since he calls believers 'the temple of the living God'" in the previous clause, imagery he uses elsewhere in his writings (1 Cor 3:16; Eph 2:21–22)." *Net Bible Notes*, study note 24, 2 Corinthians 6:16

12 Keener, Craig S., *1 Peter: A Commentary* (Baker Academic 2021) 1 Peter 2:4-5, p. 128

13 The glory of God is seen in those who are redeemed. See for example: 2 Corinthians 3:18. *NIV Study Bible* (Zondervan Publishing 1995) study note Isaiah 40:5, p. 1064

them he ordered them not to depart from Jerusalem, but to wait for the promise of the Father, which, he said, "you heard from me; for John baptized with water, but you will be baptized with the Holy Spirit not many days from now." Acts 1:1-5 ESV

When the day of Pentecost arrived, they were all together in one place. And suddenly there came from heaven a sound like a mighty rushing wind, and it filled the entire house where they were sitting. And divided tongues as of fire appeared to them and rested on each one of them. And they were all filled with the Holy Spirit and began to speak in other tongues as the Spirit gave them utterance. Acts 2:1-4 ESV

Luke records the amazing fact that God's *Shekinah* glory visibly descended on the waiting disciples. Not only did God's glory come down, it descended in a manner similar to His glory descending on the Tabernacle in the wilderness and on Solomon's Temple. In this case, His glory came to rest on His waiting *talmidim*. Before we can understand how those standing there would have viewed this event, we need to add a historical fact. In the book of Isaiah, as well as other ancient writings, God's heavenly Temple is in part pictured by tongues of fire.[14] As a result, the tongues of fire that descended on Pentecost provided clear visible evidence to those who experienced it and those who saw it that these disciples were now the new spiritual Temple and God would dwell among them! The promised latter-day glory had begun to

---

14 "Since the heavenly temple is partly pictured by 'tongues of fire', it might be appropriate that the descent of that temple would be pictured with the same thing." Beale, G. K., *The Temple and the Church's Mission: A Biblical Theology of The Dwelling Place of God* (InterVarsity Press 2004) p. 206. Beale points to Isaiah 5:24-25; 30:27-30 and 1 Enoch 14:8-25; 71:5 as sources which connect tongues of fire with God's heavenly Temple. See also: Perrin, Nicholas, *Jesus the Temple* (Baker Academic 2012) p. 63

manifest itself in the form of living stones in God's new Temple.[15] God had chosen to come to live in (and among) the community of Christ-followers. As we have noted, it is the fact that His Spirit lives *in* them (1 Corinthians 3:16; Ephesians 2:22) which makes them the new Temple God Himself created.

On that same day, the day of Pentecost, about 3,000 more living stones were added to this new form of Temple (Acts 2:41) and the glory of the new Temple increased. Luke tells us that growth continued, "And the Lord was adding to their number day by day those who were being saved (Acts 2:47b)." To this very day new living stones are continually being added around the world.

In its present form, it is appropriate to think of the Temple as a synonym for God's Kingdom on earth. As His Kingdom advances, His Temple grows. Wherever His Temple is, there we find His Kingdom and wherever we find His Kingdom, we see His Temple. The living stones being put in place function as proper building materials by fulfilling their calling. They grow in Christ-likeness and then, as well trained *talmidim*, they put God on display for the rest of the world to see. In fact, as disciples of Christ, we are to become so saturated with Him that we can't help but put Him on display to the world. He expects every disciple to live under His Kingly rule. Each one is to obey His commands and live a life that RE•presents[16] Him for who He *really* is to the

---

15 Scholar Gordon Fee points out that it is quite possible Paul understood the new Temple to be a fulfillment of the restored Temple Ezekiel saw (Ezekiel 40-48) "where God promised 'to live among them forever' ([Ezekiel] 43:9) and out of which flowed the river of fresh water that restored the land ([Ezekiel] 47:1-12)." Fee, Gordon D., *The First Epistle To The Corinthians*, New International Commentary on the New Testament (Eerdmans 1987) 1 Corinthians 3:16, p. 147

16 I am intentionally repurposing the word "represent" by making a clear separation between the prefix "re" and the remainder of the word "present." The prefix "re" indicates repetition and has an ordinary meaning of "again" or "back." My goal in showing the word in this unique form is to highlight the truth that one who is God's "representative" does not act on his own accord, that representative is actually commissioned by God to "repeat" what God has done, to show "again" who God is. I have placed the prefix

My Dwelling Place   151

lost and dying world around them. By our obedience we are the living stones forming a Temple for God's dwelling place on earth in the present age.[17]

The word "church" throughout the New Testament is a translation of the Greek word *ekklesia*. In the first century Greco-Roman world *ekklesia* was a political term, not a religious one. Jesus was the promised King in the line of David and the New Testament used the term *ekklesia* for good reason.[18] In the days of the early church, the civic *ekklesia* was comprised of citizens who met regularly. They were convened by the civic counselors at specified times and locations so they could handle specific governmental functions relating to judicial proceedings and the administration of the law. For example, in Athens they met every thirty-six or thirty-nine days. A typical meeting location would be the city's *agora* which was the civic market place in the city.[19] In short, the *ekklesia* functioned as the ruling council in the city. As noted by scholar Ralph Korner, "There is a long history of interaction between *boulai* [civic counselors] and *dēmoi* [common people who were citizens and therefore had the rights of citizenship] within *ekklēsiai*." Because the early *talmidim* were called the *ekklesia* they must have understood their role to govern, to be co-regents with King Jesus and bring to earth the will of God as it is in heaven! In other words, we find the concept of ruling, reigning and Kingdom citizenship inherent in the very definition of the word we translate

---

"re" in all caps to indicate the emphasis on that syllable when pronouncing the word.

17 Perrin, Nicholas, *Jesus the Temple* (Baker Academic 2012) p. 117

18 Scholar Ralph Korner asserts that the Jewish background for the term *ekklēsia* is of equal importance as the Greco-Roman background "in providing missional relevance" for its use in the New Testament. In addition to its common use as a Greek civic term, *ekklēsia* was the word used for a Jewish synagogue/community. Korner, Ralph J., *Reading Revelation After Supersessionism: An Apocalyptic Journey of Socially Identifying John's Multi-Ethnic Ekklesiai with the Ekklesia of Israel* (Cascade Books 2020) p. 25

19 Korner, Ralph J., *Reading Revelation After Supersessionism: An Apocalyptic Journey of Socially Identifying John's Multi-Ethnic Ekklesiai with the Ekklesia of Israel* (Cascade Books 2020) p. 23

as "church." We pointed out in Lesson 6 that a properly functioning church is an outpost of God's heavenly Kingdom. As we are going to learn, being an effective Kingdom outpost is precisely the mission statement recorded for the *ekklesia* in our Key Scripture.

Paul had just revealed the mystery that through the work of the cross Christ created one new man out of two. Paul was speaking about Jewish Messiah-followers and Gentile Messiah-followers becoming one in Christ. Historically they had been two distinct and separate people groups accustomed to hostile division. Paul reveals that while their individual heritage may have been of Jewish or Gentile origin, as followers of Christ they now belong to the same body – together they are building the same living Temple. Because they share the high status of saints [set-apart ones][20] they have a "correspondingly high responsibility and task."[21] They were called to be a holy alternative to the ways of the world in keeping with the fact that "God's temple is holy (1 Corinthians 3:17)."

Paul informs the *talmidim* that God's plan calls for apostles, prophets, evangelists, pastors and teachers within the *ekklesia* to train Christ-followers as living stones in the work they are called to do. The goal is to build them up into full maturity in Christ – becoming holy (set-apart) "in the moral-ethical sense."[22] The call to maturity puts them on notice that a "radical reorientation [is] involved in their commitment to Christ."[23] It will not be enough

---

20 They are "set apart from that which is secular, profane, and evil and on the other hand dedicated to worship and service of God." *Ephesians 3:8-9 Commentary*, Precept Austin. Retrieved from https://www.preceptaustin.org/ephesians_38-9 (last accessed October 27, 2023)
21 Barth, Markus, *Ephesians: Translation and Commentary on Chapters 4-6*, The Anchor Bible Vol. 34 (Doubleday 1974) Ephesians 4:1-16, under *Comment II Proclamation, Exhortation, and Vocation*, p. 454
22 Fee, Gordon D., *The First Epistle To The Corinthians*, New International Commentary on the New Testament (Eerdmans 1987) 1 Corinthians 3:17, p. 149
23 Zoccali, Christopher, *Reading Philippians After Supersessionism: Jews, Gentiles and Covenant Identity*, The New Testament after Supersessionism (Cascade Books 2017) p. 76, citing Nebreda

to be advocates of Christ-likeness, they will need to outwardly display the likeness of Christ for all the world to see. In this way, they are "the *manifestation of Christ to the world*"[24] and evidence of His Kingdom rule. No matter where they physically reside in the world, by their obedience they demonstrate their submission to the rule of the one true King! They are citizens in the growing *Kingdom within other kingdoms* living a style of life which is invariably "at odds with current society."[25]

God had given Israel two historical contexts for understanding what this looks like in real life. The first began way back in the restoration period following the Babylonian exile. You'll recall that the people who returned to Jerusalem were the remnant of God's Kingdom, the ones who had chosen to live under His Kingdom rule. However, they resided in the larger kingdom of the Persian Empire. A more current context in Paul's day was the experience of Jews living in the Roman Empire where those in God's Kingdom were permitted an exemption from total assimilation into the larger kingdom of the Roman Empire. "As the Roman Empire expanded .... [o]nly the Jews retained a distinctive communal identity. And what is more remarkable, the Romans accepted the Jewish self-understanding and allowed them to be exempt from the religious obligations that were imposed on other inhabitants of the cities. Jews did not have to worship the Roman gods, and they responded with gratitude by offering sacrifices and prayers for the emperor in the Temple in Jerusalem."[26] There were

---

24 Barth, Markus, *Ephesians: Introduction, Translation, and Commentary on Chapters 1-3*, The Anchor Bible Vol 34 (Doubleday 1974) Ephesians 1:15-23 under *Comment VI Head, Body, and Fullness B. The Body*, p. 198, italics in original

25 Zoccali, Christopher, *Reading Philippians After Supersessionism: Jews, Gentiles and Covenant Identity, The New Testament after Supersessionism* (Cascade Books 2017) p. 77, quoting Nebreda, *Christ Identity*, p. 63

26 *Jews as the Romans Saw Them by Robert Louis Wilken*, First Things, Articles, May, 2008 citing the work of Martin Goodman, *Rome and Jerusalem: The Clash of Ancient ¬Civilizations* (Vintage 2008). Retrieved from https://www.firstthings.com/article/2008/05/jews-as-the-romans-saw-them#:~:text=Jews%20did%20not%20have%20to%20worship%20the%20

Jewish people in Jesus' day who had chosen to live in the Kingdom of God while residing in the larger kingdom of the Roman Empire.

We have one remaining matter to address in this lesson. It will be instructive for our study to carefully consider what Paul meant when he referred to the heavenly citizenship of Christ-followers. Our key text is found in what Paul wrote to the Philippians:

> Only **conduct yourselves in a manner worthy of the gospel of Christ**, so that whether I come and see you or remain absent, I will hear of you that you are standing firm in one spirit, with one mind striving together for the faith of the gospel. Philippians 1:27, bold added

> Brethren, join in following my example, and observe those who walk according to the pattern you have in us. ... For **our citizenship is in heaven**, from which also we eagerly wait for a Savior, the Lord Jesus Christ .... Therefore, my beloved brethren ... in this way stand firm in the Lord, my beloved. Philippians 3:17-4:1, bold added

To rightly understand Paul's instruction, we will be greatly aided by supplying some historical context that provided Paul with a unique backdrop. Paul was writing to Philippi. It was a Roman colony that had been given a distinct status which permitted the city to be treated as if it was actually on Italian soil.[27]

Roman,for%20the%20emperor%20in%20the%20Temple%20in%20Jerusalem (last accessed October 24, 2023). Katell Berthelot, a French historian who specializes in ancient Judaism, points out that the sacrifices and prayers were a Jewish response to Roman imperialism which accommodated Roman rule "by means of sacrifices or prayers *on behalf of* the ruler rather than *to* the ruler." Berthelot, Katell, *Jews and Their Roman Rivals: Pagan Rome's Challenge to Israel* (Princeton University Press 2021) p. 87, italics in original

27 Garland, David E., "Philippians," in *The Expositor's Bible Commentary: Ephesians ~ Philemon*, Vol. 12, Revised Edition, edited by Longman III and Garland (Zondervan Academic 2006) Philippians 1:27, p. 208

My Dwelling Place

Only four other cities in Macedonia had this special designation by Rome.[28] As a Roman colony, Philippi was formed largely by Roman soldiers. Those soldiers had been given land grants in that area after the territory had been conquered and became part of the expanding Roman Empire. "Roman colonies were set up as 'miniatures' of Rome to foster the majesty of Roman culture, religion, and values."[29] The former Roman soldiers – now colonists – lived in that newly acquired territory as Roman citizens to govern the territory on behalf of Rome. They were considered to be full citizens of Rome, sharing all the rights and privileges held by Roman citizens.[30] In return for their privileges as colonists, they were expected to show complete loyalty to the Roman Emperor.[31] We have a modern-day example of such colonization in American history. The British Empire sent colonists to the land we now call America with the purpose of settling it on behalf of Britain. The colonists were expected to remain loyal to Britain's ruling power while they lived in a land that was far away from their British homeland.

Colonists kept strong links with their previous "country" (in the first century that meant Rome)[32] while they formed an out-

---

28 Thielman, Frank., "Philippians," in *Zondervan Illustrated Bible Backgrounds Commentary*, Vol. 3, edited by Clinton E. Arnold (Zondervan 2002) Philippians 1:27, p. 353

29 Garland, David E., "Philippians," in *The Expositor's Bible Commentary: Ephesians ~ Philemon*, Vol. 12, Revised Edition, edited by Longman III and Garland (Zondervan Academic 2006) Philippians 3:20, p. 248, citing Gellius, *Attic Nights* 16.13.9

30 Keener, Craig S., *The IVP Bible Background Commentary: New Testament* (Intervarsity Press 1993) Philippians 3:20, p. 564

31 Garland, David E., "Philippians," in *The Expositor's Bible Commentary: Ephesians ~ Philemon*, Vol. 12, Revised Edition, edited by Longman III and Garland (Zondervan Academic 2006) Philippians 1:27, p. 208

32 The Roman Empire began with Rome as a city. The expansion from city to empire began with the conquest of the Italian peninsula and the areas surrounding the Mediterranean Sea. As they expanded territory they colonized to secure the new territory. One author notes, "The story of Roman colonization is the story of the growth of the Roman Empire." MacKendrick, P. L., *Roman Colonization*, Phoenix Vol. 6, No. 4 (Winter

post in a separate geographic location on behalf of their home "country" (in the first century that meant Rome). That new territory was fully subject to the ruling power of Caesar. Let me add two more relevant facts which help supply context for us. The first fact is that in the culture of Paul's day "the ruler was frequently called 'savior.' This term was especially common for Roman emperors."[33] The second relevant fact is that according to the Roman Empire, the good news "gospel" (same word used in the New Testament for the gospel of Christ) was inscribed on a stone in Priene, in the province of Asia Minor. The inscription announced that the emperor Augustus Caesar brought peace and benefits to Rome therefore the new gospel of Rome is that Augustus was a Savior.[34]

Keeping in mind that background, let's look carefully at the word "citizenship" in Philippians 3. It is a translation of the unique Greek verb *politeuma* {pol-it'-yoo-mah}. The term "was sometimes used generally to speak of the political rights of a particular group.... The same word could also refer to a distinct ethnic group that lived away from its homeland and was governed by

---

    1952) pp. 139-146, at p. 139. Retrieved from https://www.jstor.org/stable/1086829?origin=crossref (last accessed October 27, 2023)

33 Thielman, Frank, "Philippians," in *Zondervan Illustrated Bible Backgrounds Commentary*, Vol. 3, edited by Clinton E. Arnold (Zondervan 2002) Philippians 3:20 under *We eagerly await a Savior from there*, p. 362

34 The Priene [Calendar] Inscription, Biblical Criticism & History Forum, earlywritings.com. Retrieved from https://earlywritings.com/forum/viewtopic.php?t=3255 (last accessed October 12, 2023). "Augustus was worshiped throughout the empire as the savior and benefactor of the entire world, as the one who had rescued the world from the evils of war and chaos. And the proclamation of his heroic deeds and extraordinary benefactions constituted the essence of the new gospel of Rome." Bonz, Marianne P., *The Gospel of Rome vs. the Gospel of Jesus Christ: Two New Testament Responses from the Churches Founded by Paul*, Symposium - The Gospel Of Rome Vs. The Gospel Of Jesus Christ, From Jesus To Christ, Frontline, PBS, May 30, 1998 under *The Gospel of Rome*. Retrieved from https://www.pbs.org/wgbh/pages/frontline/shows/religion/symposium/gospel.html (last accessed October 12, 2023)

My Dwelling Place 157

its own constitution—'a city within a city.'"[35] Paul is reminding the Philippians that they may physically live in a Roman colony, but the real ruler of their "city" (*politeuma*) "is none other than Jesus, who will bring 'everything under his control' (Philippians 3:21)."[36]

Paul knew that God's rule and authority transcends every geographic boundary established by a kingdom on earth. His audience may presently have dual citizenship (Rome and heaven) but their highest call is to be colonists of heaven. That is why Paul instructed them to "conduct yourselves (*politeueomai*) in a manner worthy of the gospel of Christ (Philippians 1:27)." Paul employed a term *politeueomai* (conduct yourselves) related to *politeuma* (citizenship) which presents the image of a person fulfilling their duties as a citizen.[37] (Both *politeueomai* and *politeuma* derive from *polis* which refers to "the political community"[38] – a city that is the ruling center along with the wider area that the city governs.)[39] When Paul wanted to speak about the responsibilities of Christ-followers to live as Christ he typically employed the verb *peripateo* {per-ee-pat-eh'-o}. For example, in Philippians 3:17 he instructed the disciples to "*walk* [*peripateo*] according to the pat-

---

35 Thielman, Frank., "Philippians," in *Zondervan Illustrated Bible Backgrounds Commentary*, Vol. 3, edited by Clinton E. Arnold (Zondervan 2002) Philippians 3:20 under *Our citizenship is in heaven*, p. 362. Thielman gives credit for the phrase "a city within a city" to E. Mary Smallwood, *The Jews under Roman Rule from Pompey to Diocletian: A Study in Political Relations* (Brill 1981) p. 225

36 Thielman, Frank., "Philippians," in *Zondervan Illustrated Bible Backgrounds Commentary*, Vol. 3, edited by Clinton E. Arnold (Zondervan 2002) Philippians 3:20 under *We eagerly await a Savior from there*, p. 362

37 Garland, David E., "Philippians," in *The Expositor's Bible Commentary: Ephesians ~ Philemon*, Vol. 12, Revised Edition, edited by Longman III and Garland (Zondervan Academic 2006) Philippians 1:27, p. 208

38 Barth, Markus, *Ephesians: Translation and Commentary on Chapters 4-6*, The Anchor Bible Vol. 34 (Doubleday 1974) Ephesians 4:1-16 under *Comment II Proclamation, Exhortation, and Vocation*, p. 455

39 Bromiley, Geoffrey W., *Theological Dictionary of the New Testament*, Abridged in One Volume (Eerdmans 1985) entry for *polis* under *A. Nonbiblical Greek*, p. 906

tern you have in us." The fact that Philippians 1:27 is his only use of the word *politeueomai* highlights an intentional purpose for this specific word choice. Its only other use in the New Testament is found in Acts 23:1 which has been understood to refer to "living in allegiance to a community and authority."[40] It seems that this type of political connotation fit perfectly with the contrast Paul has in mind.[41]

In the first century, it was fully expected that a citizen should seek to profit the city in which he lived by placing the interests of the city above his own interests.[42] Paul's word choices point to the fact that he expected his readers to draw the appropriate contrasts that naturally exist for those who have chosen to be a spiritual colonist of heaven (on behalf of King Jesus) while at the same time they are a physical colonist living in Philippi (on behalf of Rome). Heaven "has a different constitution and different laws, and [those who follow Christ] are to exemplify the values of the heavenly realm. Christ's resurrection establishes a new city (*polis*) [political community] and an alternative political jurisdiction that challenges the values and the methods of the [Roman] empire."[43]

In other words, Paul calls their attention to the reality that they are living in a *Kingdom within a kingdom* and in essence had dual citizenship. It is because they physically resided in a Roman colony that Paul's audience "understand quite well what it means

---

40 Garland, David E., "Philippians," in *The Expositor's Bible Commentary: Ephesians ~ Philemon*, Vol. 12, Revised Edition, edited by Longman III and Garland (Zondervan Academic 2006) Philippians 1:27, p. 208
41 Garland, David E., "Philippians," in *The Expositor's Bible Commentary: Ephesians ~ Philemon*, Vol. 12, Revised Edition, edited by Longman III and Garland (Zondervan Academic 2006) Philippians 1:27, p. 208, quoting Doble, Peter, '*Vile Bodies*' or *Transformed Persons? Philippians 3:21 in Context*, JSNT 24, 2002, p. 18
42 Garland, David E., "Philippians," in *The Expositor's Bible Commentary: Ephesians ~ Philemon*, Vol. 12, Revised Edition, edited by Longman III and Garland (Zondervan Academic 2006) Philippians 3:20, p. 248
43 Garland, David E., "Philippians," in *The Expositor's Bible Commentary: Ephesians ~ Philemon*, Vol. 12, Revised Edition, edited by Longman III and Garland (Zondervan Academic 2006) Philippians 3:20, p. 248

to be citizens of the supreme city while not yet living there."[44] In the present they are to live "in a manner worthy of the gospel of Christ" not the false gospel of the Roman Empire. Their Savior is Christ, not the Roman Emperor.[45] "They are Christ's colony, and he is their [true] Emperor."[46] Of course, this leads to a clash of kingdoms and we'll have more to say about that in our last lesson.

We will conclude this lesson with documented evidence that the early church fully understood and was living out the mission she had been given. *The Epistle to Diognetus* was written as an early Christian apology. While the author, recipient and date are uncertain (likely written between 150 to 225 A.D.)[47] the goal is easily recognizable. The author makes his purpose clear in the first section of the epistle. He indicates that he is answering questions posed by "most excellent Diognetus" related to the God of the Christians, how they worship, the nature of their love for each other and why this new way of life has been introduced in the world. Quite germane to our discussion in this lesson, as well as the next, is Chapter 5 of this epistle. We will conclude our lesson by quoting that entire Chapter.[48]

Chapter 5. The Distinctiveness of Christianity

---

[44] Keener, Craig S., *The IVP Bible Background Commentary: New Testament* (Intervarsity Press 1993) Philippians 3:20, p. 564

[45] "There is wide agreement in contemporary New Testament scholarship that Paul's gospel challenges the imperial pretenses of the Roman Empire …." Zoccali, Christopher, *Reading Philippians After Supersessionism: Jews, Gentiles and Covenant Identity, The New Testament after Supersessionism* (Cascade Books 2017) p. 78, footnote 77

[46] Garland, David E., "Philippians," in *The Expositor's Bible Commentary: Ephesians ~ Philemon*, Vol. 12, Revised Edition, edited by Longman III and Garland (Zondervan Academic 2006) Philippians 1:27, p. 208

[47] Holmes, Michael W., *The Apostolic Fathers In English*, 3rd edition (Baker Academic 2006) p 290

[48] *The Epistle to Diognetus*, 5:1-10, Michael W. Holmes, translator, editor, quoted in Holmes, Michael W., *The Apostolic Fathers In English*, 3rd edition (Baker Academic 2006) pp. 295-296

For Christians are not distinguished from the rest of humanity by country, language, or custom. ²For nowhere do they live in cities of their own, nor do they speak some unusual dialect, nor do they practice an eccentric way of life. ³This teaching of theirs has not been discovered by the thoughts and reflections of ingenious people, nor do they promote any human doctrine, as some do.[49] ⁴But while they live in both Greek and barbarian cities, as each one's lot was cast, and follow the local customs in dress and food and other aspects of life, at the same time they demonstrate the remarkable and admittedly unusual character of their own citizenship.[50] ⁵They live in their own countries, but only as nonresidents; they participate in everything as citizens, and endure everything as foreigners. Every foreign country is fatherland, and every fatherland is foreign. [Every foreign land is to them as their native country, and every land of their birth as a land of strangers.][51] ⁶They marry like everyone else, and

---

49 "The course of conduct which they follow has not been devised by any speculation or deliberation of inquisitive men; nor do they, like some, proclaim themselves the advocates of any merely human doctrines." *Epistle of Mathetes to Diognetus*, translation from Roberts-Donaldson English Translation. The anonymous author of the *Epistle of Diognetus* gave himself the title (Mathetes) meaning "a disciple of the Apostles" and in his translation Roberts-Donaldson adopts that title as the author's name believing it serves a useful end. Retrieved from https://www.earlychristianwritings.com/text/diognetus-roberts.html (last accessed February 5, 2024)

50 "But, inhabiting Greek as well as barbarian cities, according as the lot of each of them has determined, and following the customs of the natives in respect to clothing, food, and the rest of their ordinary conduct, they display to us their wonderful and confessedly striking method of life." *Epistle of Mathetes to Diognetus*, translation from Roberts-Donaldson English Translation. Retrieved from https://www.earlychristianwritings.com/text/diognetus-roberts.html (last accessed February 5, 2024)

51 *Epistle of Mathetes to Diognetus*, translation from Roberts-Donaldson English Translation. Retrieved from https://www.earlychristianwritings.com/text/diognetus-roberts.html (last accessed February 5, 2024)

have children, but they do not expose [destroy⁵²] their offspring. ⁷They share their food, but not their wives. ⁸They are in the flesh, but they do not live according to the flesh. ⁹They live on earth, but their citizenship is in heaven. ¹⁰They obey the established laws, indeed in their private lives they transcend the laws. ¹¹They love everyone, and by everyone they are persecuted. ¹²They are unknown, yet they are condemned; they are put to death, yet they are brought to life [restored to life].⁵³ ¹³They are poor, yet make many rich; they are in need of everything, yet they abound in everything.¹⁴They are dishonored, yet they are glorified in their dishonor; they are slandered, yet they are vindicated. ¹⁵They are cursed, yet they bless; they are insulted, yet they offer respect. ¹⁶When they do good, they are punished as evil doers; when they are punished, they rejoice as though brought to life. ¹⁷By the Jews they are assaulted as foreigners, and by the Greeks they are persecuted, yet those who hate them are unable to give a reason for their hostility.⁵⁴

May the same be said of us in the culture of our day.

Hear What The Spirit is Saying to the Church: *Yes, yes, yes! A thousand times yes. Open your hearts to new understanding. Refuse to be stuck in old ways of thinking. Learn anew what has been written in My Word. See anew with open eyes what my plan has been all along. Wake up and see as I unveil the true meaning of my word. And so it shall be.*

---

52 *Epistle of Mathetes to Diognetus*, translation from Roberts-Donaldson English Translation. Retrieved from https://www.earlychristianwritings.com/text/diognetus-roberts.html (last accessed February 5, 2024)

53 *Epistle of Mathetes to Diognetus*, translation from Roberts-Donaldson English Translation. Retrieved from https://www.earlychristianwritings.com/text/diognetus-roberts.html (last accessed February 5, 2024)

54 *The Epistle to Diognetus*, 5:1-10, Michael W. Holmes, translator, editor, quoted in Holmes, Michael W., *The Apostolic Fathers In English*, 3ʳᵈ edition (Baker Academic 2006) pp. 295-296

LESSON 12:

THE CLASH OF KINGDOMS

 "I did not see a sanctuary [temple] in [the New Jerusalem], because the Lord God the Almighty and the Lamb are its sanctuary [temple]." Revelation 21:22 HCSB

THERE IS ONE remaining Temple form to consider in this study. It is the true Temple which has always been and will last for all eternity! We begin this lesson with our Key Scripture. One of the last visions the Apostle John records in what we call the book of Revelation is a vision of New Jerusalem.[1] John informed his audience he did not see a temple. If John were to stop there it would have sounded very odd to his first-century listeners because "all normal Greek and Roman cities included temples."[2] As we read on in our Key Scripture, however, we learn that it's not that John saw no temple. The new city did not contain a made-with-

---

1. John saw New Jerusalem come down from heaven (Revelation 21:21). As was pointed out in Lesson 2, in ancient Jewish thought, after Adam and Eve sinned and were banned from the Garden of Eden, "this Edenic paradise was then taken up to heaven to await the faithful .... Here in Revelation it has once more come down to join the renewed earth and is now part of the eternal city. Eden has not only been restored but has been elevated and expanded for the people of God in eternity." Osborne, Grant, *Revelation* (Baker Academic 2002) Revelation 22:1-5 under *C. New Jerusalem as the Final Eden*, p. 768, citing *T. Levi* 18.10-11; *T. Dan* 5.12-13; *2 Bar.* 4:3-7
2. Keener, Craig S., *Revelation*, The NIV Application Commentary (Zondervan 2000) Revelation 21:22-22:5, p. 497, citing Arrian, *Indica* 7.2; Kraybill, *Imperial Cult and Commerce*, p. 213

human-hands temple *because* the Temple standing in the New Jerusalem is none other than God Himself and the resurrected Lamb, Jesus Christ. Before we move on, let me point out that the title "Lord God the Almighty" is the equivalent of the title "LORD of Hosts"[3] which we learned in Lesson 9 is a title emphasizing God's Kingship.

It is not that God and the Lamb *became* the Temple, they always were the Temple. However, once sin existed on earth the Holy Presence of God could not dwell on earth among His people without sufficient sacrifice to cover the sin. Jesus provided that sacrifice enabling a renewed type of dwelling which would be accomplished through the Holy Spirit abiding in God's Covenant people. The new form of Temple He had inaugurated was a bridge leading to the ultimate end-time Temple – "the true temple on which the [Tabernacle and the] temple 'made by human hands' was based."[4] As summarized by G. K. Beale:[5]

> ... God created the cosmos to be his great temple, in which he rested after his creative work. His special revelatory presence, nevertheless, did not yet fill the entire earth because his human vice-regent [Adam] was to achieve this purpose. God had installed this vice-regent in [Eden] the garden sanctuary to extend the boundaries of God's presence there worldwide. Adam disobeyed this mandate, so that humanity no longer enjoyed God's presence in the small Garden. As a result, all humanity and all creation became contaminated with sin.... The successful fulfillment of the Adamic commission awaited the presence – and obedience – of the last Adam, Jesus Christ. Thus, the redemptive-historical development

---

3 Osborne, Grant, *Revelation* (Baker Academic 2002) Revelation 1:7-8, p. 72. Osborne points out that the Greek translation of the Old Testament frequently translates "LORD of Hosts" with *ho pantokratōr*, the Almighty.
4 Perrin, Nicholas, *Jesus the Temple* (Baker Academic 2012) p. 117
5 Beale, G. K., *The Temple and the Church's Mission: A Biblical Theology of The Dwelling Place of God* (InterVarsity Press 2004) pp. 392-393

may be explained as proceeding from God's unique presence in the structural temple in the Old Testament to the God-man, Christ, [who is "the image of the invisible God (Colossians 1:15)." "The fullness of all that God is was present in Jesus (Colossians 1:19)"] the true temple. As a result of Christ's resurrection, the Spirit continued building the end-time temple, the building materials of which are God's people, thus extending the temple into the new creation in the new age. This building process will culminate in the eternal new heavens and earth as a paradisal city-temple. Or, more briefly, the temple of God has been transformed into God, his people and the rest of the new creation as the temple.

Now we can more fully understand God's Sanctuary-Presence with Israel during the period of her exile from the Promised Land. You may recall that in Lesson 6 we discussed God's promise in Ezekiel 11:16 that He would personally be a Sanctuary for His exiled people *for a little while.* I had suggested God's intention was to inform Israel He would be that Sanctuary in the absence of a physical Temple for a short period of time. I believe it is in light of our Key Scripture that understanding comes full circle. Let me explain. After God allowed Babylon to conquer His people, He would be a Sanctuary for them for a little while in a foreign land where He had exiled His people. However, after God decisively conquers symbolic Babylon (as portrayed in Revelation) He will be a Sanctuary for His people forever! All the barriers between God and His Covenant people have at last been removed. His unrestricted fixed Presence is now forever with them.

In Lesson 11 we looked at a contextual understanding of Paul's instruction to new followers of Christ to be like colonists and settle new Kingdom territory on behalf of God's heavenly Kingdom. We recognized that directive would inevitably lead to a clash of kingdoms and promised to explore that inescapable collision in this lesson. We also noted that we would return to the notion of suffering in this last lesson. Those two remaining topics fit together like a hand in a glove. As we have witnessed throughout this study, there is a perfection to God's eternal plan that is beyond human understanding. The matter of persecution and suffering as a part of God's divine plan is no exception. It too seems beyond our capacity to fully understand. Even so, it is important to acknowledge that there is a recurring theme of persecution and suffering that begins prophetically in the Old Testament and runs from Matthew to Revelation in the New Testament.

It may be helpful for us to think of an imaginary suffering/persecution timeline that extends from Christ's first coming to His second coming. The personal suffering of Christ, who fulfilled the role of Isaiah's Suffering Servant, is seen at the beginning of our imaginary timeline. The Bible reveals that suffering/persecution will continue all the way to the end of the timeline we have imagined. That reality highlights the fact that someone must pick up where Christ left off and fulfill that suffering role all the way to the end of the timeline. According to the Bible, the suffering shown on our imaginary timeline between the two advents of Christ is divinely ordained to be shouldered by those who chose to follow Christ.[6] The starting point of this thematic thread of suffering is found in the words of Jesus.

> [3]As [Jesus] was sitting on the Mount of Olives, the disciples came to Him privately, saying, "Tell us, when will these things happen [when the Temple in Jerusalem will be destroyed], and what will be the sign of Your coming, and of the end of the age?" [Jesus then described various types of trials, tribulations and suffering that will be endured on earth during His absence. Included

---

[6] This period has been referred to as the time of "Messianic Woes." The idea originates from the book of Daniel. See for example: Daniel 7:25–27, 8:9–14, 9:24–27, and 11:31–12:3. Daniel's vision is thought to provide a recurring pattern which indicates God's Covenant people will be persecuted and suffer. Only after their suffering will they be vindicated through resurrection in order to receive the promises of God.

within His description is that they will experience tribulation, martyrdom and be hated by all nations because of His name.] ²¹"For then there will be a great tribulation, such as has not occurred since the beginning of the world until now, nor ever will. ²² Unless those days had been cut short, no life would have been saved; but for the sake of the elect those days will be cut short.... ²⁹But immediately after the tribulation of those days THE SUN WILL BE DARKENED, AND THE MOON WILL NOT GIVE ITS LIGHT, AND THE STARS WILL FALL from the sky, and the powers of the heavens will be shaken. ³⁰ And then the sign of the Son of Man will appear in the sky, and then all the tribes of the earth will mourn, and they will see the SON OF MAN COMING ON THE CLOUDS OF THE SKY with power and great glory. ³¹ And He will send forth His angels with A GREAT TRUMPET and THEY WILL GATHER TOGETHER His elect from the four winds, from one end of the sky to the other." Matthew 24:3,21-31, uppercase text in original

The New Testament authors do not express alarm at persecution and suffering. Instead they present tribulation for Christ-followers as temporary, but "necessary" (cf. 1 Peter 1:6). They seem to accept as fact that suffering must be precede (and in fact advance) the consummation of God's Kingdom. Luke informs us that Paul told Christ-followers they enter the Kingdom of God, "[t]hrough many tribulations (Acts 14:22)." When encouraging the Thessalonians in the midst of the affliction they were enduring, Paul reminded them not to be disturbed because they already knew that they had been "destined for [trials and suffering] (1 Thessalonians 3:3)." The all-inclusive reality of tribulation for Christ-followers is made clear in 2 Timothy 3:12 when Paul writes, "Indeed, all who desire to live godly in Christ Jesus will be persecuted."

Paul affirmed his part to play in this theme of suffering when he told the Colossians that his own suffering was "filling up what is lacking in Christ's afflictions (Colossians 1:24)." To use our imaginary timeline analogy, Paul said his suffering was fulfilling the part he was assigned on that timeline. He assured the Christ-followers in Rome that he "consider[ed] that the sufferings of this present time are not worthy to be compared with the glory that is to be revealed to us (Romans 8:18)."

Peter taught that one "finds favor with God" any time they "[bear] up under sorrows when suffering unjustly. ... For [they] have been called for this purpose, since Christ also suffered for [them], leaving [them] an example ... to follow in His steps (1 Peter 2:19,21)." The author of Hebrews repeatedly encourages his audience toward steadfast endurance when they face temptation to compromise in times of persecution and hardship. In Revelation John speaks of trials, suffering and persecution. In fact, in Revelation 6:11 he refers to an appointed number of martyrs. Even so, John encourages all Christ-followers to persevere through the persecution of these end times in order to receive the promises of God.

We have learned that Jesus both preached and embodied (through His lifestyle) the righteousness God expected in Covenant relationship. In this way, He was a new heaven-sent Temple. His death ushered in a Temple form which as we have just noted above would be a bridge leading to God's intended end-time Temple. Until the full manifestation of that temple, "a temporary dwelling-place of God [will continue] to be carried along on the shoulders of the suffering faithful ...."[7] According to the Bible, "For Jesus and his followers, suffering was no random happenstance but the very means by which God's people, his chosen priests, would help usher in the [K]ingdom of God."[8] As to this purpose of suffering, I will simply echo the wisdom of Nicholas Perrin in his book, *Jesus the Temple,* "I decline to be much more specific than this, for I confess, as to precisely how suffering helps

---

7   Perrin, Nicholas, *Jesus the Temple* (Baker Academic 2012) p. 115
8   Perrin, Nicholas, *Jesus the Temple* (Baker Academic 2012) pp. 187-188

advance the divine purpose remains something of a partially veiled mystery to me."[9]

The primary motivation for Christ-followers to endure any present distress is the hope that Christ will soon return and when He does He will "fully establish his [K]ingdom *from* heaven ... *on* earth."[10] In the present age we live with the promise. But we aren't there yet. As we wait for its fulfillment, we must take seriously the words of Jesus:

> You will be hated by all because of My name, but it is the one who has endured to the end who will be saved. Matthew 10:22

The need for this type of endurance is echoed by virtually every New Testament author. It is particularly prevalent in Paul's writings, but is also found in 1 Peter 5:9,12 and in Hebrews 3:6,14; 4:14 and 10:23 (among other places in that epistle). The idea of persevering to the point of being a victorious overcomer is a key concept in the book of Revelation. As shown below, it is found in every one of the seven letters in Revelation 2 and 3 (bold added in each).

1. Letter to Ephesus – The one who **overcomes** will be granted the privilege of eating from the tree of life. Revelation 2:7b
2. Letter to Smyrna – The one who **overcomes** will not experience the second death. Revelation 2:11b
3. Letter to Pergamum – The one who **overcomes** will be given hidden manna and a white stone with a new name. Revelation 2:17b
4. Letter to Thyatira – The one who **overcomes** and remains faithful to God's commands will be given authority over the nations and the right to rule over them just as Jesus has received authority from His Father. Revelation 2:26-27

---

9   Perrin, Nicholas, *Jesus the Temple* (Baker Academic 2012) p. 188
10 Zoccali, Christopher, *Reading Philippians After Supersessionism: Jews, Gentiles and Covenant Identity, The New Testament after Supersessionism* (Cascade Books 2017) p. 78, italics in original, cites in quote omitted

5. Letter to Sardis – The one who **overcomes** will be clothed in white garments. The overcomer's name will never be erased from the book of life. Jesus will confess that person's name before His Father and before the angels. Revelation 3:5
6. Letter to Philadelphia – The one who **overcomes** will become a pillar in the new temple and will never go out from that temple. Jesus will write a new name on that person. Revelation 3:12
7. Letter to Laodicea – The one who **overcomes** will be given the right to sit with Jesus on His throne. Revelation 3:21

This is a good place for our first Word Study in this lesson. It is important that we understand what Jesus meant when he referred to those who *overcome*.

Word Study

In each of these quoted verses from Revelation, the Greek word translated as **overcomes** *is nikao {nik-ah'-o}. It refers to one who has prevailed by conquering and therefore, nikao is frequently translated with the word "victorious."*

The verb itself implies a battle and indicates triumph in battle.[11]

Biblically, *nikao* refers to achieving victory over whatever resists the promises or the preferred will of God.[12] In other words, each of these churches was facing God-ordained testing which

---

11 Hill, Gary, *The Discovery Bible*, HELPS Ministries, Inc., [G]3528 *nikáō*, citing K. Wuest; Zodhiates, Spiros, *The Complete Word Study Dictionary: New Testament* (AMG Publishers 1992) word #3528, p. 1011
12 Hill, Gary, *The Discovery Bible*, HELPS Ministries, Inc., [G]3528 *nikáō*

included a temptation to terminate their participation in the test before victory was obtained.

In his letter to the Ephesians, Paul had identified for his audience the victory and power available in Christ. He then informed them their mission is to actively put Christ on display in their world. He had outlined for them how to do that by living a life worthy of their calling. However, Paul did not want his readers to be caught by surprise. He knew all too well how the powers of darkness intrude on life in this present world – especially when the goal is to advance God's Kingdom rule on earth as it is in heaven! After all, Paul was imprisoned at the hands of the Roman Empire as he penned the words of that letter. His crime? Spreading the gospel message – extending God's Kingdom rule on earth! The kingdom of darkness hates to lose subjects whom it has held captive and the ruler of that kingdom fights back. The result is war!

In fact, in the Bible eternal salvation is pictured as a literal rescue from the captivity of the kingdom of darkness resulting in a new citizenship in the Kingdom of Light. Paul said it this way:

> For He rescued us from the domain of darkness, and **transferred** us to the kingdom of His beloved Son. Colossians 1:13, bold added

WORD STUDY

*The word **transferred** in Colossians 1:13 is a translation of the Greek verb methistemi {meth-is'-tay-mee}. It is a compound term which results from combining meta (referring to a change of place or condition) + histemi (to place or stand).[13] The resulting word literally means to transfer or remove from one place to another,[14] but it is*

---

13 Zodhiates, Spiros, *The Complete Word Study Dictionary: New Testament* (AMG Publishers 1992) word #3179, p. 953

14 The idea of a change of situation or place aligns with the idea of Jubilee.

used figuratively as causing someone to change sides either in a mental or spiritual sense.[15]

Paul's choice of this particular word is interesting. *Methistemi* described the common ancient Near Eastern practice whereby a powerful conquering ruler would uproot defeated people groups and resettle them elsewhere in his kingdom.[16] We see a biblical reference to this practice in 2 Kings 16, "So the king of Assyria attacked the Aramean capital of Damascus and led its population away as captives, resettling them in Kir...."[17] What a perfect image to explain how new Christ-followers are uprooted from the kingdom of darkness and resettled into the Kingdom of Light! When Jesus commissioned Paul as an Apostle to the Gentiles, He spoke in terms of these two opposing kingdoms.

> I have selected you [Paul] out of the people and the nations to whom I am sending you. You are to open their eyes, to turn them around from darkness to light, and from being under Satan's authority to being under God, that they might receive the forgiveness of sins and an inheritance among those who are made holy by faith in me. Acts 26:17-18 MIT[18]

That means Paul's mission, along with every other *talmid*,[19] is to build up God's Kingdom as a *Kingdom within a kingdom*

---

15 *Deuteronomy 30 Commentary*, Precept Austin. Retrieved from https://www.preceptaustin.org/deuteronomy-30-commentary (last accessed August 26, 2022)
16 Arnold, Clinton E., "Colossians" in *Zondervan Illustrated Bible Backgrounds Commentary*, Vol. 3, edited by Clinton E. Arnold (Zondervan 2002) Colossians 1:13 under *Brought us into the kingdom*, p. 378
17 2 Kings 16:9 NLT
18 *MacDonald Idiomatic Translation*, translated by William G. MacDonald
19 Remember *talmid* is the Hebrew word for the student of the rabbi who is learning to be like his teacher.

My Dwelling Place 173

by fighting the good fight.[20] However, we might protest, "Doesn't Scripture say that Jesus defeated Satan?" Again, I'll turn to G. K. Beale whose description of the tension which exists in the present age is useful.

> Despite defeat, the devil and his forces continue to exist.... [The devil and the beasts depicted in Revelation] have no authority over the saints and no authority but what God gives them. Nevertheless, the dragon and the beast deceptively cover up the fact that their authority has been removed.... The beast's wicked activities ... stretches from Christ's death and resurrection all the way to his final coming again.[21]
>
> Christ's defeat of the devil was like D-Day [in World War II] and the subsequent existence of the devil (and his servant beast [in Revelation]) like the subsequent resistance of the Germans to the Allies' inevitable advance.[22]
>
> ... Oscar Cullmann has metaphorically described Jesus's first coming as "D-day" because this is when Satan was decisively defeated. "V-day" is the second coming,

---

20 The phrase *fight the good fight* is employed by Paul twice in 1 Timothy 6. This phrase was a frequently used ancient idiom to denote good and faithful character. It speaks of the honorable character of a citizen who has demonstrated his loyalty to his king and his kingdom. Of course, Paul uses this "patriotic warfare idiom" in reference to Timothy (with implication that it is equally applicable to all Christ-followers) to indicate the character of a person who is loyal to Christ and His Kingdom. Beale, G. K., *The Greco-Roman Background to "Fighting the Good Fight" in the Pastoral Epistles and the Spiritual Life of the Christian*, Themelios Volume 48, Issue 3 (The Gospel Coalition December 2023). Retrieved from https://www.thegospelcoalition.org/themelios/article/the-greco-roman-background-to-fighting-the-good-fight/ (last accessed December 5, 2023)
21 Beale, G. K., *The Book of Revelation*, The New International Greek Testament Commentary (Eerdmans 1999) pp. 688-689
22 Beale, G. K., *The Book of Revelation*, The New International Greek Testament Commentary (Eerdmans 1999) p. 689

when Jesus's enemies will totally surrender and bow down to him.[23]

[In the book of Revelation] the beast's resuscitation [is linked] to the repeated rise and fall of oppressive states, world systems, or social structures that continue because the devil continues to inspire opposition to God's people, even though he has been decisively defeated by Christ.[24]

The period of time described by Beale overlaps perfectly with the time period on the imaginary timeline of suffering we discussed earlier in this lesson. Theologians call this in-between stage in which we presently live the "already and not yet" Kingdom. Some scholars suggest a more accurate term is: "already, not full."[25] That said, we are experiencing a *foretaste* of God's Kingdom now, as we await a *full taste* in the future.[26] We are not yet delivered from the *presence* of evil in this age, but every Christ-follower "can experience deliverance from the *power* of this present evil age right now."[27] One of the best practical descriptions I've seen of the

---

23 Beale, G. K., *A New Testament Biblical Theology: The Unfolding of the Old Testament In the New* (Baker Academic 2011) p. 17
24 Beale, G. K., *The Book of Revelation*, The New International Greek Testament Commentary (Eerdmans 1999) pp. 691-692
25 I credit R. T. France with the phrase "already, not full." It speaks to an inaugurated invisible version of the kingship of God in Messiah, and the fact that we are seeking and praying for the visible fullness of the kingship of God to come on earth, as it is in heaven.
26 Henri Goulet, my friend and research mentor, is among those scholars like R. T. France who believe a far more accurate reference for this stage of God's advancing Kingdom is "already, not full." The essence of this phrase speaks the fact that we've had a "foretaste" God's Kingdom, but we have not yet experienced the "full taste."
27 Guzik, David, *Galatians 1 – Challenging a Different Gospel*, Enduring Word, bold omitted. Retrieved from https://enduringword.com/bible-commentary/galatians-1/ (last accessed July 22, 2021)

"now, net yet" understanding of the present age is found in Lynn Cohick's commentary on Ephesians.[28]

> Christ's cross brings forgiveness of sins, his resurrection brings hope of inheritance, and his ascension opens the heavenly realms with their plethora of spiritual blessings ([Ephesians] 1:3). Yet there is more to come, as Christ will bring unity to all things in heaven and on earth ([Ephesians] 1:10). Paul declares that Christ is seated "now" in the heavenly realms, ascended to the greatest place of honor ([Ephesians] 1:20; 2:6). Yet Paul introduces the "not yet" component, that in these coming ages God's grace will be magnified in Christ Jesus. Paul applies this same principle to believers. They are now seated with Christ in the heavenly realms ([Ephesians] 2:6) and also must walk daily in the light ([Ephesians] 5:1-10).

Jesus already achieved a decisive victory by His death and resurrection. However, until He comes again, that victory must be continually repeated in the present by those who have chosen to follow Him.[29] Clear biblical instruction for gaining personal victory in spiritual battles is provided in Ephesians 6.

> Finally, be strong in the Lord and in the strength of His might. Put on the full armor of God, so that you will be able to stand firm against the schemes of the devil. For our struggle is not against flesh and blood, but against the rulers, against the powers, against the world forces of this darkness, against the spiritual *forces* of wickedness in the heavenly *places*. Therefore, take up the full armor of God, so that you will be able to resist in the evil day,

---

28 Cohick, Linn H., *The Letter To The Ephesians*, The New International Commentary on the New Testament (Eerdmans 2020) Ephesians 6:13, pp. 414-415

29 Bauckham, Richard, *The Theology of the Book of Revelation* (Cambridge University Press 1993) p. 67

and having done everything, to stand firm. Stand firm therefore, HAVING GIRDED YOUR LOINS WITH TRUTH, AND HAVING PUT ON THE BREASTPLATE OF RIGHTEOUSNESS, AND HAVING SHOD YOUR FEET WITH THE PREPARATION OF THE GOSPEL OF PEACE; in addition to all, taking up the shield of faith with which you will be able to extinguish all the flaming arrows of the evil *one*. And take THE HELMET OF SALVATION, and the sword of the Spirit, which is the word of God. With all prayer and petition pray at all times in the Spirit, and with this in view, be on the alert with all perseverance and petition for all the saints. Ephesians 6:10-18, italics and uppercase text in original

In typical Paul fashion, he relied on direct quotations from the Old Testament (shown in the Ephesians 6 quote in UPPERCASE TEXT) as well as images that have Old Testament background. The armor imagery is supplied by the typical Roman soldier of the day. However, long before there was a Roman Empire with a Roman Legion there was Yahweh's army! As a well-trained student of the biblical text, Paul turns to Isaiah for the meaning he attaches to each piece of armor.[30]

Paul says our "struggle is ... against the world forces of this darkness, against the spiritual forces of wickedness in the heavenly places (Ephesians 6:12)." The word *pale* {pal'-ay} (translated here as "struggle") is the Greek word for wrestling. In those days, the common sport of wrestling was a violent and potentially deadly competition. Most opponents chose to fight to the death rather than leave the match defeated. Strangling, chocking, breaking fingers, using a waist lock to break ribs, gashing the face and

---

30 Ephesians 6:14 " having girded your loins with truth" see Isaiah 11:5; "and having put on the breastplate of righteousness" see Isaiah 59:17; Ephesians 6:15 "and having shod your feet with the preparation of the gospel of peace" see Isaiah 52:7; Ephesians 6:16: "taking up the shield of faith" see Isaiah 21:5; Ephesians 6:17: "And take the helmet of salvation" see Isaiah 59:17

My Dwelling Place   177

gouging eyes were just some of the permissible tactics.[31] Beyond that powerful word picture, *pale* was a natural word choice for Paul because it also referred to the hand-to-hand combat of an individual soldier which required both speed and skill.[32]

Paul then identifies our opponent. He first made it clear that we don't fight against other people. Satan's schemes may involve another person (or even governments like the Roman Empire). However, the people involved are functionally doing the work of Satan. They not the "enemy" we are to battle against. Paul points out that we are in a spiritual battle. He specifically identifies our struggle as being "against evil rulers and authorities of the unseen world, against mighty powers in this dark world, and against evil spirits in the heavenly places (Ephesians 6:12 NLT)." We can learn more about our spiritual enemy by considering the Greek words Paul used in Ephesians 6:12.

> The first two words [are] *archais* ("rulers") and *exousiais* ("authorities") … [i]n the present context they refer to heavenly beings not earthly rulers …. The third word, *kosmokratoras* … [is described by Paul] as "world/cosmic rulers of this darkness" to indicate "the terrifying power of their influence and comprehensiveness of their plans, and thus to emphasize the seriousness of the situation" (*TDNT* 3:914). These potentates are supernatural beings …. Their leader is the Devil ([Ephesians 12:] v.11) and they are in direct conflict with Christ and believers.[33]

Having identified our true enemy, Paul then highlights the supernatural power God has made available for our fight with the

---

31 Renner, Rick, *Sparkling Gems from the Greek* (Harrison House Publishers 2003) June 9, p. 395
32 Zodhiates, Spiros, *The Complete Word Study Dictionary: NT* (AMG Publishers 1992) word #3823, p. 1091
33 Hoehner, Harold W., "Ephesians," in *The Bible Knowledge Word Study Acts-Ephesians,* edited by Darrell L. Bock (Victor 2002) Ephesians 6:12 under *Against the rulers, against authorities, against cosmic potentates,* p. 477

unseen, demonic powers that war against us. In the original Greek there are three power different power words in Paul's exhortation.

> … be strong [*endunamao*] in the Lord in the strength [*kratos*] of His might [*ischus*] …. Ephesians 6:10

It will be helpful to do a Word Study on each of these Greek words I have pointed out in this quote. We will consider them in order beginning with the term *endunamoo*.

WORD STUDY

In Ephesians 6:10 the Greek verb translated as **strong** *is endunamoo {en-doo-nam-o'-o}. It is a compound word combining en (in) + dunamis (power) resulting in a verb that literally means to give power to enable one to be "in-strengthened, inwardly strengthened."*[34]

The emphasis of endunamoo is on being able, having ability or capacity to act.[35] *This power is given to one as a" right" because of the position he holds.*[36] *Greek verbs like*

---

34 Bromiley, Geoffrey W., *Theological Dictionary of the New Testament*, Abridged in One Volume (Eerdmans 1985) entry for *dynamai*, p. 186; Wenstrom, William E., *Greek Word Studies*, entry for *endunamoo*. Retrieved from https://www.wenstrom.org/downloads/written/word_studies/greek/endunamoo.pdf#:~:text=The%20verb%20endunamoo%20is%20a%20compound%20word%20and,something.%E2%80%9D%20God%20is%20often%20the%20source%20of%20power (last accessed March 7, 2024)

35 Bromiley, Geoffrey W., *Theological Dictionary of the New Testament*, Abridged in One Volume (Eerdmans 1985) entry for *dynamai*, p. 186; Wenstrom, William E., *Greek Word Studies*, entry for *endunamoo*. Retrieved from https://www.wenstrom.org/downloads/written/word_studies/greek/endunamoo.pdf#:~:text=The%20verb%20endunamoo%20is%20a%20compound%20word%20and,something.%E2%80%9D%20God%20is%20often%20the%20source%20of%20power (last accessed March 7, 2024)

36 Wenstrom, William E., *Greek Word Studies*, entry for *endunamoo*, quoting Liddel and Scott, *Greek-English Lexicon*, New Edition, pp. 561. Retrieved from https://www.wenstrom.org/downloads/written/word_studies/greek/

> *endunamoo* which end in *"oo"* denote not just being strength-
> ened but to prove that strength by putting it on display.[37]

In the Greek translation of Judges 6:34 the word *endunamoo* was chosen to translate the Hebrew *lavesh {law-bashe'}* (meaning dressed, be clothed). The text employs *endunamoo* in the figurative sense of being clothed with power by the Holy Spirit.[38] In similar fashion, Paul commands the Christ-followers in Ephesus to be empowered by means of God's Spirit. His expectation is that the *talmidim* keep walking a life worthy of their calling, however, they do not have to depend on their own resources. This power comes from an external source not an internal source.[39] It is "*a power whose purpose is to infuse a believer with an excessive dose of inward strength*" so they can endure any attack and oppose whatever comes against them.[40] Paul knows that God's goal is for the community of Christ-followers to rest "in God's saving power."[41] He chose a word that was used by ancient Greek writers to denote

---

endunamoo.pdf#:~:text=The%20verb%20endunamoo%20is%20a%20compound%20word%20and,something.%E2%80%9D%20God%20is%20often%20the%20source%20of%20power (last accessed March 7, 2024)

37 Barber, Wayne, *Ephesians 6:10 Commentary*. Retrieved from https://www.preceptaustin.org/ephesians_610 (last accessed March 7, 2024)

38 Wenstrom, William E., *Greek Word Studies*, entry for *endunamoo*. Retrieved from https://www.wenstrom.org/downloads/written/word_studies/greek/endunamoo.pdf#:~:text=The%20verb%20endunamoo%20is%20a%20compound%20word%20and,something.%E2%80%9D%20God%20is%20often%20the%20source%20of%20power (last accessed March 7, 2024)

39 Barth, Markus, *Ephesians: Translation and Commentary on Chapters 4-6*, The Anchor Bible Vol. 34 (Doubleday 1974) Ephesians 6:10 under *Notes, become strong*, p. 760

40 Renner, Rick, *Sparkling Gems from the Greek* (Harrison House Publishers 2003) May 20, p. 346, italics in original

41 Bromiley, Geoffrey W., *Theological Dictionary of the New Testament*, Abridged in One Volume (Eerdmans 1985) entry for *dynamai* under *D. The Concept of Power in the NT, 4. The Community*, p. 191

special individuals like Hercules who was thought to have been handpicked by the gods and supernaturally invested with superhuman strength in order to accomplish a superhuman task.[42] Paul appropriates this ancient belief to his own use in order to say God has made *that* kind of supernatural strength available to those who trust in Jesus Christ!

The last two words we want to consider are *kratos* {krat'-os} and *ischus* {is-khoos'} which function as additional descriptive synonyms.[43]

> **WORD STUDY**
>
> In Ephesians 6:10 the Greek word translated as **strength** is kratos {krat'-os}. As a power word, kratos includes the idea of rule/victory. One source refers to it as "power that brings dominion."[44]

The Greek word *kratos* describes what Rick Renner calls "demonstrated power." As he notes, "It almost always comes with some type of external, outward manifestation that one can actually see with his or her eyes. This means that *kratos* power is not a hypothetical power; this is real power!"[45] Paul employed *kratos* to describe manifested or demonstrated power that is exerted until it

---

42 Renner, Rick, *Sparkling Gems from the Greek* (Harrison House Publishers 2003) May 20, p. 347
43 Cohick, Linn H., *The Letter To The Ephesians*, The New International Commentary on the New Testament (Eerdmans 2020) Ephesians 1:17-19, p. 121
44 Hill, Gary, *The Discovery Bible*, HELPS Ministries, Inc., [G]2904 *kratos*
45 Renner, Rick, *The 'Kratos' Power of God!* Retrieved from https://renner.org/article/the-kratos-power-of-god/ (last accessed March 7, 2024)

My Dwelling Place 181

prevails.[46] Ephesians 1:19,20 affirms that when God raised Jesus from the dead He used *kratos* power! Paul says that power is the very same power that is now at work in us. As followers of Christ we have resurrection power working in our lives![47]

> **WORD STUDY**
>
> In Ephesians 6:10 **might** *is the Greek word ischus {is-khoos} which denotes endowed strength or power.*[48] *Ischus is part of a Greek word group that overlaps with dunamis but "with greater stress on the power implied."*[49]
> *The core meaning refers to "force that overcomes immediate resistance."*[50] *Ischus is "combative strength" which stands ready for direct, immediate encounter.*[51]

Paul makes clear it is *God's ischus* at work. God is the One who stands ready for direct and immediate resistance which enables every Christ-follower to overcome. Therefore, Christ-followers battle against the kingdom of darkness not by their own strength but by the ever-ready combative strength [*ischus*] which God supplies.

---

46 Hill, Gary, *The Discovery Bible*, HELPS Ministries, Inc., [G]2904 *krátos*; Renner, Rick, *Sparkling Gems from the Greek* (Harrison House Publishers 2003) May 20, p. 347
47 Bromiley, Geoffrey W., *Theological Dictionary of the New Testament*, Abridged in One Volume (Eerdmans 1985) entry for *dynamai* under D. *The Concept of Power in the NT, 4. The Community*, p. 191
48 Zodhiates, Spiros, *The Complete Word Study Dictionary: New Testament* (AMG Publishers 1992) word #2479, p. 787
49 Bromiley, Geoffrey W., *Theological Dictionary of the New Testament*, Abridged in One Volume (Eerdmans 1985) entry for *ischys*, p. 378
50 Hill, Gary, *The Discovery Bible*, HELPS Ministries, Inc., [G]2479 *isxýs*
51 Hill, Gary, *The Discovery Bible*, HELPS Ministries, Inc., [G]2479 *isxýs*

The goal of each battle we face is "to stand firm against the schemes of the devil (Ephesians 6:11)." "Paul stresses the fact that there is a supernatural being who is bent on promoting the demise of God's people."[52] But, like Peter (1 Peter 5:8-9) and James (James 4:7), Paul advises followers of Christ to submit to God and resist the devil! Immediately we can take comfort in the fact that Christ-followers are never given biblical commands without the assurance that God's grace will supply all we need to obey.

"The verb 'stand firm' ... 'belongs to the language of war' ... and either means 'to take over,' 'to hold a watch post' ... or 'to stand and hold out a critical position on a battlefield.'"[53] Roman soldiers were expected to stand their ground in the day of battle and never retreat. By standing together and not breaking rank, a Roman legion was considered to be virtually unconquerable. Relying on this imagery, Paul is not describing a "passive posture; [standing] is more akin to maintaining one's balance and remaining upright while knee deep in an angry sea."[54]

Next, Paul describes the enemy's plan of attack. The word "schemes" is the Greek word *methodeia* {meth-od-i'-ah} which refers to an orderly, logical, effective arrangement, implying the use of clever methods or strategies to attain the desired end. "Satan's attacks are 'tailor made' ('the schemes') carefully and methodically selected to attack each person's specific weaknesses and vulnerabilities. His wiles and methods are usually attractive, always deceptive and often ensnaring."[55] Now we know why we

---

52 Arnold, Clinton E., "Ephesians," in *Zondervan Illustrated Bible Backgrounds Commentary*, Vol. 3, edited by Clinton E. Arnold (Zondervan 2002) Ephesians 6:11, p. 337

53 Barth, Markus, *Ephesians: Translation and Commentary on Chapters 4-6*, The Anchor Bible Vol. 34 (Doubleday 1974) Ephesians 6:11, under *Notes, in order to be able to stand firm*, p. 762

54 Cohick, Linn H., *The Letter To The Ephesians*, The New International Commentary on the New Testament (Eerdmans 2020) Ephesians 6:10-13, p. 410

55 *Ephesians 6:11 Commentary*, Precept Austin, bold omitted. Retrieved from http://www.preceptaustin.org/ephesians_611 (last accessed July 10, 2021)

My Dwelling Place

need to be armed and prepared for battle using the power made available to us.

In order to stand firm, every Christ-follower must put on the "full armor of God (Ephesians 6:11,13)." The phrase "full armor" is a translation of the Greek word *panoplia* which denotes all the weapons, whether offensive or defensive, that are necessary for victory in battle.[56] Paul employs it here in a figurative sense to refer to spiritual armor.[57] Notice that truth, righteousness, faith, the gospel message and effectively employing God's Word all have a spiritual component. I'll point out here that they are also connected to Christ-like character. As we will see, that's the key to understanding Paul's instruction about putting on the armor.

When Paul counsels Christ-followers to put on the whole armor of God he is advising them to walk out their identity as "holy ones" who are "children of God." He is admonishing them to become exemplary protypes of what it looks like to be a true disciple of Christ. It will be helpful to add a bit of background in order to better understand that last statement.

The Bible sometimes uses clothing in the sense of what someone is actually wearing. As an example, in John 21:7 we read that Peter wrapped his outer garment around him and jumped into the water. There John is talking about an actual piece of clothing that Peter put on. However, the Bible often uses clothing in another way. It is frequently used as a metaphor. In its figurative use, it refers to a person's character, their commitment, or being enabled to do the task at hand.[58] For example, in Zechariah 3 we read about the priest Joshua who was dressed in filthy rags but then given clean clothes to wear. In that narrative, replacing the

---

56 Renner, Rick, *Sparkling Gems from the Greek* (Harrison House Publishers 2003) May 9, p. 319, italics omitted; Hill, Gary, *The Discovery Bible*, HELPS Ministries, Inc., [G]3833 *panoplia*
57 Zodhiates, Spiros, *The Complete Word Study Dictionary: New Testament* (AMG Publishers 1992) word #3833, p. 1092
58 Motyer, J. Alec, *The Prophecy of Isaiah: An Introduction & Commentary* (InterVarsity Press 1993) Isaiah 59:17-18, p. 491

filthy clothing of Joshua, the high priest, with clean clothing is a metaphor for the unrighteousness of the people that is covered by God's forgiveness. One additional contextual fact is that in the first century Roman Empire dress was used to indicate societal status.[59] That is to say you could tell where a person fit in the Roman society by the clothing they wore.

Paul appears to have creatively drawn on both of those realities – the fact that clothing is often used figuratively to speak of character and commitment, as well as the fact that dress was an indication of societal status. He is informing those first-century disciples to recognize the societal status they had as followers of Christ. Because they are God's ambassadors, His representatives in Roman society, they are to be dressed in a way that they display character consistent with *that* identity. That's why each piece of armor is tied to character traits consistent with Christ-likeness: 1) truth (being authentic, not fake as well as speaking the truth), 2) righteousness (doing what is expected in Covenant relationship), 3) the gospel message of peace (a fruit of the Spirit), 4) faith (steadfastly trusting in God's promises), 5) salvation (unwavering confidence that you have been saved, are presently being saved and will be saved)[60] and 6) knowing and applying God's Word which never changes and judges the thoughts and desires of the heart.

In Ephesians 6 Paul's primary goal is not to outline a technique for putting on pieces of spiritual armor. He is counseling Christ-followers about their personal character. Paul exhorts every follower of Christ to be who you really are, to manifest the dis-

---

59 Cohick, Linn H., *The Letter To The Ephesians*, The New International Commentary on the New Testament (Eerdmans 2020) Ephesians 6:14-17, p. 416
60 The Bible reflects three tenses of salvation: past (what God has already saved us from), present (what God is presently saving us from) and future (what God will save us from in the future). See for example: Ephesians 2:8-9 (past salvation); 1 Corinthians 1:18 (present salvation); Romans 5:9 (future salvation)

My Dwelling Place   185

tinctive character of Christ in all you do.[61] Paul advises us to be dressed from head to toe in these "spiritual weapons" which will equip us for victory in every battle. He understood that collectively the armor "testifies to the person's identity and loyalty.... Wearing the armor of God . . . distinguishes [the disciples] from those around them, as ones who seek holiness and justice, who practice kindness and forgiveness, [those who love their enemies] and who humbly serve others above themselves."[62]

I view Paul's counsel as an exhortation to walk in Christ-like behavior in all we do so that we can take an unwavering stand against our enemy, Satan. Another similar way to view Paul's armor analogy is presented by Steven J. Cole when he writes:[63]

> The armor is just a graphic way of saying what Paul says in Romans 13:14, "But put on the Lord Jesus Christ, and make no provision for the flesh in regard to its lusts." In other words, Christ Himself is our armor. He is the belt of truth (John 14:6). He is our breastplate of righteousness (2 Cor. 5:21). He is the gospel of peace that we stand on (Eph. 2:13-14,17). He is the shield of our faith (Heb. 12:2). He is our helmet of salvation (Titus 3:6). He is our sword, the word of God (John 1:1). He

---

61 An example of this figurative understanding for putting on clothing can be found in Isaiah 52:1 which speaks of Zion putting on her strength and Jerusalem as putting on her beautiful garments. In Isaiah 52:1, "*Clothe yourself* and *Put on* are the same verb twice, 'Put on ... put on'. The metaphor of clothing ... means 'be what you really are'; it is not an exercise in pretense or a 'cover-up' but a manifestation of character." Motyer, J. Alec, *The Prophecy of Isaiah: An Introduction & Commentary* (InterVarsity Press 1993) Isaiah 52:1, p. 416, italics in original

62 Cohick, Linn H., *The Letter To The Ephesians*, The New International Commentary of the New Testament (Eerdmans 2020) Ephesians 6:14-17, p. 417

63 Cole, Steven J., *Lesson 55: Standing Strong, Standing Firm (Ephesians 6:10-11)*, Bible.org. Retrieved from https://bible.org/seriespage/lesson-55-standing-strong-standing-firm-ephesians-610-11 (last accessed November 3, 2023)

is our full armor, capable of protecting us from every onslaught of the devil. Putting on God's armor means that in every trial and temptation by faith you appropriate Christ's strength in place of your weakness. By faith you cry out to Him for deliverance and strength to persevere. By faith you rely on His promises, even as Jesus defeated Satan by quoting Scripture (Luke 4:1-13).

Said either way, a good present-day analogy is to think about fans at a sporting event. As the camera pans the audience, the viewer sees sports apparel of all kinds that reveals identity. What fans are wearing is a testimony that shouts loud and clear which team they support. When we are properly wearing our spiritual armor, we are like a walking billboard for Christ – looking like Him and acting like Him in a lost and dying world that needs to meet Him!

As we've been learning, God created an *ekklesia* to rule on earth in between the two advents of Christ (His first coming and His second coming). Although the work of Jesus soundly defeated the kingdom of darkness, Paul understood evil would be present on earth until the end of the age. The fact that God is carving out His *Kingdom within other kingdoms* places His *ekklesia* in the crosshairs of war!

> Paul therefore desires … Christ allegiants to emulate his own uncompromising commitment to the gospel …. By doing so, they themselves would become models for imitation ….. This required him to seek [their] *empowerment* in their allegiance to Jesus Christ, which he knew quite well could only be sustained amidst counter-pressures to the degree that the community fully recognizes

and lives out their own creative yet prototypical[64] identity as 'holy ones' … and 'children of God'….[65]

The kingdom of darkness does not want to relinquish its rule in spite of the reality that Satan has actually lost his *right* to rule. It is only when a person believes Satan's lies and falls into the temptations he offers that Satan has power of any kind. His rule is retained only through the cooperation of people through which he can work. Even Christ-followers who are not consistently vigilant can get caught up in his deceptive schemes and end up functionally doing the work of their spiritual enemy. This then is the clash of kingdoms and one of its most common expressions takes place in what we have come to term "the culture war." Satan is not going down for the final count without a fight! But we are assured God *will* reign as King. The Apostle John recorded what he heard and saw:

> Then I saw a new heaven and a new earth; for the first heaven and the first earth passed away, and there is no longer *any* sea. And I saw the holy city, new Jerusalem, coming down out of heaven from God, made ready

---

64 Prototypical can refer to "illustrating the typical qualities of a … group." *Dictionary.com*, entry for *prototypical*. Retrieved from https://www.dictionary.com/browse/prototypical (last accessed November 7, 2023). It also denotes a "a first example from which all later forms can be developed." *Cambridge Dictionary*, entry for *prototypical*. Retrieved from https://dictionary.cambridge.org/dictionary/english/prototypical (last accessed November 7, 2023)

65 Zoccali, Christopher, *Reading Philippians After Supersessionism: Jews, Gentiles and Covenant Identity, The New Testament after Supersessionism* (Cascade Books 2017) pp. 75-76, italics in original, Scripture citations and other references omitted. "Research … has demonstrated that prototypical group members tend to demonstrate greater loyalty to the group when it is under significant threat, whereas peripheral members are far more unpredictable in their response—a social psychological reality that Paul surely understood intuitively." Ibid. p. 94, citing Jetten et al., *Distinctiveness Threat and Prototypicality*, pp. 635-57

as a bride adorned for her husband. And I heard a loud voice from the throne, saying, "Behold, the tabernacle of God is among men, and He will dwell among them, and they shall be His people, and God Himself will be among them, and He will wipe away every tear from their eyes; and there will no longer be *any* death; there will no longer be *any* mourning, or crying, or pain; the first things have passed away." And He who sits on the throne said, "Behold, I am making all things new." And He said, "Write, for these words are faithful and true." Revelation 21:1-5

Hear What The Spirit is Saying to the Church: *Yes, My dwelling place is once again being established on the earth as it is in heaven. All over the world I have faithful people who hear my voice and obey. They are the ones who are the living stones in My present-day Temple. They are the ones I call my talmidim – my sheep who know my voice and will not listen to the voice of a stranger. At the end of the age I will separate the sheep from the goats – each person will have made their choice and I will honor that choice. Oh, how I wish for all to choose me as I alone know what is best for my creation.*

Appendix

How to do basic WORD STUDIES when you don't read Hebrew or Greek

To understand why Word Studies are important refer to "Preface: About Word Studies."

Begin with prayer

The best counsel I have seen from anyone about how to do Word Studies on the internet comes from the Precept Austin website, "And so as you begin your word study, remember to begin with prayer beseeching our Father to grant that our Teacher, the Holy Spirit might guide us into all truth (Jn 16:13), for spiritual truth is spiritually revealed by the Spirit."[1]

There are multiple ways to do word searches using internet reference tools. As you become proficient at using these tools you will develop your favorites and find shortcuts to locating the information you are seeking. I am providing a basic starting point here for those just beginning.

As an initial matter, don't forget to check the English Dictionary for how your word of interest is defined in the English language. You may not be aware of all the nuances of a given English word. As a result, sometimes that research alone provides greater clarity to a word's usage.

Next, read your targeted Scripture in multiple Bible translations. Reading your passage in several translations may provide you with all the information you need.

---

1 *How to Perform a Greek Word Study*, Precept Austin. Retrieved from https://www.preceptaustin.org/greek_word_study#web (last accessed January 24, 2022). Note, as with the other materials on this website, this is an overall helpful article regarding Word Studies.

As a general rule of thumb, I "over research" my word of interest to be as assured of accuracy as I can possibly be. When I am in doubt I check with someone more knowledgeable than I am.

STRONG'S NUMBERS ARE THE STARTING POINT FOR YOUR RESEARCH

When you've decided to proceed with an internet search the Strong's number associated with your word of interest is a must! A Strong's Number is the unique number that has been assigned to a word used in the Bible.[2] For example: the Hebrew word יָשַׁע *yasha`* {yaw-shah'} has been assigned the number: 03467. The Greek word δοῦλος *doulos* {doo'-los} has been assigned the number: 1401. Each number links the root meaning of the word back to the original meanings in the Hebrew and Greek manuscripts from which they were translated. *NOTE: When you use this number in internet searches you will generally need to add a "H" before the number for a Hebrew word or a "G" before the number for a Greek word.*

Caveat: Strong's concordance, keyed to numbers for roots in the original languages, is a valuable resource. Users need to be aware of some issues: 1) Strong's is old enough to almost be outdated. Because it is keyed to the language of the KJV it is advisable to check your results against more modern commentaries and other Bible translations. 2) Strong's provides glosses (words or phrases proposed as possible translations of a particular Greek or Hebrew word) rather than definitions.[3] That's because those Greek and Hebrew words have many potential meanings in differ-

---

[2] Strong's Numbers originate from a reference book known as *Strong's Exhaustive Concordance of the Bible.*

[3] When a Greek student is taught that *"pistis"* means "faith" what he is learning is a "gloss." Contrast that with the following from the *Greek-English Lexicon of the New Testament Based on Semantic Domains*: "that which is completely believable—'what can be fully believed, that which is worthy of belief, believable evidence, proof'" [Louw, J. P., & Nida, E. A. (1996, c1989). *Greek-English lexicon of the New Testament: Based on semantic domains* (electronic ed. of the 2nd edition.) (Vol. 1, p. 370). New York: United Bible societies)].

The Power of Hope   191

ent contexts. It is imperative that you check carefully which word definition works best for the passage you are studying.

HOW TO LOCATE A STRONG'S NUMBER ON THE INTERNET USING FREE RESOURCES:

1. Go to https://biblehub.com.

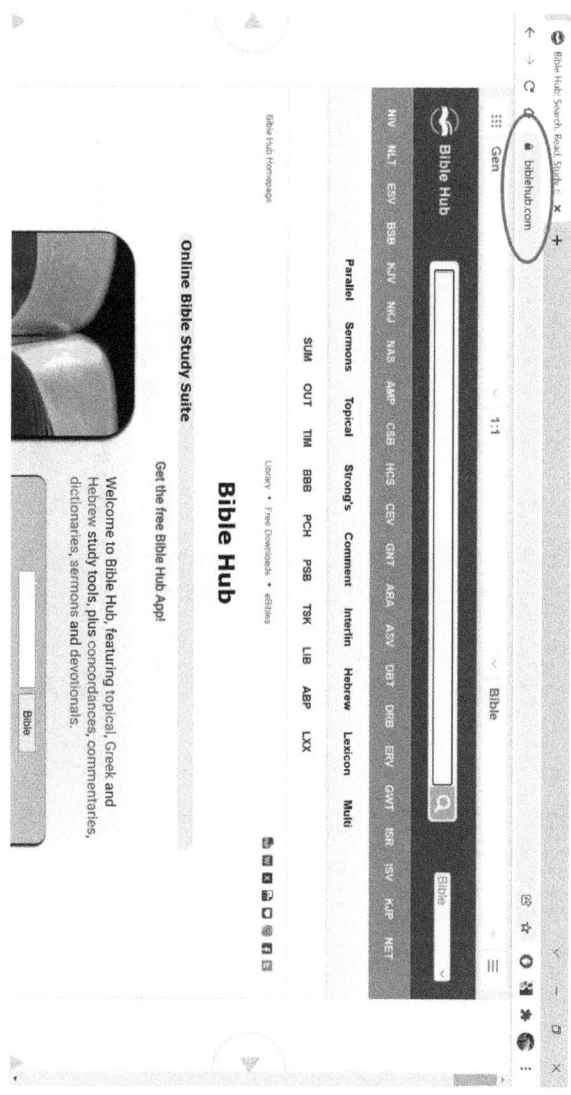

How to do basic WORD STUDIES when you don't read Hebrew or Greek

2. Across the tool bar find the header for "Interlin."

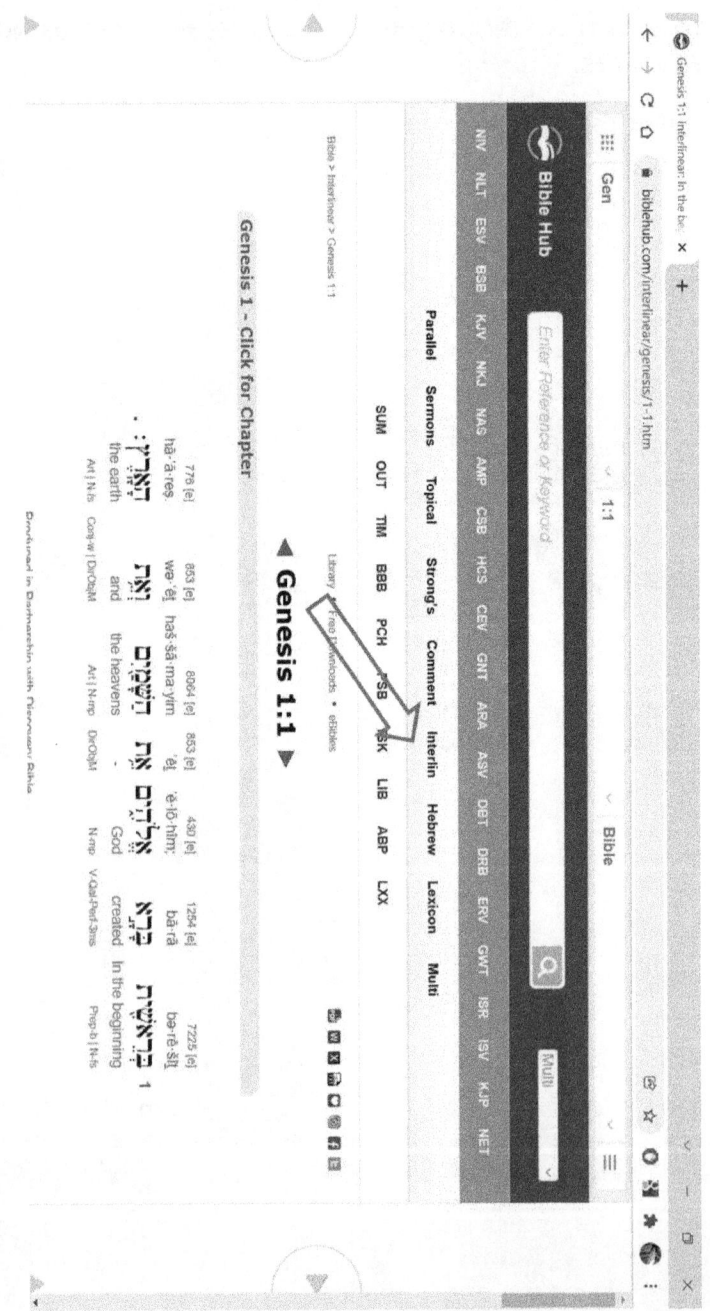

The Power of Hope   193

3. When you click that header, it will take you to the Interlinear page for Genesis 1:1. Find the search box at the top of the page and enter the verse address containing your word of interest. The search engine will take you directly to the Interlinear entry (either Hebrew or Greek) for that verse.

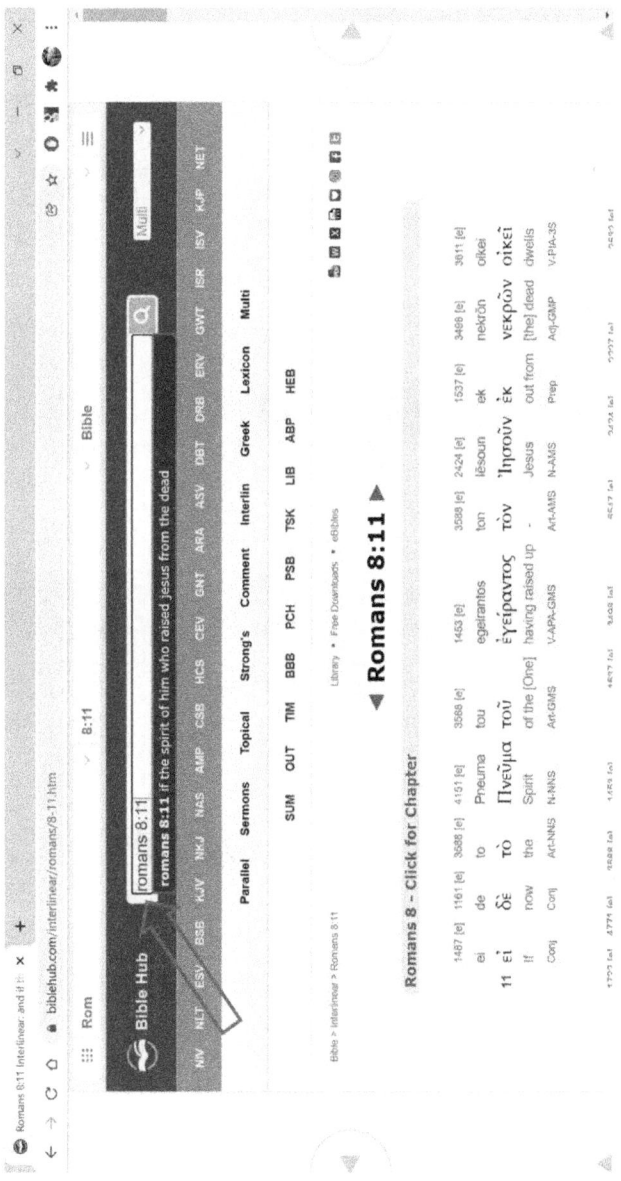

4. The numbers in blue across the top of each word is the Strong's number. You can click on that blue number and it will take you to a page with the Strong's Concordance information and other Bible Dictionary entries for that word. However, once you have the Strong's # you can research in a wide variety of other reference sources as well.

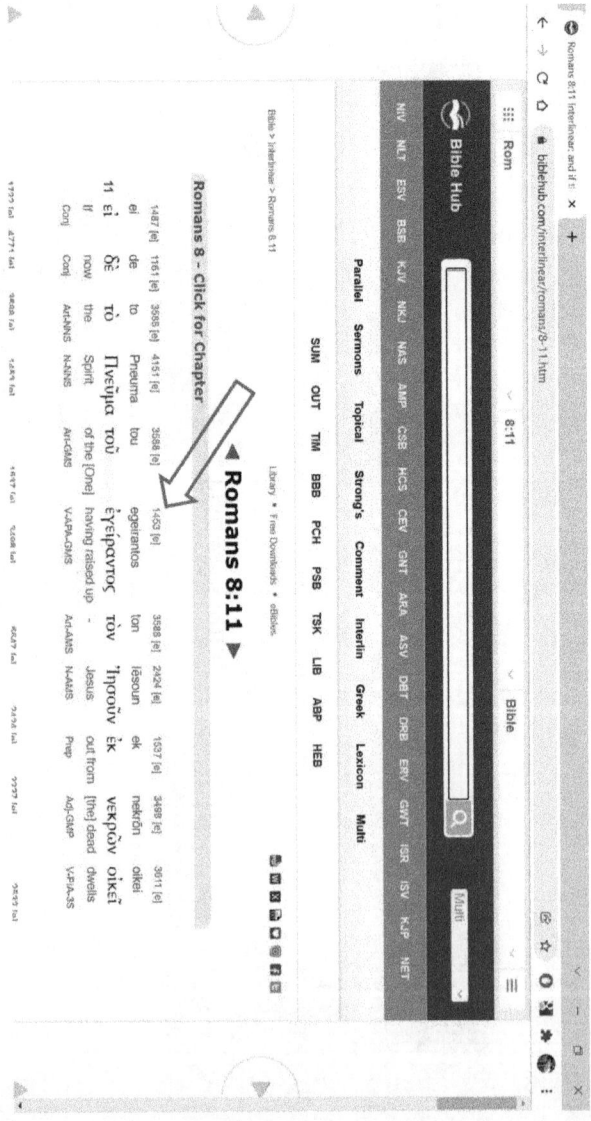

COMMENTARIES CAN BE A GREAT SOURCE OF INFORMATION IN UNDERSTANDING HOW A WORD IS USED

Often the Commentary will define the word itself, but even if no definition is provided checking a variety of Commentaries for that particular verse/section of Scripture is a good way to gain additional understanding regarding the context surrounding your word of interest.

Bible Dictionaries and Bible Encyclopedias are another free resource worth searching to view any entries that might be available for the word you are studying.

Caveat: As you consider broadening your internet search a quote from Yale University Library helps us place the usefulness of internet resources in their proper context.[4]

> 1. Searching on the Internet. Care must be taken in searching for information on the Internet .... [F]reely available Internet resources have not necessarily been published by reputable academic publishers nor have they been selected by librarians with expertise in their subject area. Nearly anything can be posted on a website, and just because it is available online does not mean it is valid or authoritative. **However, this does not mean that you cannot find good resources on the Internet; the key to doing so is to carefully evaluate what you find on the web.** If you use web resources, be sure to ask these questions:
>
> - Who is the author of the website? Are the author's credentials listed?
> - What institution or organization is behind the website?

---

4 Yale University Library, *Biblical Studies Guide: Websites*, Yale University Library Research Guides at Yale University, bold added. Retrieved from https://guides.library.yale.edu/c.php?g=295834&p=1972575 (site last updated Apr 30, 2021 1:08 PM) (last accessed January 24, 2022)

- When was the website created or last updated?
- Who is the intended audience for the website?
- Is the information provided objective or biased?
- How does information provided by the site compare to other works, including print works?

There are times when a website you are viewing provides you with the opportunity to view the beliefs and doctrines behind those who post articles on that particular site. Taking the time to read that information can provide valuable insight about the biases the author(s) may have about biblical points of view. Understanding the framework (lens) though which the author is operating may explain cases where their viewpoint is radically different than others you have read in your research efforts. It helps you evaluate the weight you may want to give to their characterization of your word of interest or its biblical context.

A Caution Regarding Commentaries: The advice provided by the Yale University Library quote above concerning internet searches is equally wise counsel when using Commentaries.

A Few Remaining Observations

Words can have multiple meanings. As an example, the word "dig" has a wide range of meanings in the English language. It can refer to excavation (for archaeological or other purposes); an insult, taunt or sarcastic remark; a jab or nudge; to tunnel, to burrow or mine; or to plow a field. Dig can imply using large commercial equipment, a simple hand trowel or shovel; or it can refer to words that come out of your mouth. The same is true in Greek and Hebrew. However, generally speaking a word only carries one specific meaning at a time.

Caveat: Without getting too complicated, let me add one quick caveat to my last statement. The Apostle John is well known for using a word to mean two things at once (known as double entendre).[5]

The goal in a Word Study is to determine the author's originally intended meaning. It is a fundamental principle for Word Studies that the author's usage determines the word's meaning. In other words, the author's original intent, as determined by context, must be the guide you use to choose the most applicable meaning from the range of possible word meanings. The goal of your research is to find a working definition that fits precisely in the specific context. As my Publisher warns, "Most errors in interpretation come from focusing too narrowly on a single verse or even phrase. If you come up with an understanding of the meaning of a particular word that contradicts the teaching of that author in the rest of his writings, you might want to reconsider. Who is more likely to have made a mistake?"

A research technique I often use in Word Studies is to locate the first use of that word in the Bible. Let me first explain why I do that and then I'll provide an easy way to locate that first biblical usage for your word of interest.

---

5   Keener, Craig S., *The Gospel Of John: A Commentary*, Volume Two (Hendrickson Publishers 2003) John 19:30b, p. 1148; Levison, Jack, *Filled with the Spirit* (Eerdmans 2009) p. 245. "One of the unique devices used by the author of the Fourth Gospel is that of double meaning. The author uses two meanings of a word, both of which are distinct enough that they could not convey one aspect of thought. He probably did not intend to present an either/or situation wherein a Christian must make a choice of meaning. More likely he was following a pattern of usage found in Qumran and the Old Testament wherein two meanings were intended to be conveyed through one expression." Wead, David W., *The Johannine Double Meaning*, Restoration Quarterly, 13 no 2 1970, pp. 106-120. Language: English; Publication Type: Article; (AN ATLA0001588405), citing 1. S. Cohen, "The Political Background of the Words of Amos," Hebrew Union College Annual 36 (1965) pp. 153-160

Reason First Occurrence Can Be Important

The first time a key word or concept is mentioned in the Bible "gives us important details or facts regarding the subject, which will, of course, help us understand the person or thing introduced."[6] It is notable that "ancient Jewish commentators call special attention to [first mentions in Scripture], and lay great stress upon them as always having some significance. They generally help us in fixing the meaning of a word or point us to some lesson in connection with it."[7]

An Easy Way to Locate First Usage

Using https://www.blueletterbible.org/lexicon/index.cfm enter the Strong's number for your word of interest, remember to use the "H" before the number for Hebrew words or the "G" before the number for Greek words. The search will take you to the Lexicon entry for that word. Scroll down past the definitions and reference section to the header: Concordance Results Shown Using the KJV. The first text box under this heading will show you how many times that particular word was used in WLC (Westminister Leningrad Codex) Hebrew. Following that entry will be a list of the verses where that word is used. You will be able to identify your word of interest by the superscript Strong's number next to the word. The first verse listed is the first instance of that word's biblical use.

---

6   Sheets, Dutch, *A Serpent In The Garden*, GiveHim15, February 20, 2021. Retrieved from http://gh15database.com/2021/02/february-20-2021/

7   Bullinger, E. W., *Number in Scripture: Its Supernatural Design and Spiritual Significance*, 4th Ed. (Eyre & Spottiswoode (Bible Warehouse) Ltd. 1921) Part II Its Spiritual Significance, One under *First Occurrences of Words*. Retrieved from https://www.levendwater.org/books/numbers/number_in_scripture_bullinger.pdf (last accessed January 25, 2022)

Some online sources of commentaries (and other valuable research resources) are:

Biblehub.com Retrieved from https://biblehub.com/ (last accessed January 24, 2022). From the Home Page, find the tool bar that lists resources. Select the header for "Comment" which will open a page containing Commentaries for Genesis 1:1. You can enter your verse in the search box on that page and it will take you to the available Commentaries for that verse.

BibleStudyTools.com Bible Versions and Translations Online (biblestudytools.com). Retrieved from https://www.biblestudytools.com/bible-versions/ (last accessed January 24, 2022). From Home Page, locate study menu, drop down menu lists available resources such as: Commentaries, Concordances, Dictionaries, Encyclopedias, and others.

BlueLetterBible.org Bible Search and Study Tools - Blue Letter Bible. Retrieved from https://www.blueletterbible.org/study.cfm (last accessed January 24, 2022). This page lists Bible Commentaries, Bible References, Topical Indexes, among other resources. Blue Letter Bible also permits you to research a specific Hebrew or Greek word if you know the Strong's "G" or "H" number. By the way, this site provides you with the opportunity to hear how the word is pronounced. It's a great tool if you are planning to teach and need to say the Greek or Hebrew word.

NetBible.org Net Bible Translation with Notes. Retrieved from https://netbible.org/ (last accessed January 24, 2022). The NET Bible is a Bible translation containing almost 61,000 translators' notes from over 25 scholars. The translator's notes (identified with a number followed by the letters "tn" like this, [175] **tn)** document the decisions and choices they made for how/why they translated the original text. The notes make the original languages accessible to the reader who does not know Greek and Hebrew. Study notes (identified with a number followed by the letters "sn" like this, [2] **sn**) are often added to the notes section providing an additional layer of helpful information.

PreceptAustin.org Retrieved from https://www.preceptaustin.org/ (last accessed January 24, 2022). Home Page tool bar contains drop down menus for Commentaries, Verse By Verse (Commentaries), Study Tools with options for Greek or Hebrew Word Studies, among other resources. On the Home Page there is a search box that allows you to search for a particular Hebrew or Greek word using the common form transliteration (without markings) and/or search for a particular Bible verse. When you locate the verse you are studying, it will often have word study links to a particular Greek or Hebrew word used in that Scripture. You will also find a treasure trove of quotes from various Bible Dictionaries and Commentaries related to that verse.

Note: A transliteration is the form of a Greek or Hebrew word translated into letters in the English language making the word readable to one who does not read Hebrew or Greek. When you locate the Strong's number you will see your word of interest in its original language form and you will also see the common form transliteration for that word. It is important to point out that occasionally a given word has more than one acceptable transliteration. In those cases, you may need to research the alternate forms of transliteration. To be clear, let's use the examples I used above.

Hebrew word יָשַׁע *yasha`* {yaw-shah'} has been assigned the Strong's number: 03467. In this case "*yasha`*" is the transliteration; while {yaw-shah'} provides the reader with a key to pronunciation.

Greek word δοῦλος *doulos* {doo'-los} has been assigned the number: 1401. In this case "*doulos*" is the transliteration; while {doo'-los} provides the reader with a key to pronunciation.

StudyLight.org Retrieved from https://studylight.org/ (last accessed January 24, 2022). From Home page, the tool bar contains an option for "Bible Study Tools" that will take you to a list of available Bible Commentaries, Concordances, Dictionaries and Encyclopedias.

The Power of Hope

If you plan to do word studies often and have the ability to invest in a few published resources my recommendation for Greek words: Geoffrey W. Bromiley, *Theological Dictionary of the New Testament*, Abridged in One Volume (Eerdmans 1985)[8] and Hebrew words: Harris, Archer, and Waltke, editors, *Theological Wordbook of the Old Testament* (Moody Press 1999).[9] Additional valuable resources for your personal library include: Baker and Carpenter, *The Complete WordStudy Dictionary of the Old Testament* (AMG Publishers 2003) and Spiros Zodhiates, *The Complete Word Study Dictionary: New Testament* (AMG Publishers 1992) – both are keyed off of the Strong's Number. Suggestion: Search Amazon or eBay for used copies in very good / good condition to purchase these materials at a lower cost.

---

8   When you know the Strong's word number you can enter it in the search box on BlueLetter Bible website. You will have to inform the search as to whether you are looking for a Hebrew Strong's number or a Greek Strong's number. To locate a Greek # place a "G" in front of the number with no spaces. The TDNT Reference (if applicable) will be provided under the header "Dictionary Aids." For example, G42 will be listed as: TDNT Reference 1:114,14. In this case, you would go to page 14 of the Abridged Volume to find the TDNT entry for your word. Note: the first part of the TDNT Reference [1:114] is given for the unabridged volumes of *The Theological Dictionary of the New Testament*.

9   When you know the Strong's word number you can enter it in the search box on BlueLetter Bible website. You will have to inform the search as to whether you are looking for a Hebrew Strong's number or a Greek Strong's number. To locate a Hebrew # place a "H" in front of the number with no spaces. The "TWOT" (*Theological Wordbook of the Old Testament*) Reference (if applicable) is listed under the header "Dictionary Aids." For example, H3467 is listed as: TWOT Reference:929. In this case, you turn to word #929 on page 414 of *The Theological Wordbook of the Old Testament*.

INDEX TO THE WORD STUDIES

Note: Words are alphabetized according to their transliterations under the English alphabet.

Greek
dunamis 178
endunamoo 178
ischus 181
kainos 93
kratos 180
methistemi 171
nikao 170
skenoo 7

Hebrew
'eth 120
chadash 93
chayil 114
kabod 50
koach 114
menuha 16
miqdash 10
shakan 4
Shekinah 5
shuwb 64

Meet the Author: Deborah L. Roeger

I confessed Christ as my Lord and Savior in 1962 when I was 9 years old. I was baptized the same day and I can still visualize that experience clearly in my memory. When God knit me together He did so in a way that blessed me with a deep love for research. It is one of the reasons I excelled in academic study resulting in a Bachelor's degree in Business Administration, Master's in Human Resources Management and Juris Doctor – all with highest honors. All glory belongs to God that my research skills and giftedness as a quick learner brought me out on top in every academic environment and led to an extremely successful professional career.

In the months leading up to February, 1999 God was drawing me closer and closer to Him through worship and His Word. That season culminated in an earnest prayer to *know* Him more. On my knees I offered to *go wherever* He sent me or *do whatever* He asked me to do that I might truly *know* Him. God answered that prayer in a most unanticipated way. Seven months later He shockingly led me to resign from my job with a large wireless phone carrier. At that time, I was employed as a regional Senior Counsel, overseeing the company's legal resources for the Eastern region of the United States. Little did I know that at only 46 years old I had just *retired* from the professional work world. Before a full year elapsed God had unexpectedly reconnected my heart to something He had buried deep within me when I had visited a men's medium security prison as a young college student. He then divinely arranged an invitation from the Christian Warden of that same prison to serve there as a volunteer working with both inmates and staff.[1] Nine years later God called me to lay down the prison ministry work which had by that time expanded into other men's prisons, the women's prison and Ohio's juvenile correctional facilities. His astonishing instruction was that I begin teaching Bible studies in our local church. It was an extremely challenging transition for me to make. However, looking back I see that my love for learning, commitment to advance on my knees in prayer and my well-developed research skills gave me a jump start on lesson preparation.

I cut my teeth on facilitating DVD-driven Bible studies others had written, supplementing those lessons with historical and cultural background information. From there God began to give me assignments to teach various books of the Bible verse by verse. The next step was to instruct me to begin writing Bible studies I would then teach. Eventually teaching assignments grew to include an international teaching ministry. From the rearview mirror, I can see that the progression was a natural one. Each step along the way was undertaken cautiously and prayerfully – undergirded by my own prayers, times of prayer with my husband and the prayer covering of our faithful prayer partners.

At the Lord's direction, my husband and I co-founded Hope of the Nations International Ministry, Inc. a nonprofit ministry with a goal to disciple others. Our earnest desire is to see the body of Christ mature by growing up in the grace, knowledge and love

---

1   In my first meeting with the Warden she asked me if I knew anything about mediation. I was in fact an experienced mediator and was presently mediating disputes for the Equal Employment Opportunity Commission. That began our working relationship which blossomed into a wide variety of ways in which God enabled me to serve both inmates and staff.

of God through the study and application of His Word. Every Bible Study I've written is well researched and profits from the fact that I whole heartedly embrace the goal of being a life-long learner who seeks to apply the truth I teach others. I love drawing fellow Christ-followers into the biblical text for the purpose of life transformation.

My husband and I presently reside in Florida. We have celebrated over 50 years of marriage and are blessed with two married children, Jeremy and Kimberly, daughter-in-law Jennifer, son-in-law Nathan and six amazing grandchildren: Jordan, Jackson, Hannah, Caleb, Jacob and Abigail.

www.ingramcontent.com/pod-product-compliance
Lightning Source LLC
Chambersburg PA
CBHW032041150426
43194CB00006B/376